Prophecies and Predictions

*Dedicated to
the One I love*

PROPHECIES & PREDICTIONS
Everyone's Guide to the Coming Changes

Moira Timms

Previously published in Britain as
The Six O'Clock Bus

Unity Press   **Santa Cruz**

This book was previously published in Britain by the title *The Six O'Clock Bus*. This edition has been revised and updated.

Published by Unity Press, Santa Cruz, California, 95065

Cover design by Bill Prochnow. Images by Aurora Borealis, San Francisco.

Library of Congress Cataloging in Publication Data

Timms, Moira, 1938–
    Prophecies & predictions

    Edition of 1979 published under title: The six o'clock bus

    Bibliography: p.
    1. Prophecies (Occult sciences), Futurism I. Title.
BF1809.T55   1980   133.3   80-25137
ISBN 0-913300-55-1 (pbk.)

PRINTED IN THE UNITED STATES OF AMERICA

Cover photograph courtesy of NASA

Itinerary

Foreword

"I invite you to the Great Adventure,
and on this adventure you are not to
repeat spiritually what others have done
before us, because our adventure begins
from beyond that stage. We are for a new
creation, entirely new, carrying in it all
the unforseen, all risks, all hazards – a
true adventure . . . . of which the way is unknown and has to be traced out step by
step in the unexplored. *It is something
that has never been in the present universe
and will never be in the same manner.* If
that interests you, well, embark."

– The Mother
Auroville, India

Preface

What you are about to read is a book about the true nature of things. 'In the beginning was the word...' and in the beginning truth was. It was not until fairly late, as we judge time, in the history of humankind that things began to go wrong.

The following pages will help clarify what went amiss and what can happen as a result of our individual and collective errors. The future may look bleak, desperate even, but there *is* a light at the end of the tunnel. If we can but recognize the obstacles between ourselves at this point of the dark passage and its end, we shall be able to negotiate the course with courage and understanding of what is ahead, and finally emerge into the light. Indeed, all of evolution has been progressing through this tunnel toward the light. It will not be long now until we are free of the darkness.

There has never been a period in human history when the stakes were so high or the rewards so great. In cosmic history as in the affairs of humanity there comes a time for the consummation of the Age and the restitution of all things. Quite simply, this means that we're rapidly approaching a great era when the chaotic quality of life as we now know it will cease to exist on the planet: a transmutation will have taken place.

Readers of this volume should fully understand that what is happening at this moment is part of a plan which has been unfolding for a very long time, or since the beginning – whenever that was. Our free will has been allowed to weave the fabric of our present circumstances around the strands of our destiny. The guidelines have always been there but somewhere along the way we decided to play by our own rules and lost sight of the original 'master plan'. It got mislaid, overlaid; laid to rest you might say, by most of us. Nevertheless, it is still there to guide us if we can re-learn the original rules and recognize that the correct path lies not within the grasp of our present technologies and ideologies but within our Selves, our inner beings. An outline of the master plan is presented in the following pages. It is hoped that readers will discover their own resonance with it. It may be hard to recognize at first, but it has not been permanently lost. All that is required to perpetuate our successful evolution as individuals and as a planet is still here. It always has been, and we must simply – but quickly – re-discover it. That's all. We do have everything we *need*. I say, we do have *everything* we need.

You will not find within these chapters the ultimate solution to the world's problems or society's ills. But you may gain some perspective on the signs of the times, the pattern of prophecy and current events and the promise of the future. Also, you can expect to experience the odd rush of adrenalin which can provide the energy to help you make some constructive changes in your life while time permits. Tension, after all, keeps us alert, stimulated and ready to act.

It is not the author's intention to motivate the reader by fear, but rather to educate us to the urgency of the times in which we live. To be enlightened on the subject may give many the necessary insights to reassess some priorities, restrain some compulsions, release the hold of the past over some fixed attitudes and venture out into the real world of newfound opportunity and challenging potential. So, take responsibility for your own judgement of the following and use as seed or catalyst those aspects which suit your own reality and needs, now.

This is not a 'religious' book. Religion, based on the word 'religâre' (ironically) 'to bind back', has become associated over the years with time-honoured and man-made dogmas, pedantic power-trips and limited vision. 'Spiritual' is a more appropriate description; the distinction being that an athiest can actually be more 'spiritual'

than a religious person. Spirituality is only peripherally related to religion in that its essence is more clearly defined in terms of laws and principles as they relate to the flow of nature and life, and the harmony which permeates the universe. Because the full import of spiritual information often fails to penetrate the filter of the mind, until the guard of intellect has been satisfied by the pass-words of 'logic' and 'reason', the book you now hold attempts to pass through this frontier of intellect on its way to the heart.
heart.

With us or without us, a cosmic timetable is unfolding on schedule, and to understand something about it is to have the kind of overview which will provide maximum benefit as it does unfold. In the meantime, please know that this information is offered as a blueprint, a guide and tool for safe conduct to the end of the tunnel. We have been taught to listen with our ears and not to hear with our heart. There are many ways of knowing and we can learn them all. There are many blueprints; seek them out. They are but a 'via' to help the real guide within you to awaken and show the way. Once there, you will be free of all vias. You will be the one who shouts back into the tunnel, 'Come on out, the Light is fine! . . . . '

Part One
Tools for the Journey

Introduction

Cosmic Primer

Science is still divided in its opinion of how the universe originated, but on one thing there is agreement – that there is order in the universe. Webster defines order as 'conformity to law' and orderly as 'well managed'. Just what is the order of the universe? We know that it does conform to law and that it is certainly well managed. What is the meaning of life? What is the nature of WoMan, of the universe? What's for dinner?

Ever since we became intelligent enough to ask these questions they have intrigued each generation, and the answers are still unclear. One thing we can know, however, is that all manifestations of nature are governed by cosmic laws which are simple and immutable. Cosmic law is the common denominator of the shifting spectrum of physics versus metaphysics. Reality, as we understand it, is only what the majority (influenced by the whims of fashion and the growing edge of science) agrees upon at any given time. In perpetual motion, it changes from generation to generation. But set apart from all of that are seven first-cause principles, or laws, which form the dynamic matrix of all existence. They never change.

We shall talk about them a little as preface to the rest of the book so that we may share a common understanding of the elements upon which the subject is based. Individual belief systems, especially those pertaining to established theisms, are particularly difficult to reconcile because they each stubbornly stake their claim to the ultimate truth. Therefore, if we can find common ground upon which to work, collectively, toward a more complete understanding of ourselves and our universe, we shall come much closer to the truth. Violation of these laws and indifference to their importance is what has caused most of the trouble in the world today. Because the Christian tradition is familiar to Westerners, and readers may relate more easily to that source than those of other cultures, Biblical references have been drawn upon in many instances. However, it is definitely not the author's intention to promote any one religious point of view, but rather to emphasise the similarity of many religious belief systems where truth is concerned and to show that the divergence of the material world can be reconciled to the subtler world of spirit. A continuum exists. Physics and metaphysics are different stages of the one science.

Each of the following Laws is an aspect of that primal energy in which absolutely everything we can name (and even those things we cannot) evolves and has its being. Just as Deity can only be interpreted in terms of attributes, these Laws defy exclusive definition and must be described by arbritary illustration, as they mix and merge with each other in diffuse juxtaposition.

The Law of Mentalism

This refers to the creative force of thought. Things, events, all words, took seed in thought. Thoughts are the underlying causative principle which humans have to work with in creating and contributing to the physical universe.

Uri Geller, the Israeli psychic, has been generally astounding audiences and scientific researchers by using mental energy to bend metal, to stop or start time-pieces, and so forth. One would like to believe there are more creative ways of using this energy, but in the meantime he is showing what can be done by the mind. After one television appearance the station's lines were flooded by calls from parents whose children were suddenly able to duplicate the pheno-menon they'd just seen. This has led to the theory that children between the ages of seven and ten are psychically receptive and have not yet developed the screening mechanism of self-imposed

limits about what is, or is not, possible. The Universities of London and South Africa are now studying these children.

We have all experienced mind over matter to some extent and, hopefully to a lesser degree, its opposite, in the form of psychosomatic illness. Bio-feedback is a recently developed technique for electronically monitoring the body's responses in relation to altered states of consciousness. As thoughts decrease, the mind becomes calmer and remarkable success has been experienced in 'uncreating' symptoms. Eastern philosophy teaches that it is the impressions we receive from the outside world via the five senses which create seed patterns for thought. A healthy environment, therefore, contributes to healthy thoughts, and healthy thoughts contribute to a healthy environment.

The Law of Polarity

This is the law of gender and opposites, male-female, negative-positive, yin-yang, matter-antimatter, etc. Based on this principle, nature is able to perpetuate herself. The apparent opposites we observe, when reconciled, help our spiritual growth and provide understanding of the phenomenal world.

Many opposites we encounter are analogous to points upon a circle, or opposite ends of a spectrum, and their interpretation is a matter of subjective translation.

Consciousness of reality is something like a small night-light in a huge, dark room. As the wattage of the lightbulb is increased, more of the room can be seen in detail. The room itself never changes, but only the observable reality, according to the intensity of the light. Things are seldom as simple as they seem when they appear in contradiction, and values like 'good' or 'bad' can fade into nonexistence when resolved in the light of greater understanding. Really, there are no opposites, only reality. It appears to change according to how we perceive it.

Unless something is experienced first, its opposite is not recognisable. Since there is no sweet without sour or joy without sorrow,

these extremes are only illusions which serve to facilitate our experiential existence. In natural healing it is necessary to understand the Law of Polarity in order to restore harmony to the body's imbalanced energies. All antagonisms are complementary; the 'good' in life depending for its very existence upon its polar opposite of 'evil'. (Interestingly, evil is 'live' spelled backwards.) The separation and fragmentation of life into aspects of good and bad vary in individuals and cultures and change with historical perspective. If life is approached with flexibility and sensitive awareness, rather than rigidity and blind faith, it becomes apparent that

17

fear and ignorance incline us toward suffering, whilst love and awareness draw us toward happiness or the 'good'.[1] By increasing the light of our understanding we can dissolve ignorance and penetrate the illusions which bind us.

The Law of Vibration

After the Creator, the Great Spirit, the Supreme Intelligence, or whatever name one can best relate to, conceived the idea (as in Law of Mentalism) of the universe, it went something like this: 'In the beginning was the Word . . . ' (John 1 : 1). 'And God Said, "Let there be light" and there was light.' (Genesis 1 : 3). When the words were spoken, causing vibration, duality and the Law of Polarity came into existence because movement creates opposites (i.e. opposite movement).

The spoken word is a vehicle of power, giving form and expression to thought. If you don't want something to become a reality, don't verbalise it, for by so doing you set in motion the forces which create circumstances. Words clothe a thought with a matrix of vibration, amplifying and easing it out into the physical world of matter and action. Floating there like a tangible echo, this bubble of spoken thought has an inherent creative and magnetic quality.

We're told that the purpose of a *kiai* (a fighting cry used in Japanese martial arts) uttered in a minor key is to effect partial paralysis of one's opponent by abruptly lowering the arterial blood pressure. Many people creating and sharing the same thoughts and words generate a force-field of energy. This is the power of chanting, whether it be for prayer and devotion, or for negative ends as in 'Heil Hitler!'. American Indians, of course, used this principle to build courage before battle through their war dances and songs, and for healing.

We usually think of vibration as the kind of sound heard only through the ears, which pick up but a minor fraction of the auditory

[1] Superior figures indicate references which are listed at the end of each chapter.

spectrum. The vibration of each thing forms its own energy pattern: rocks, insects and plants differ from each other because of their vibrational rate. Each molecule of the body is held in place, keeping its relationship to all the others, because of its programmed frequency. We know that subtle matter, once believed to be composed of finite particles, is now identified as a wave-form process. Faraday first conceived the electro-magnetic field as the lowest element of physical reality and now this invisible principle of non-linear bonding is recognized by science as 'resonance.' Pitched to a certain note, a tuning fork will cause to resonate other objects of the same fundamental frequency and harmonics with which it comes in contact, just like a smile, a yawn or anger. In this sense like attracts like and objects of disparate vibration gravitate to their own frequency as they are held in orbit around their common principle, the resonance factor. On a human level, it is love which is the creative force and cohesive element. Without it we become isolated and out of harmony with others. Using this model, it is easy to see how individuals, held together by a common positive goal and rightly motivated can, like the wave-form, transform others around them; even (would you believe) the world. A wave of dissonance can generate destructive force to the same power.

I CHING: Pi/Holding Together

.... Water flows to unite with water, because all parts of it are subject to the same laws.
So too should human society hold together through a community of interests that allows each individual to feel himself a member of the whole.

'Matter is energy becoming spirit'
– Paolo Soleri

'Time dissipates to ether the shining angularity of fact'
– Emerson

The molecules of an ice-cube vibrate faster when it is heated and transform it into water, steam and then vapour. Its changing form is due to melting and then evaporation, which is simply the excitation

"MIGHTY THICK FOG COMING IN, MRS. QUINCE!"

Gahan Wilson

of its molecules to a faster dance. None of us questions this, and yet some people cannot understand that matter is itself a condensation of an energy which is usually referred to as spirit; a state to which it eventually returns by way of evolution. The frozen world of ice is like the material world; the invisible world of vapour, the spirit. The physical world is created by spirit extruding itself into matter. All matter is composed of energy and all energy is manifested by consciousness.

The Law of Karma

This is the Law of Cause and Effect: cosmic justice. The word 'karma' means action. And for each and every action there is an equal and opposite reaction to the same power, whether we notice it or not. That's Newton's Law of Motion. The Bible refers to it: 'as ye sow, so shall ye reap'. Nowhere is this law more clearly illustrated than in the planet's disturbed ecology. Whole species are missing and a profusion of deadly substances within the bodies of all living organisms is a dismal testimony to humanity's trying to outsmart nature in lieu of understanding, or caring, to live within its flow. These pollutants, so harmful to all life, are our karmic heritage until we can desist or find new ways.

The word karma usually carries a negative connotation because when we violate the natural order of things some form of distortion or confusion is always the result. Good karma passes unnoticed most of the time, or disguised as good luck, because it is a continuation of the harmony in our lives. 'Luck' never hits a random target, but there would be more of its good side in evidence if we only knew what natural law was all of the time and how to build our lives around it.

Several kinds of karma are common to everyone: personal, family, national and planetary, and each of us is responsible for all of them in varying degrees. Dues have to be paid when a lesson of life remains unlearned. Moses brought the basics of the Law and later on the example of the life of Christ showed folks how to live it and help straighten out the world-muddle. We are told the suffering of His death paid off the negative karma accumulated by the entire planet to that time. He left behind a clean karmic slate and this was the Law of Grace in action. Without that all karmic debts are due and payable upon cosmic demand unless a period of grace is extended, or a divine waiver bestowed!

Edgar Cayce the American prophet had some interesting things to say about this Law, 'In the last analysis, it must be realized that all karma is mind-created. An error of conduct arises from an error of consciousness. Hence, unless a person can understand his own mental relationship to creative energy, he can not hope to redeem his negative karma. Man constantly meets himself. "Do good" then, as He said, "to those who have despitefully used you" and you overcome then in yourself what you have done to your fellow-man.'

The Law of Rhythm

Rhythm can be described as organized vibration. Vibration is to musical notes what rhythm is to melody. Rhythm has to do with repetition and cycles. 'Superimposed on the cosmic chaos are rhythms and harmonics that control many aspects of life on Earth by a communication of energy made possible by the shape of things here, and their resonance in sympathy with cosmic themes,' says Lyall Watson in *Supernature*. In American Indian healing rituals, drums are paced to the rates of the sick body's rhythms. By gradually adjusting their beat to that of the optimum life force the sickness can be normalized. By adjusting lifestyles, sickness can be avoided.

IT'S PLAYING ITSELF AGAIN, SAM!

Brahma,
in breathing world conceiving.
  Brahma exhales and the world
    issues out in a shower of . . .
      stars.
    and when the Great One sleeps
  our world becomes
quiescent
translucently suspended within the
void,
  within the cosmic bubble of
    consciousness.
      circadian rhythms um-
        bilically tie
      pulsating flesh to time
    tables of the sky.
  expanding and contracting,
liquid life-force flowing
  around the freeways of our free
    form flowing . . .
      ebb and flow
        in breath
        reflecting
        tide rhythms and

      small rockpools
      awash.
    new cells: regeneration
  every seven years.
    the cycles of celestial spheres
      needlepoint the heaven.
      changing faces of the
      moon and
      sunspots each eleven.
    precession of the equinoxes,
  a tilting wheel
of twenty six thousand
earth years.
    around its mighty center
      slowly turning . . .
      the galaxy yawns
      silently digesting
      eons
      within its center point.
    two hundred million years
  round trip
repeating itself
eternally. . . .
and again

                    Moira Timms

22

According to philosopher Alan Watts, 'Whatever we experience as existing, as continuing in time, is not so much persistent stuff as repetitive rhythm or vibration.'[2] The still frames of a film reel are accelerated to form the illusion of movement. In the same sense, light is both particle and wave, giving a clue to the real nature of time and space, based on the Laws of Vibration and Rhythm. On/off, in/out, hot/cold, day/night, rain/shine, appear as contradictory pulsations, but because each is an aspect of an existing continuum, a cyclical wave, and is *periodic* in its separation from the whole, it becomes fused at the interface of time and eternity by the Law of Rhythm.

The entire universe can be defined in terms of vibrations, rhythms and waves; a sequence of structured phases implicit in every process. The oneness of creation, in its continual expansion, is always manifesting perfectly in divisions of itself and this creates two basic forces – expansiveness (centrifugality) and contraction (centripetality). The oriental cultures have long understood this process and have identified as Yin and Yang these shifting forces which complement yet repel each other, which merge and transmute in continual spirals of power and inertia.

The Law of "As Above, So Below"

The systems governing both macrocosm and microcosm are the same. In the miniature solar system of the atom we see the sun/nucleus. The heart is the nucleus of the body and is known as the sun-centre in yoga. Trees and forests draw in energy to the Earth, transforming poisons of the atmosphere into usable oxygen. They also provide coolness, warmth and protection. Is it not remarkable that those fine capillaries at the interface of our internal and external environment, the hairs of our body, perform the same function. Like tiny antennae, they attract cosmic energies (prana) to the plexi of the body's autonomic nervous system and siphon off toxins. St. Barbe-Baker, the man who reforested two million square

23

miles of the Sahara, says, '... a human being cannot survive unless the body surface is covered with at least one third of intact skin, and the planet cannot survive unless its land surface has one third of tree cover.' Shaving one's body hair can be like clear-cutting a forest! Volcanoes vent the Earth's disturbed interior in the same manner as the human organism rids itself of waste through boils and 'eruptions'. Revolutions, the temper-tantrams of the populace, play the same role on the emotional level.

Osmosis The system of osmosis within our bodies interchanges nourishment and waste, positive and negative. It can be observed from the universe in its myriad, multifaceted manifestations that every apparent separation is only a semi-permeable membrane capable of osmosis; an interface. The free flow and exchange of excess and inadequate energies produces equilibrium. This mechanism is consistent on every level of life. Socially, blocked or congested energies become the symptoms of hate, separations, unrest, scarcity, etc., which touch our lives daily. Blocked impurities on the cellular scale create organ mal-function and sickness of the body. The most subtle energies are the first to become congested, beginning within ourselves and radiating out like the proverbial pool ripples to the external environment. Today's world-dilemma is but a very real magnification of humanity's inner state.

Black Holes Right at the outermost reaches of space the osmosis format still applies because the Law of As Above, So Below is absolute. For instance, if our universe is expanding, what are the ones next to us doing? Are galaxies separated by the osmotic membranes of space? Black Holes in deep space are totally invisible, but they gobble up any stellar material in their vicinity like cosmic vacuum cleaners. Where does this material go? And what about the inevitable White Holes? Intense amounts of energy and radiation appear to be enamating from distant Quasars located in the centres of other galaxies, and our own Milky Way. Their energy output, versus distance from the Earth, is something of a paradox as it is greater than can be accounted for by any known methodology of science. Astronomers say this is indicative of White Hole phenomena where energy sweeps in ... presumably from other universes. Our Black Holes would be their White Holes and vice versa. Thus the flow of stellar matter and particles between universes is kept in balance. When this was just the author's hypothesis it could have sounded, literally, pretty far-out. Now British theorist Roger Penrose and astrophysicist Robert M. Hjellming of the National Radio Observatory at Green Bank, West Virginia, have postulated the same theory.

Neuro-logic The scientists who are becoming intrigued enough to study such things now know that expanding one's consciousness (increasing the light in that dark room) and raising one's vibration are synonymous. Yoga, meditation, breathing exercises, pure diet, body work and so on help cleanse mind and body of the impurities which keep it gross. They prepare it to receive higher vibration. In fact, physicist David Finkelstein of New York's Yeshiva University has been searching for a link between particle physics, relativity and human consciousness. He says, 'The way has been prepared to turn over the structure of present physics to consider space, time and mass as illusions in the same way that temperature is only a sensory illusion.' Meanwhile, Dr. Timothy Leary, in his work of inner research, *Neurologic,* declares, 'The neurological transformation [of these formulae] substitutes number of neurons-firing-per-second as the velocity factor in the relativity formula.' Similarly, the Castaneda books on becoming a 'man of knowledge' speak of increasing one's 'speed'. In other words, to attain the breakthrough from the ordinary, mundane consciousness as we know it, to that of direct perception of Reality, enlightenment, self-realization, one must first attain within one's self the microcosmic equivalent of the macrocosmic speed of light. The less external chatter in the mind and the slower the brainwaves (alpha, delta) the closer the approach to higher spiritual vibration and ultimate transcendence.

The higher the vibration of human consciousness the more time and space condense. Get it?

The Law of Correspondence

The Law of Correspondence is simply the fact of the interdependence of everything. In relation to nature, we speak of this concept as ecology: the study of the interrelationships between organisms and environment. The web of life sustains all things in its fragile balance and violation of natural law leads to imbalances which create more and still more imbalances in an attempt to maintain a working harmony. Extinction or disruption of one form calls for adjustment and compensation by all forms.

Relating the Law of Correspondence to the experiences of life means cultivating the facility of overview. This way we can understand the wholeness of things and fill in the details and formulae later. Predicating life entirely upon the demand for facts, scientific proof and practicality prior to acknowledging something as valid has brought our culture to its present dismal circumstances. And individually we find ourselves perplexed, confused and surrounded by failing systems.

The quality of daily life can't be removed from the arena of nature, although for the past 150 years (specifically with the advent of the industrial revolution) we've been trying real hard to do just that. Humankind's impact upon the planet has finally become overwhelmingly evident as our species has learned to tilt the dynamic balance of nature ever more irrevocably in its favour. '...And God said unto them, "Be fruitful, and multiply and replenish the earth, and subdue it, and have dominion over the fish. of the sea, and over the fowl of the air, and over every living thing that moveth upon the earth"' (Genesis 1 : 28).....and sure enough, we *did*!

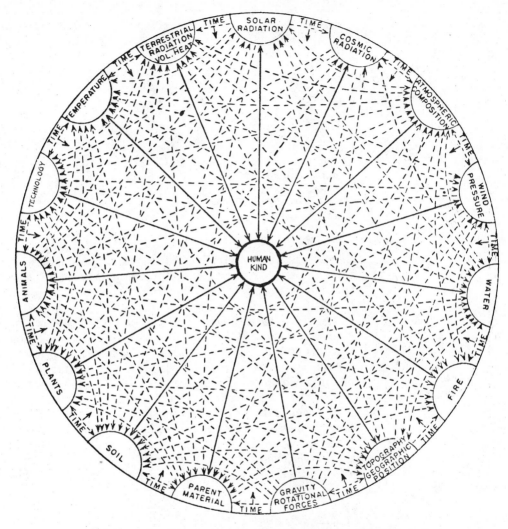

A holocoenotic environmental complex. *Solid lines show factor-humankind relationships. Dashed lines show relations between factors. Arrowheads show the general direction of the effect. If the effect is reciprocal, arrowheads are placed at both ends of the line.* [Adapted from W. D. Billings, "The Environmental Complex in Relation to Plant Growth and Distribution," *Quarterly Review of Biology*, 27:251–264 (1952).]

Spirals

'Being great, it passes on;
Passing on, it becomes
remote; Having become
remote, it returns.' (Lao Tsu,
describing the Tao)

Spirals are very interesting. Things, and the energies that cause them to be, expand and contract in a progression of cycles which are spiral in nature. Everything eventually changes into its opposite.

According to philosopher Michio Kushi, 'Because the laws of change are the order of the universe, electrons may slowly spiral towards the nuclei of their atoms and change into protons. In a like manner, we may imagine our sun to be the melting point of a solar spiral in which comets change into planets and planets eventually refuel the sun.' Galaxies are spirals, of course, as are cloud formations and weather patterns photographed from high altitudes. The wind itself, cyclones, hurricanes and tornadoes; water down a drain swirls away spirally; and then there are fingerprints and hair growth patterns. Crystals are formed from molecular spirals. Living cells, protein molecules and that tiniest seed of intelligence, the DNA, are all spirals.

The centripetal (clockwise) spiral of natural things has the cohesive force of uniting and drawing together – holding from the centre. We see this within the healthy cell and also the solar system as the planets are held in orbit around the sun. The ancient swastika symbol representing the sun and the harmony of the universe was a motif of clockwise direction. The centrifugal spiral is basically counter-creative and its spin creates disbursement and separation, which is why the leaders of Nazi Germany appropriated the original sun-symbol swastika and reversed it to represent their quest for world domination as they spread out over Europe to divide and conquer. This phenomena can also be observed within the cancer cell: the nucleus, like a group of tiny spinning tops, is polarized in a counter-clockwise direction which allows reproduction without restriction.

Not only have we been accustomed to thinking of history as that linear progression, the 'march of time', but Western culture as a whole has unfolded in a very yang way (the positive, masculine principal in nature characterized by direct energy and straight lines). Certainly this has been partly because it was men who ran the world, a symptom of the age of reason and rational thought which led to materialistic focus and technological prowess, all of which are yang attributes. Philosophically speaking, masculine energy is like the sun which appears to move across the sky in a linear direction. Yin, or negative, feminine energy, is cyclical like the moon, and revolves around the sun.

Feminine Influence   To illustrate this point a little further, it could be said that when the sea becomes stormy its waves have very little, really, to do with the surface wind, but are responses to the deeper stirrings within the ocean's depths itself. Similarly, the over-reactive element which has characterized early feminist activity should not be allowed to becloud the movement. Social change and feminine freedoms are crucial issues in themselves but on a cosmic level the movement is vital. Its ultimate function is to yin up the planet sufficiently to create the necessary pro-evolutionary synergy of balanced male and female energies. (See New Age chapter for fuller development of this theme related to the feminine ray.)

The picture of electron tracks in a bubble chamber shows a direct analogy of this process. Linear, positive, energies collide with negative, feminine energies moving in a circle. From this union a spiral is born inheriting the forward progress of the line while maintaining the conserving principle within its cyclic wave. Clearly, such a union in human affairs will steer humanity away from its present illogical and dangerous course. We have only a short time to give up our mission of 'search and destroy' before every last resource has been ripped from the Earth to sustain the counter-evolutionary priorities of material progress and military might. There are other kinds of progress and other kinds of might.

Right now our world is approaching the centre of an evolutionary spiral which will culminate in a new direction for human development. Instead of 'forward, march!' how about 'onward, flow . . . .'!? flow . . . . . . '!?

References
1.   From the teachings of The Church of the Tree of Life, 405 Columbus Avenue, San Francisco, CA 94133.
2.   Alan Watts, *Cloud Hidden, Whereabouts Unknown* (Pantheon Books, 1977).

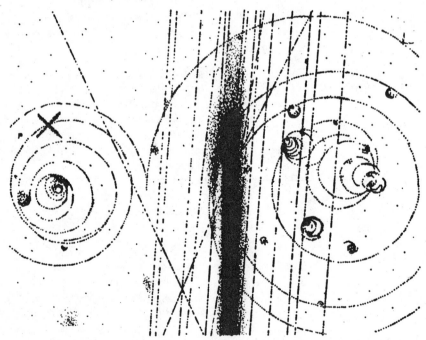

Part Two
Outward Bound

1. A Different Theory of Evolution

'But the natural man recei-
veth not the things of the
spirit of God, for they are
foolishness to him; neither
can he know them because
they are spiritually dis-
cerned.' (1 Corinthians 2 : 14)

A different theory...isn't that what has prefaced all major scientific breakthroughs and inventions throughout history? We discover a set of rules, formulae or theories that apply and serve a purpose up to a certain point, and then discover that they must be modified or changed in order for us to progress further. It would seem that laws of logic are inviolate, yet they can, on occasion, be eclipsed by others that supersede them. The higher principles govern the lower ones and foster the progression of human knowledge. One thing is certain, however, understanding the higher laws makes the lesser ones easier to deal with.

For instance, simple arithmetic formulas work fine until the need for more complex computations poses a problem. Then one can turn to calculus, or computers. The flat world theory was OK too until men's curiosity drew them to the known edges of the world. They must have found it very remarkable that the world gradually became round to accommodate their quest for new lands. Later, it seemed impossible for a plane to fly faster than the speed of sound because as the craft approached the necessary speed it would dive out of control. Finally, contrary to the logic of such an emergency, one test pilot accidentally reversed the 'joy stick' while in the spin and found that it brought the plane out of its dive and penetrated the sound barrier in the process.

A synopsis of the alternative theory of evolution is presented here in brief outline as just such a case. Because of evolutionary dictates and the momentum of human energy patterns like politics, technology, economics and the material needs of civilization today the progression of world events cannot be altogether avoided. However, constructive changes in the mass consciousness can ameliorate or modify their intensity and avert total catastrophe.

The chapters which follow are, at worst, undoubtedly disturbing, but at best they show that taking full responsibility for one's individual life and creations will enable us collectively to 'pull out of our spin'.

Three Cycles   At this time in the twentieth century humankind approaches the end of a minor cycle: the passing from the Age of Pisces to the Age of Aquarius. The events between now and the end of the century will be most transformational and prepare us all for the culmination of a major cycle, the precession of the equinoxes. These two cycles happen to coincide with the repolarization point of a final cycle of human history, the end of the Yuga. So, with three cosmic cycles about to end you can be sure we're in for a period of heavy changes. (Explanation of these cycles comes later.) In order to be clearer about what all this means, let us go back to the beginning (an arbitrary definition) and see how it all started:

The evolution of cosmic time is divided into sections known in the Hindu tradition as Yugas. At the end of each Yuga – a period of hundreds of thousands of years – there occurs a phenomenon known as 'the progression of the life waves', or the graduation from the Earth plane of all human souls in existence during a given Yuga. All of us here now are at varying stages of our own personal unfoldment, but we're all part of the same life wave.

The 'Fall'   A long time ago, as individual extensions of the Creator, we were really very happy, but after the 'Fall' from that idyllic state we descended into physical form here on planet Earth in order to exercise our free will between the ways set out by Lucifer and those of the Creator. (Lucifer, apparently, had challenged Him, and in the ensuing power-struggle was vanquished and cast out of the celest-

34

ial realms into the grosser vibration of the physical plane accompanied by his followers.) In His infinite wisdom, the Creator indulged the wilful departure from divine harmony and leased out the Earth 'reservation' until humanity came to the realization that the only way to go while allowing negativity to control, was down. Naturally, returning home to the source is the brighter alternative and we now find it necessary to free ourselves from all the tricks and illusions of matter (maya) before we can graduate back to that original state of perfection with full God-power. That old black magic has mesmerized the Earth for so long that it is no longer so easy to just pack up and go back home to the Father.

As time went by, each Age became less conducive to mastering this task. This, the Kali Yuga, is the most negative of all the cycles. There is very little perception of the true nature of reality and chronic ignorance of the Law (i.e. cosmic, natural or divine law) seems to be humanity's natural state. However, because all things eventually come full circle, (or, more correctly, full spiral), and we now approach the closing phase of the Yuga,[1] a human and planetary transition between the old age of darkness and the new upswing of consciousness toward the New Age of light is coming about. It is sometimes called the Golden Age. With this passage the sun will be influenced by changing cosmic energies which will project rays of transformed energy to the entire solar system. This will be a period of great positive influence and understanding because it represents the highpoint and culmination of civilization this time around.

The human race will be fully equipped to complete the remainder of this Earth sojourn in a state of perfection: harmony with each other, nature and the Creator. By gaining mastery over the physical plane this life-wave will then be ready to progress to a higher sphere of existence on its evolutionary journey.

Earth-School Life on Earth is a school for God's co-creators, and the souls who fail to learn their karmic lessons before the coming 'graduation' will be held behind after the transition to populate yet another Yuga at another time in the future where they will 'do it again and again until they get it right'. In fact, it's pretty certain that most folks are

35

laggards held up from the last cycle. Before the change to the new harmonious state can happen, though, some very drastic events are in store.

A Healing Crisis International chaos, distress of nations, famine, natural and man-made catastrophes, geophysical and celestial anomalies are the outward appearance of these events which are prophesied by many cultures and many religions. However, they can more accurately be described as a cleansing of the Earth, the karma of which is due and payable before the new phase can become operable. Only the purest water can become vapour, and this is how it will be with us humans caught up in this evolutionary process. Chances of survival are related to the state of one's inner being and its relative purity. If a person wishes to explore more of his or her divine potential there must first be an attunement with that higher frequency, which is spiritual in nature. This divine radiation comes from universal life energy and can be personally contacted by a number of disciplines and paths. Everyone needs, most urgently, to purify – physically, mentally and spiritually. Techniques for purification and service to humanity (karma yoga) will help one work off negative karma. (Negative karma represents unlearned lessons.) Therefore, progress to a more elevated condition is only possible as quickly as this backlog can be worked through, gaining new understanding and insights of past mistakes as we go.

Planetary Stress The planet itself has been badly dealt with by modern man, precisely because civilized cultures, as presently defined, are out of harmony with the universe. Production and technology needs and effluent have desecrated and polluted the planet in the process of sustaining this particular model of culture. These conditions, in particular, will be karmically rectified in ways appropriate to those conditions. The planet kept a pretty low profile in the past, quietly sustaining, gently nurturing, and getting ripped off in the bargain. But all that is about to change: diverse disturbances of nature, geographical shiftings, eruptions and earthquakes will be but symptoms of the planet's reaction to manmade ecological imbalances which can no longer be sustained. Like a sick body, the Earth will rebel in its attempt to regain equilibrium. The Hopi Indians refer to this phenomenon as the time of the great purification.

Central Sun   We know from Kirlian photography that there is a body of energy surrounding all living forms. This is a significant step in understanding that all natural forms have a refined energy form or spiritual counterpart. Our own planet, and the others of this solar system also have a spiritual body. Our sun receives its radiant energy from a larger, more powerful sun in deep space. It radiates beyond the ultra-violet end of the spectrum and, because its light is scientifically undetectable at this time and its emanations so refined, we refer to it as the Central Sun or Spiritual Sun. Its light is referred to as spiritual light or energy. This Central Sun is energized by yet another intradimensional sun blazing with unimaginable radiance from another level, and so on through a series of supraphysical suns.

The elliptical revolution of our solar system around the Central Sun produces spiritual seasons on Earth and within ourselves, just as revolution around our solar system's sun causes the mundane seasons of spring, summer, autumn and winter. We are now entering the invisible aura of the Central Sun, the influence of which is responsible for the new consciousness that everyone is experiencing to some degree. As the light becomes stronger it affects our spiritual bodies, displacing the accumulated clouds of negative karma and thus purifying our planet and our beings. Hard times, sickness and adversity in many forms on mental, physical and emotional levels are the physical way these clouds are dissipated. None of us can do anything to avoid the process or prevent it. Through Grace and the right kind of aspirations, though, it can be lessened both individually and collectively. And that's why understanding the significance of the coming changes and flowing along with them will enable us to enter into greater acceptance of them, knowing that purification is the positive side of hardship.

The Bible speaks of 'signs and wonders in the heavens' in the last days. Whatever form they take, they will undoubtedly be related to many other phenomena taking place within and around the Earth and affecting its stability. The globe's axial spin is slowing down and contributing to weather changes right now, prior to a reversal of the poles. This particular phenomenon has occurred before and it will happen again at some indeterminate time in the near future. This is because pole reversal represents a principal phase of cosmic evolvement for our solar system and all its life forms. Subsequent to the events culminating in the Earth's polar shift, a new sun and moon will govern our planetary system. You'll be relieved to know that this heavy change does not represent the 'end of the world' but the end of the *present world system* and the beginning of the New Age. 'And I saw a new heaven and a new Earth; for the first heaven and the first Earth were passed away' (Revelation 21:1). With a change in the positions of the poles the map of the heavens viewed from Earth would certainly appear as a 'new heaven' and the Earth changes accompanying an event of such magnitude would assuredly create the geography of a 'new Earth'.

Although the above might sound like a very spacey science-fiction notion, this book is devoted to proving its reality to readers in a practical way. Each of the following chapters represent a piece of the total picture, fleshing out the various aspects of this synopsis. Cosmic and astrological cycles, the matrixes within which this drama unfolds, are explained, in addition to the significance of weather changes and Earth anomalies related to the polar shift. Prophecies are also a part of the future which will be explored, together with insights into our environment, food and financial crises. It is important to keep in mind that the promise and aspirations of the New Age are scheduled to stabilize the planet within our own life-time, and bring to a close the errors of the past.

Physical preparation has its place in terms of surviving the future transitional phase, but it is the change of consciousness and spiritual attitude that is the real focus of this particular crisis. It cannot be emphasized too strongly that attunement to the higher principles and the One/God will be the ultimate protection, and that forming supportive groups of good, close, loving friends will generate much creative energy and offset despair and fear. This is a time for the members of the planetary family to get to know each other.

References
1.   Lt. Col. Arthur E. Powell, *The Solar System* (Theosophical Publishing House, London, p. 89).

2. Cosmic Cycles

Within the legends, histories and religious folklore of almost all ancient peoples there is contained some reference to varying numbers of previous world ages, or civilizations, which flourished for millenia and ended in cataclysm.

Here in the Western world we are both sceptical and intrigued about the Biblical flood and the lands of Atlantis and Lemuria which disappeared in the big splash. Did these events really occur, and if so, why? Since our own civilization is destined in the course of the ensuing years to face the same kind of changes experienced by many past 'mythical' cultures, it is not without relevance to dip far back into history for an overview of just what went on, and see whether it provides any clues to our own situation today.

Yugas   According to the Hindu tradition of cosmology, we are now nearing the end of the Kali Yuga (the Age of Iron) which is the final and most negative of four evolutionary Yugic cycles. Each Yuga is like the season of a super-cosmic year, even greater than the cosmic year of the precession of the equinoxes. When the Earth came into its current phase of manifestation and the first Yuga began ('Satya' Yuga, meaning 'Purity') humanity was barely removed from its original state of God-like innocence. This was the original Golden Age. As time progressed the planet underwent the influence of a negative descending spiral, and the quality of life in each successive Yuga became further and further removed from the knowledge of truth and natural law (in other words, 'Reality'). In the second, Treta Yuga (silver age) spiritual awareness decreased by one fourth and by the time of Dvapara Yuga (copper age) negativity

39

had a 50% holding. In the Kali Yuga the vibration has become pretty murky and humanity is labouring against heavy odds. Righteousness (right-use-ness) has diminished to a scant one fourth of its original strength. Throughout our current history we have created and been assailed by all the evils of Pandora's box. No wonder the human race is having such a difficult time. But the turning point has now arrived, and the dawn once more sheds its light on a confused and ignorant planet.

Division of Time

18 Nimeshas (Twinkling of an eye)	= 1 Kashtha (3⅕ sec.)	3600 Years of the Gods	= 1 Treta Yuga
30 Kashthas	= 1 Kala (1⅗ min.)	2400 Years of the Gods	= 1 Dvapara Yuga
30 Kalas	= 1 Muhurta (48 min.)	1200 Years of the Gods	= 1 Kali Yuga
30 Muhurtas	= 1 Day and Night	12000 Years of the Gods	= 1 Mahayuga (4 Yugas) or an Age of the Gods
30 Days and Nights and odd Hours	= 1 Month	1 Age of the Gods multiplied by 71	= 1 Manvantra
12 Months	= 1 Year (Human)	4380 Millions of Human Years or 1000 Divine Ages	= 1 Kalpa or Day of Brahma (the night of Brahma is of equal duration)
1 Year (Human) or 365 Days and Nights	= 1 Day and Night of the Gods		
365 Human Years or 365 Divine Days and Nights	= 1 Year of the Gods	36000 Kalpas	= Maha Pralaya
4800 Years of the Gods	= 1 Satya Yuga		

(According to the Hindu tradition, this is the 28th Yuga under the laws of Manu Vyvaswata, seventh Manu, who reigns over this Manvantara)

The *Vishnu Purana,* one of the oldest sacred texts of India says about the Kali Yuga, 'The leaders who rule over the Earth will be violent and seize the goods of their subjects... Those with possessions will abandon agriculture and commerce and will live as servants, that is, following various possessions. The leaders, with the excuses of fiscal need, will rob and despoil their subjects and take away private property. Moral values and the rule of law will lessen from day to day until the world will be completely perverted and agnosticism will gain the day among men.'

There are many other references to this division of time. For instance, in the Bible, Nebuchadnezzar's dream (Daniel 2:31-45) was of a bright and terrible image with a head of finest gold, chest of silver, hips of brass and legs of iron. The feet and toes were of iron mixed with clay. This image was destroyed by a stone, unmade by human hands, which crushed the feet to dust and the pieces blew away in the wind. Although Daniel the prophet interpreted the various metals as the world empires which succeeded Babylon, the head of gold, the dream also has a more cosmic meaning. It represents the great yugas. The iron legs are the Iron Age or Kali Yuga which deteriorates at the end of its cycle into the present unstable civilization symbolized by the feet of iron and clay. (The toes represent the intended ten countries of the Common Market. See chapter on Bible.) The prophet interpreted the stone as the true kingdom of God which would replace the other civilizations as the real and lasting Kingdom.

Four Worlds, Four Suns In the Americas, the Hopi Indians' creation story tells of four successive worlds (identified with gold, silver, copper and a mixed-mineral) which were destroyed because people had grown away from the Creator's instructions. They say we inhabit the fourth world which is about to be 'purified' again by the Great Spirit.[1]

Amongst the Incas, records remain of cosmic upheavals which also ended previous world ages.[2] Brasseur, in his *Histoire des Nations Civilisées du Mexique* recounts that Mexican chronicles state, 'The ancients knew that before the present sky and earth were formed, man was already created and life had manifested itself four times.' Researching the same subject, the author in a later work says that the Mayas counted their ages by the names of their consecutive suns: Water, Earthquake, Hurricane and Fire Sun. 'These suns mark the epochs to which are attributed the various catastrophes the world has suffered.'[3] The famous Mayan calendar forecasts the end of the present cycle on December 24,

41

2011. Gomara, the sixteenth century Spanish writer, said that according to their hieroglyphic paintings, the nation of Culhua or Mexico believed that four previous suns had already been extinguished. The four suns were as many ages, in which the human species was wiped out by inundations, earthquakes, general conflagration and tempests.[4] In the *Visuddi-Magga*, sacred book of the Buddhists, a section on world cycles speaks of seven suns or ages, which each terminated with fire, water or wind. Meanwhile, Aborigines of British North Borneo still hold that the sky was originally low, and that six suns have already shone in the sky prior to this one.[5] One of the earliest Greek authors, Hesiod, wrote in his *Theogony* about four ages and generations of men that were destroyed by the anger of planetary gods, the fifth and current one being the Age of Iron.

As the current cycle reaches its final phase and Earth draws closer to the light region of the galaxy, negativity in all its forms is being revealed in the 'purging' brought about by the higher vibration of the light. Earth is progressing toward a higher orbital frequency. This process is already affecting psyches and bodies in many ways, helped along by new solar activity which is not yet fully understood.

Sunspots According to extensive research published by the Foundation for the Study of Cycles,[6] sunspot activity is intimately related to important mass historical events, epidemics and cycles of human behaviour (as also are weather cycles). Records from 72 countries were studied, back to 500 BC, which showed periods of minimum, maximum and declining excitability in human affairs during the eleven year cycle of sunspotting. It is thought that the influence of the sun's maximum vivacity upon the centres of the nervous system lends energy to impulses arising from the mass unconscious and transforms potential energy into especially significant forms of action. However, since humanity as a whole takes the path of least resistance, it all too often has led to bloodshed. Soviet research using Kirlian photography to study the bright electrical energy field around living things has found that the fields flare up brightly to correspond with flares on the sun's surface. The magnetic field of the entire planet reacts to solar flares in various ways, just as the human organism does, via its own aura. In later chapters we will explore the nature of sunspots, their influence on Earth's conditions and their unusual intensity in recent years.

In discussing an increase of light/vibration upon human behaviour and consciousness, it is useful to refer again to Eastern philosophy.

Gunas In nature there is a combination of three basic manifestations. The Hindus call these manifestations the Three Gunas: Sattva (purify) which concerns aspects of perfection, rhythm, harmony, self-realization and a healthy nature. Rajas (inertia) has to do with the passions, attachment, egocentricity and so on. Tamas (regression) is related to ignorance, darkness, degeneracy and the grosser tendencies. Each person fluctuates between each of these three expressions. Here are just a few examples:

Actuating force	Predominance of Sattva/Purity	Predominance of Rajas/Inertia	Predominance of Tamas/Regression
Expression	Firmly confident but not egotistical. Unchanged by success or failure.	Swayed by emotions and motivated by ego.	Inert, selfish, stubborn, malicious.
Action	Unattached to the result.	Attached to results. Ego involvement.	Indifferent to loss or injury to others. Self centred.
Knowledge	Sees the unity of all beings and things.	Sees only the separateness and differences.	Insists his/her view is the only one.
Reason	Knowledge of power and right action.	Indifferent to ethics or morals.	Morally and ethically indifferent and confused.
Pleasure	Knowledge of the true self. Knows how to accept a disadvantage in order to enjoy its advantage.	Primarily enjoys only the senses. Unwilling to tolerate a negative to get to a positive.	Thrives on discord and negativity. Enjoys grossness. Takes pleasure at others' expense.
Food	Live, raw organically grown foods. Fresh fruit and vegetables, nuts, seeds, grains. Unprocessed foods.	Dead, overcooked, flesh foods. Bitter, sour, too hot/cold, pungent, processed, sprayed or chemicalised foods.	Stale, flat, putrid, leftovers, plus all the inertia producing foods of the previous column.

Because of the influence of increasing light vibration upon mass consciousness now, it becomes very important to understand its effect upon these three aspects of human nature. Persons of a basically Sattvic or pure disposition will gain in wisdom and understanding as the vibration continues to increase. Predominantly Rajas persons (the average state of 'the masses') will suffer dissipation of vital energy, becoming restless as negative qualities surface to cause anxiety, disorientation and confusion. Those undeveloped personalities of Tamasic (regressive) inclination do not have much to look forward to as the higher frequency triggers inertia, delusions, sickness and violence. It could be said, more simply, that the awakening is like the two-edged sword and that vibrational acceleration nourishes a pure condition but badly over-amps fair to middling characters. *The light that illumines also blinds.*

In recent years the intensifying rays from the Central Sun have been responsible for a polarization in human consciousness. A growing spiritual awakening is one effect while the disturbing rise in crime and general confusion is the other. Surely this is incentive enough to get our trip together, spiritually, mentally, physically, socially and in all ways. For in our direst projections of a catastrophic future, with major breakdowns of the system and societal panic, it is not the ensuing events themselves which most people fear (the hardship, deprivation and confusion). What we really fear most is other people and what they will do!

References
1. Frank Waters, *Book of the Hopi* (Ballantine, 1963).
2. H. B. Alexander, *Latin American Mythology* (1920, p. 240).
3. Brausseur, *Sources de L'Histoire Primitive du Mexico* (p. 25).
4. Humboldt, *Researches 11* (p. 16).
5. Dixon, *Oceanic Mythology* (p. 178).
6. Foundation for the Study of Cycles, 124 South Highland Avenue, Pittsburgh, PA 15206, *Cycles* (Jan. 1971).

3. Astrological Cycles

Within the major cosmic cycles are minor ones intrinsic to the course of history. Specific expressions of celestial influence are now affecting the Earth very strongly as it progresses from one astrological sign to the next. Astrology is still a controversial subject to established ways of thinking because many people have only limited acquaintance with its more sensational aspects or have been disappointed with their daily horrorscopes. However, sceptics who believe astrology to be folklore or fancy frequently shift to neutral when they gain some insight into the logic of its deeper laws.

As little as a decade ago astrology was still in the closet. But today it is regaining recognition as a true science, along with the other branches of occult knowledge. Could this be because we're entering the two millenia period of the Age of Aquarius which governs astrology and metaphysics?

In order to understand fully the influences which are now operating upon the Earth, a basic knowledge of astrological fundamentals is helpful. Here's a very brief summary:

The Zodiac   The word 'zodiac' is Greek for 'living creatures'. These equally spaced signs are a series of twelve star groupings circling the sky in a 16° belt. Sun, moon and planets appear to be 'in' these constellations as they move against the background of these star clusters. Each sign of the zodiac makes a brief and regular appearance with the passing months of the year. Summer and Winter divide the year into a combination of darkness and light. The Earth rotates on its axis, 23° to the plane of its orbit, bringing about our seasonal changes. (Without this tilt there would only be a single season as the sun's rays would always fall directly at the equator.) The elliptical orbit of the Earth's annual rotation around the sun warms and lengthens the days approaching the Summer solstice, shortens and chills them around the Winter solstice. Spring and Autumn equinoxes mark the mid-point between these two extremes; then, day and night are of equal duration.

Celestial 'Ages' This model of the celestial timetable applies on a much larger scale, too. 2152 years comprise an astrological 'age'. An age is the duration of each zodiac sign, and represents a month of the cosmic year which consists of the twelve zodiacal ages and lasts for 25,826 years. During this great cosmic year, the Earth's axis will have pointed to each zodiac constellation in turn, and this is called the Precession of the Equinoxes, or the equinoctial cycle. (The exact number of years in an Age and an equinoctial cycle is the subject of disagreement among experts. The figures quoted here are based upon the measurements given in the geometry of the Great Pyramid.[1])

The Age of Pisces has been with us for the past two thousand years or so. Pisces is known as the house of 'self undoing'. We've been trapped in orbit, as it were, around the materialism, competitiveness and limitation generated by Piscean energy (and are certainly almost undone). What we are now experiencing is all the surface instability, precariousness and velocity needed to break away from that confining matrix to an expanded state of harmony and wisdom, consistent with the influence of that benevolence which is Aquarius. No birth pangs are completely painless and the mighty labour now being generated to wrest new life from the clutches of the old will not be easy. In human affairs, age tends to crystallize one's ideas, and our culture is now cracking under the weight of its own senile tenacity to status quo. The task at hand is to sustain, for just a little longer, the best from all that we have built and accomplished to serve as a platform upon which the 'New Order of the Ages' will be secured.

Equinoctial Cycles As the Earth traverses the heavens during the great cycle of 25,826 years, it passes through the cosmic year's equivalent of the four

46

seasons, which produce spiritual changes in the state of evolving humanity. As the tilt of Earth's axis allows its North magnetic pole to align with a particular constellation of the heavens, cosmic energies are drawn to the Earth from that region. This in turn directly influences the spinal energy channel of Earthlings, who receive these same energies through their major energy centre, the Crown Chakra. It is the body's equivalent of the Earth's North magnetic pole! Scientific studies reveal that the bioelectric force field of the body profoundly influences the entire nervous system and that the field itself responds to changes in the Earth's magnetic field. Life on this planet is spiritually impoverished during its sojourn in the 'Winter' season, at its darkest in the constellation of Draco the Dragon. It is able to flourish in the light of the spirit while in the 'Summer' region, peaking closest to the Milky Way. The Age of Light began in 1931. Pisces represents the dark before the dawn, and we are at the turning point of the circle, the cusp, merging into Aquarius.

The symbolic and mythical characters depicted by the constellations around the wheel of the Zodiac are codes, metaphors for the evolutionary stages of progression since the beginning of the present cycle. Whether they were named by ancient or modern astronomers is not so relevant as the fact that they were accurately named. (Mars' satellites Demos and Phobos (Rout and Terror) were named by a modern scientist who much later, and to his own amazement, discovered that those were the exact names given in ancient documents.) The links with the past are still there, and are expressed intact, through the medium of the unconscious.

Evolution and Historical Pole Stars

When the Earth passes closest to the Milky Way, through the Ages of Sagittarius and Scorpio during the cosmic Summer, civilization recurrently attains its highest peaks. As the Zodiacal wheel turns the planet's North polar region slowly toward the constellation of Cygnus the Swan, the dying beauty (swan song....) of the pinnacle of civilization's success fades as the time of decline is traversed. Vega, the next polar constellation of this spiral, is opposite the cosmic Fall. In fact, the dictionary confirms the correctness of its position, defining Vega as the Arabic word for 'Fall' representing both the seasonal Fall, and the mythical 'Fall from

47

Astro Logic

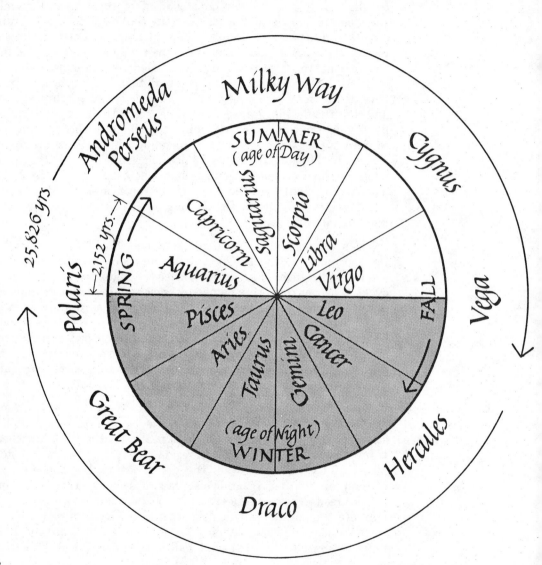

Milky Way

Andromeda
Perseus

Cygnus

25,826 yrs

2,152 yrs.

Polaris

Vega

SPRING

SUMMER
(age of Day)

Capricorn
Sagittarius
Scorpio
Libra

Aquarius

Virgo

Pisces

Leo

Aries

Taurus
Gemini
Cancer

FALL

(age of Night)
WINTER

Great Bear

Hercules

Draco

Grace' after which the first humans began to inhabit the Earth. Other 'Falls' which cycled out great civilizations were the decline of Lemuria and the sinking of Atlantis. When Vega faced the Earth 12,000 years ago, the last Age of Day ended with the Noachian flood, and the last known reversal of the planet's magnetic field (*New Scientist*, January 6, 1972).

The next constellation, Hercules, symbolizes humanity overcoming and surviving through strength and fortitude, the many difficulties of the post-flood historical period, just as the mythical Hercules did. Draco the Dragon is recognized in the Serpent of Genesis and the Dragon of Revelation. It personifies the negative force presiding over the Age of Night and deepest psychic and spiritual darkness of the cosmic Winter. The Great Bear hibernates in Winter and emerges in Spring, and the constellation of that name correlates with the Spring emergence of Aries, the first sign of the Zodiac.

Poles Today   Polaris, our pole star and marker of terrestrial North, acts as the *polarization* point between the Age of Night and the Age of Day. It governs the repolarization of the Earth's consciousness and its hemispherical poles, so that we are now experiencing the cosmic year's equivalent of the Spring Equinox. (It is both fascinating and fortuitous that the pole star of the *ecliptic*, Regulus [the regulator? possibly from the Latin roots of 'regula' to rule, or 'regere' to lead straight], will be positioning on the Leo/Virgo cusp around the turn of the century—*directly opposite* Polaris. [See Astro Logic chart.] In other words, the intense and possibly cataclysmic polarization between cosmic night and day [the Armageddon period] is being mediated, regulated by the influence of this polar opposite star.) Next, Andromeda and Perseus, the constellations toward which we are now progressing: Andromeda, wife of Perseus, was chained to a rock and rescued from the sea monster by Perseus, who, after many trials and adventures, won possession of the Golden Fleece. Here we see final freedom from the chains of the old Piscean restrictions as the feminine ray is released (see New Age chapter) and feminine energies are liberated to equal status with the male counterpart for maximum harmonizing of the Earth's energies. The pursuit of the Golden Fleece is analogous to the difficulties one experiences in attaining the Christ consciousness, the culmination of physical existence.

The Milky Way is the realm of Light itself.

Because existence is cyclical, the knowledge possessed by the ancients during the last Age of Light is being regained. Perhaps the Great Pyramid is one remaining monument of a time when the universe was understood and recorded for posterity. Great civilizations fell after the high point of achievement during the last equinoctial cycle's Age of Light. Then the Age of Night, cosmic Wintertime, again enveloped a struggling humanity and the profound knowledge of those cultures was lost. The superhuman accomplishments covered in Von Daniken's *Chariots of the Gods* may have been souvenirs of advanced space beings. But it is just as likely that many of these feats of engineering excellence and marvels of a magnitude far surpassing modern abilities are evidence of human attainments during a past cycle, more advanced than our own. In another 6,000 years we shall have reached the highpoint of this particular spiral of civilization when the progression of the life-waves, referred to earlier, occurs on the spiritual plane. It is also useful to remember that Earth is part of a spiritual/physical testing zone, the inhabitants of which have been set the task of freeing themselves from the tyranny of matter controlled by the 'fallen' hierarchies inhabiting key regions of the universe. These negative powers and principalities rule the Age of Night of Leo, Thuban – at the head of Draco the Dragon, and our pole star, Polaris. These realms contain intelligences of the negative hierarchy, administrators of Lucifer, who have used their might to establish themselves as powers over the physical plane.

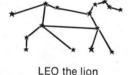

LEO the lion

VIRGO the virgin

The Battle of Armageddon, therefore, is the scene of the final conflict between the forces of good and evil described in the Bible's Book of Revelation. As the 'bad guys' are cast out of the higher heavens into the lower levels of creation, great imbalance will result

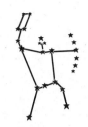

ORION the hunter

GEMINI the twins

SCORPIO
the scorpion

on the Earthplane. The great clash of celestial and demonic forces will then (as above, so below) have its counterpart on Earth. It is the great purification which all of creation must experience in order that the dark forces can be ousted and replaced by graduating beings of perfect light bodies who will preside over the Earth and restore harmony and balance to the highest purpose.

To finish up our astrological insights, let's put one big myth in the trash-can: scientists tell us the constellations do not resemble their names in anything but the most arbitrary fashion – because the way in which *they* have linked together the stars of each grouping shows a complete lack of imagination! Hans Augusto Rey has written several astronomy books for children and has rediscovered the ancient way of graphically depicting them in his stargazing book.[2]

In the writings and descriptions of almost every culture, the same creatures were used to identify the signs of the Zodiac: the American Indians, Assyrians, Chaldeans, Egyptians, Greeks, Israelites, Mayans and Romans all shared the same circle of living creatures. They probably knew something, thousands of years ago, that we have only just discovered about astrological science.

If a map of the stars is superimposed over the Earth with the Pole Star placed over the North Pole, we have a celestial clock making one revolution daily. The noon-point of that map (like Greenwich) is the Great Pyramid of Gizeh referred to by the prophet Isaiah, 'There shall be a pillar at the borders of the Land of Egypt for a sign and for a witness.' Thousands of years ago Egypt was known as the Land of Khem, and the Pleiades, a group of seven stars in the constellation of Taurus, were known as the Khema. If the map is placed with the Khema over the Land of Khem (Egypt) then Taurus falls over the Taurus Mountains of Southern Turkey; Ursa Major, the Great Bear, rambles over Russia; the head of Draco the Dragon rears itself over China; Orion over Iran; Aries the ram, over Rome, and Capricorn (identified with the god, Pan) falls over Panama, Panuco and Mayapan, the old name of Yucatan. Aquila the Eagle spans the United States. The analogies are obvious, and

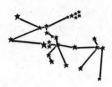

TAURUS the bull

quite impressive. This is one of the clearest examples of 'As above, so below'.

References
1. Bernard I. Pietsch, *Voices in Stone* (5353 Gates Rd, Santa Rosa, CA 95404).
2. Hans Augusto Rey, *Find the Constellations; Stars; Stargazing With Hans Augusto Rey* (Houghton-Mifflin).

4. Involution and Evolution

Having gained some perspective on the nature of cycles, relative to the coming changes, it is necessary to understand how the evolution of human consciousness fits within these matrixes. An accurate account of the descent of spirit into matter and its long journey through mass, energy, space and time, must be written at some future time by another, wiser than Darwin, more visionary than Galileo or Einstein. We cannot empirically state the exact nature of evolution in its totality, but we can discuss some general premises which stand the test of current logic and convey schematically the nature of life's progression through to completion of expression on the physical plane.

We refer to history and the origin of species as evolution, and yet it is more correctly called 'involution' as it is life in the process of becoming. It is not linear, as in the traditional 'the march of time', but cyclical, spiral.

Energy, which forms the first and most subtle wave of life, becomes progressively more intricate as it transmutes into ever more wonderful and complex forms – gases, minerals, plants, animals. The highpoint of creation is achieved at the sixth stage of development in the form of human beings who function with the privilege of erect spines and creative minds. In this sense, the human form comes out of the world, and not into it. We represent a direct metamorphosis of the soil; we are not separate. Energy gives birth to gases which form minerals. These minerals, inherent in the soil, nurture plants which feed animals. We in turn are sustained by these plants and animals. From this stage onward we can be said to

53

Involution/Evolution

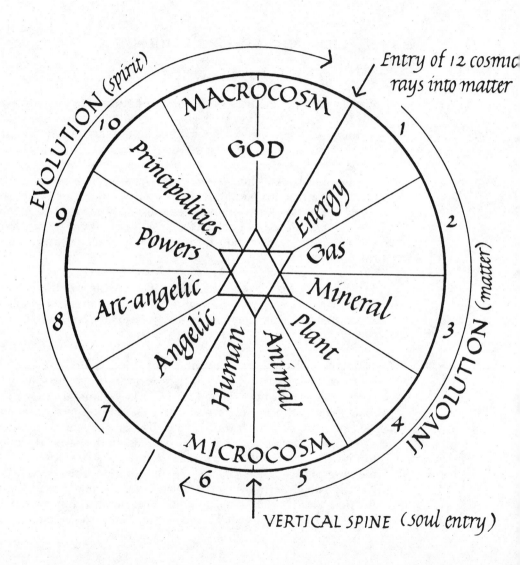

MACROCOSM
GOD

EVOLUTION (spirit)

Entry of 12 cosmic rays into matter

INVOLUTION (matter)

Principalities
Energy
Gas
Powers
Mineral
Arc-angelic
Plant
Angelic
Human
Animal

MICROCOSM

VERTICAL SPINE (soul entry)

'evolve', since matter, upon reaching its most complete expression, is at its most complex and tends to its point of origin by way of refinement; we grow up and return home as it were. The human organism, then, evolves back to its source, taking with it the entire knowledge and wisdom accumulated and integrated into its psyche during all life's experiences. Matter once again merges gently back into spirit.

Here at the sixth level of form, human beings exist at varying stages of personal development. Those whose consciousness is still in the early stages of awakening represent the human-animal nature in as much as the ego is still focused in upon itself and its own needs, largely to the exclusion of the welfare of others. It knows nothing of the higher principles nor does it care to learn, being primarily fixated upon the lower centres of consciousness characterized by security, sexual sensation and power. As life's experiences and hardships give us some social smarts and teach us to 'do as we would be done by' sensitivity grows, awareness expands and the ego gains a vested interest in the welfare of all life forms, diffusing itself vicariously as Everyman. Once the heart has become activated, creativity is expanded and knowledge of the higher wisdom is sought. As the process unfolds the human form can be said to represent God-human.

Number 6 Explained Humankind as the sixth kingdom of creation is no arbitrary definition for the purpose of explaining a chart, but enjoys the privilege of that number as a great gift. In the science of numerology, six is related to the Law of Vibration and is designated as "the number of return." The *I Ching* or *Book of Changes* is one of the world's oldest and wisest books. For more than 2,000 years it has served as a rich source of Confucian and Taoist wisdom. Here is what it has to say about the sixth stage:

24 Fu/Return All movements are accomplished in six stages, and the seventh brings return. Thus, the winter solstice with which the decline of the year begins comes in the seventh month after the summer solstice; so too, sunrise comes in the seventh double hour after sunset. Therefore, seven is the number of the young light, and it rises when six, the number of the great darkness, is increased by one.

How does this affect society today? The following ancient words could almost have been aimed at current events and the devotion to the principle of oneness which is drawing people together, away from the separateness of the old ways. Quoting from the same hexagram we read:

The Turning Point

After a time of decay comes the turning point. The powerful light that has been banished returns [the Age of Day]. There is movement but it is not brought about by force. The upper trigram . . . is characterized by devotion; thus the movement is natural, arising spontaneously. For this reason the transformation of the old becomes easy. The old is discarded and the new is introduced. Both measures accord with the time; therefore no harm results. Societies of people sharing the same views are formed. But since these groups come together in full public knowledge and are in harmony with the time, all selfish separatist tendencies are excluded, and no mistake is made.

Today we are seeing these words come to life. The time of decay is *now* in the sense of our ravished environment and the failure or decline of many traditional institutions. It is now that a great spiritual rebirth is happening with a change in consciousness which is enabling us to apply the brakes, if we so choose, to the popular notion of material progress and the havoc it has wrought. It can be reshaped to one of internal and individual progress within a minimally sustaining economic framework. We all know it's time to quit many of the old routes, and changes are occurring in our lives whether we like it or not.

Those who respond first to 'a different drummer' have always had a social stigma. In the mid-sixties, they were represented in the vanguard who reached the point of not going on with the accepted show. They needed time to re-evaluate and reorient themselves, to experiment and explore uncharted horizons. It took a certain vision and a specific kind of courage because the folks who were dedicated to the show going on, having reached the point of no return within that ethic, created unpleasant social pressures, called them dropouts and nonproductive members of society. Today, the underground flavour of those tentative explorations away from the mainstream has begun to surface and bear new and very tasty fruit. Referring to this turning point, the *I Ching* continues:

> Return always calls for a decision and is an act of self-mastery. It is made easier if a man is in good company. If he can bring himself to put aside pride and follow the example of good men, good fortune results.

Those who are still attached to the idea of executive status and corporate profits or reluctantly ensnared by dixie cups and electric can openers can ponder the oracle's words:

> When the time for return has come, a man should not take shelter in trivial excuses, but should look within and examine himself . . .

Because disaster can overtake the unprepared and those unwilling or indifferent to the needs of the times (see Chapter 23, *The Six O'Clock Bus):*

> If a man misses the right time for return, he meets with misfortune. The misfortune has its inner cause in a wrong attitude toward the world. The misfortune coming upon him from without results from his wrong attitude. What is pictured here is blind obstinacy and the judgement that is visited upon it.

You will recall that the plagues of *Revelation* are special packages of karma visited upon the obstinate, that they might awaken to their wrong attitudes. Humans are the most versatile of all the animals and yet they always resist change. As the late Dr. Jacob Bronowski described it, 'We live our past in the present from the ragbag of fixed and obsolete ideas.' Animals that don't adapt become extinct. Remember? Survival today means understanding and responding to change within the context of the 'internal revolution'. Survival tomorrow means *anticipating* the changes and preparing oneself accordingly.

Evolution from the sixth kingdom of creation takes us on to the seventh where the soul learns spirituality, finally passing from the material plane to the subtle, whence it came. In the inspired rallying song of *Woodstock* Joni Mitchell said it most poetically:

> We are stardust, we are golden, we are billion-year-old carbon, and we've got to get ourselves back to the Garden.

Seven is the number of perfection and completion, as mentioned in the first quotation from the *I Ching*. Also it is expressed in the seven symbolic days of creation, the seven days of the week, the seven rays, seven seals of Revelation which complete the action, and the seven of the Kabalistic Tree of Life where it represents victory, or the triumph of endurance.

Civilization is now at the sixth stage of evolution, the polarization point between matter and spirit, light and darkness. The seventh stage of evolution will burgeon when the necessary period of purification has passed. The Bible says that Christ will come again after the tribulation and reign for 1,000 years of peace. It has also been said that the Avatar of the New Age will not take physical incarnation but will be alive and well in the hearts of all people as the Christ consciousness, thus bringing us into perfection, and the progression of the life waves can occur. The 1,000 years of peace will provide an opportunity for spiritual development, free of the negative karmic interference which has punctuated human affairs so far. Thus, for physical plane beings, the cycle of creation will be completed.

This model for physical and spiritual evolution can also be applied to the astrological cycles (see chart, p. 48). The Fall season of the great cosmic year, 12,000 years ago, coincides with the fall or sinking of Atlantis at the end of that cycle of civilization. Beginning with the human race's new start, then, in the Age of Leo, it takes six evolutionary Ages to arrive at Pisces, where we are now. We're in the cosmic Springtime, crossing the cusp into the seventh Age, Aquarius. This impending Age will provide the tools of our ascension from the world of matter to the subtle, or spiritual, realm. Because our position now is tantamount to the cosmic time of the Spring Equinox when day and night, light and darkness are of equal power, there is a corresponding conflict on all levels for supremacy between these two forces, as the dark powers try to hold their domain and polarization occurs into an outright conflict between the light and dark force.

Creation will be fully perfected and completed upon the Earth, drawing the present era to a close. The class of the Kalu Yuga will graduate on to planes of existence more suited to its new unfoldment, 'And God shall wipe away all tears from their eyes; and there shall be no more death, neither sorrow, nor crying, neither shall there be any more pain; for the former things are passed away' (*Revelation* 21:4).

5. Weather Changes

'The global cooling presents humankind
with the most important social, political
and adaptive challenge we have had to
deal with in 10,000 years.'(Lowell Ponte
The Cooling)

If the transitional changes to the New Age are so close at hand it
seems reasonable to assume that the more Earth-shaking aspects,
that is those related to the Earth's orbital stability, would now be
building up and showing themselves as deviations from the norm.
Well, they are. When I first began researching this chapter, in 1973,
the only real clues to the pervasive weather changes we are now so
familiar with were vague references to the Gulf Stream and the
African drought. Since then we have watched the process accelerate to such immense proportions that all global cultures are
disrupted by alien weather extremes and food production everywhere is threatened.

We know that the main problem with today's delinquent weather
stems from the fact that the Earth is becoming gradually colder,
while air pollution is causing heating due to the 'greenhouse effect'.
Since 1945 temperature drops in the Northern hemisphere have
been about four times as extreme as those in the South (where
oceans predominate and absorb heat) because heat is being lost in
the North faster than the Southern hemisphere can retain it. Some
monitoring stations inside the Arctic circle report that the temperature has fallen by more than 6 degrees C during the past 30 years.
Scientists estimate that the mean global temperature of the world

dropped about 2.7 degrees and that ice and snow cover in the Northern hemisphere increased by 12% in the period 1971-72 and has remained abnormally high. Glaciers of Northwestern China have stopped receding and begun advancing according to a three-year study reported by Associated Press in 1978.

The North Atlantic Ocean has become colder and the Gulf Stream has begun shifting southward. Icelandic agriculture has been largely paralysed and Britain's growing season has declined by more than two weeks, accompanied by the worst drought conditions in 500 years. Intense drought has struck Russia, Northern Europe and many areas of the United States, attended by devastating forest fires and enormous crop losses which threaten famine if they continue. A chain reaction of secondary effects of the new intense winters and unabated drought receive daily media coverage.

Less Sunlight   The word is now out that even 1% less sunlight could trigger the next ice age (which a ripple of consensus within the scientific community says is a one in ten chance within the next 100 years). Therefore, it is pretty disconcerting to learn that pollution from the supersonic planes alone could lower the world's temperature by reducing that much sunlight, with additional disastrous effects on world agriculture. A single volcanic explosion can substantially obscure sunlight. Dust palls of the finer ash can linger in the atmosphere for years and reduce ground-level temperatures by several degrees. (It is feared that the 1980 eruptions of Mt. St. Helens in Washington State may have had this effect.) There is evidence from the Lowell Observatory that actual sunlight has increased its intensity in the last few years but a 1975 report of the National Oceanic & Atmospheric Administration indicated the duration of direct sunlight has decreased by 5%, mostly since 1964. Pollution of the atmosphere is to blame; it depletes sunlight and in subfreezing areas dust and particle matter act as nuclei to form ice crystals and seed clouds, thus increasing ice cover.

When the moon pulls close to the Earth, aligning directly opposite the sun, the combined astronomical forces produce exceptionally high tides. (Very high tides contribute to earthquakes.) This situation occurs only 20 times in each 300 years, normally,

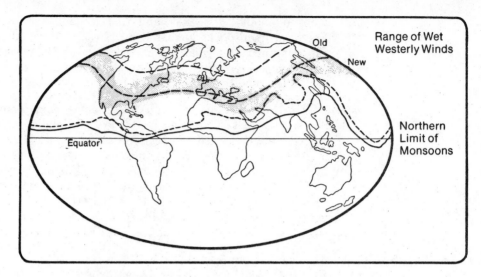

Range of Wet Westerly Winds

Old

New

Northern Limit of Monsoons

Equator

and yet it happened four times in 1974.[1] Monitors have been detecting an increase in volcanic activity since 1947, about the same time as the cooling began.[2] Since 1976 there has been a growing intensification of earthquakes around the world. In the 150 years preceding 1912 there was fairly consistent volcanic relief of the Earth's pressures, but from 1912 to the mid-1940's there was a span of phenomenally low activity.[3] This period precisely coincides with the time defined by scientists as 'normal' weather and which was really a few decades of rare and exceptionally fine, warm weather resulting in the best growing conditions to emerge in a thousand years. It was a climate upon which our entire modern agricultural technology was built. The National Academy of Sciences says that only 5% of the last 700,000 years have enjoyed such warm world weather! One is reminded of Biblical accounts of bountiful harvests before famines as God's way of providing enough to store for the hard times.

The sun is probably *the* major factor in world changes, since the dynamics of Earth's atmosphere, hydrosphere and lithosphere are all influenced by it, as well as the human impulse and behaviour referred to earlier. Certainly the recent inner changes within humanity have equalled in scope and intensity the outer events of our changing climate.

Air tides are generally related to the sun's gravitational influence and more evidence of Earth-chill is detected in the expansion of the Circumpolar Vortex, a belt of high altitude winds sweeping the North Pole in an East-West direction. This vortex has been off-course since 1975. Instead of flowing East to its African destination it veered North. Consequently, Europe has begun to receive the most intense heatwaves of the century. In this connection, British essayist Malcolm Muggeridge was moved to recall, with a sense of déjà-vu, the idyllic summers of prewar years 1914 and 1939. He wrote in the *New Statesman,* 'There seems to be something vaguely sinister in the continuing blue skies and warm, still evenings, as though they portend the coming of the positively last crisis . . . when our present way of life, so strained, so distorted, so fraudulent, finally disintegrates.'

Sunspots   Sunspots (in recent years irregular and intense as never before) also reduce sunlight reaching the Earth. These dark patches reach a maximum in number and vigour in 11-year cycles which affect the strength and direction of our planet's magnetic field. Since sunspots are associated with the sun's rotation and influence the kind of radiation produced, we can see that these phenomena are also important factors in inducing climate variables down here (and, as previously explained, changes in human consciousness). Sunspot activity of 1957-58 represented the most intense emissions ever observed up to that time. In 1972, only three years after the preceeding cycle (or 8 years early?) more solar spots reached peak animation after unusually turbulent storms on the sun. To top it all off, the solar flares of mid-1978 produced record-breaking surges of ultra-violet radiation and were *the* largest in recorded history. One effect of this activity is to slow down the Earth's rotation. (As we shall discuss in the next chapter, this decrease in spin is a major factor in producing earthquakes and vulcanism and is linked to the process of polar shifting.) Although these events occur some 93 million miles away, their influence on Earth is very real. Not only do they affect human consciousness and behaviour and cause inconvenience like radio communication disruption, power line paralysis and flamboyant Northern lights, but, if a large spot (or several) happen to face the Earth, sunlight can be reduced by up to

4%. Drastic effects upon global agriculture result, but with the crucial reduction of sunlight, premature ejaculation of another Ice Age upon our planet may be the net result. Immense solar storms are expected around 1982, due to a special alignment of planets.

It is disturbing to look back over the years and see that large-scale man-made contributions of all kinds of air pollution originated around the same time as the planet's spontaneous cooling, accelerating the process. Climate changes resulted from natural forces in historical times. We assert that the new and radical weather now prevailing *is* the result of special cyclical events of nature due to culminate in the next decades. But human causes and tampering are intricately involved in aggravating and intensifying them.

Johann Friede (1204-1257), an Austrian monk of the order of St. John, was one of the greatest seers of his time. An excerpt from one of his many revelations follows:

When the great time will come, in which mankind will face its last, hard trial, it will be foreshadowed by striking changes in nature. The alternation between cold and heat will become more intensive, storms will have more catastrophic effects, earthquakes will destory greater regions and the seas will overflow many lowlands. Not all of it will be the result of natural causes, but mankind will penetrate into the bowels of the earth and will reach into the clouds, gambling with its own existence. Before the powers of destruction will succeed in their design, the universe will be thrown into disorder, and the age of iron will plunge into nothingness.

When nights will be filled with more intensive cold and days with heat, a new life will begin in nature. The heat means radiation from the earth, the cold the waning light of the sun. Only a few years more and you will become aware that sunlight has grown perceptibly weaker. When even your artificial light will cease to give service, the great event in the firmament will be near . . . . .

The Fate of the Nations
Arthur Prieditis (Llewellyn Pubs.)

Weather Modification

Without a complete theory explaining why climate does change, human attempts to change it are certainly dangerous (very similar to drug therapy to remove symptoms without regard for their cause). Is that what Johann Friede was hinting at? – 'Not all of it will be the result of natural causes, but mankind will reach into the clouds, gambling with its own existence.' As long as the present cooling continues the ice will advance, which is why more than 60 nations have engaged in weather modification. In 1975 in the U.S. alone there were nine federal and 66 non-federal weather modification programmes operating. These programmes range from a variety of climatological research to cloud seeding to create rainfall, hail suppression, fog dispersal, hurricane manipulation, diffusing blizzards to rearrange snowfall, creation of earthquakes and tidal waves, lightning suppression, etc.[4] If the present trend of unpredictable and cool weather behaviour continues the countries who will suffer most are North America, Canada, Northern Europe and Russia. Weather-theft by sophisticated technology which can take weather from the poorer countries to sustain the richer ones may be a very real political issue in the near future as 'natural' catastrophes, famine and drought hit the lesser developed nations. It may even create international wars. Like all attempts to control natural forces, the way is fraught with multiple repercussions. No international laws have yet been established to restrict the 'monopoly' of weather – which appears to be a finite commodity. Creating weather in one place is only possible by disrupting its potential in another.

Honduras accused the U.S. in 1973 of stealing its rain and causing severe drought by artificially detouring hurricane Fifi to save Florida's tourist industry. That hurricane was the most devastating in that country's history. Drought-stricken El Salvador has made similar charges against the U.S., as has Japan who believes that typhoon seeding in Guam stole its crucial and limited rainfall. Rhodesia and Israel have both been blamed for rain-theft by neighbouring nations. No mechanism exists to prove these accusations or to compensate for their loss. The United Nations is working toward a ban on environmental warfare but this is a complex and difficult issue, and almost impossible to implement in a water-tight way. In *The Cooling* Lowell Ponte quotes military officials who

65

admitted U.S. government aircraft terminated droughts in the Philippines and Azores to protect U.S. military interests, but that a request by several other nations affected by drought and famine in the African Sahel was refused on the grounds that private American interests could be hired.

Clearly, a lot of negative karma is being created by tampering with nature on such a scale, heedless of the physical repercussions or the moral issues involved.

Weather Cycles Selby Maxwell and Raymond Wheeler were two remarkable men who came to understand the law of Spirals and As-Above- So-Below in a very practical way. In the early 1900's astronomer Maxwell (ex science editor of the *Chicago Tribune*) discovered the existence of a weather-energy cycle common to all weather, based on solar and lunar influences. He learned of the correct intervals which predetermine these changes and the fact that all cycles of the same length in nature turn simultaneously and are related in some way to the basic energy cycle. Professor Raymond H. Wheeler, head of Kansas University's Psychology Department worked for 20 years with a staff of 200 on a very unusual project. Almost two million records and 3,000 years of weather history were compiled and researched to reveal a recurring pattern of weather/culture cycles. From this data could be charted the types of government and human accomplishments, wars and cultural styles, and much more.

The two men became friends and combined their talents to form the Weather Science Foundation (now named Cyclomatic Engineering[5]). Farmers, businessmen, stock-market speculators, agricultural and industrial leaders used the predictive services of the Foundation for successful planning of their affairs. Author Brad Steiger sifted through a quarter of a ton of data to produce a fascinating book on the subject called *A Roadmap of Time.*

Substantiated research by Wheeler revealed that if a mean global temperature variation of as little as 1½ degrees F. continued for only five years it would be sufficient to influence changes in human behaviour patterns. (Scientists estimated that the mean global temperature of the world dropped about 2.7 degrees during 1971-72

66

and that the decrease has continued.) Are the recent chilly statistics responsible for the new, inner direction of Western culture? According to Wheeler, human energies increase during cool weather trends and all waves of rapid change throughout history have come because of cooling cycles.

Four phases to each bioclimatic cycle are associated with specific political, social and cultural changes:

Cold-Wet: Materialism, atheism, rising civil disorder, increased population, etc.

Cold-Dry: Anarchy, agricultural productivity decrease, social revolution and transformation, government corruption, migrations, wars, etc.

Warm-Wet: Renaissance, inspiration, idealism, increased creativity, etc.

Warm-Dry: Decline of culture, persecutions, despotism, depressions, etc.

These orderly progressions of climatic change unfold in cycles of 100, 500 and 1,000 years. Each cycle is like a small cog synchronized to a larger wheel so that the tenth 100-year cycle and second 500-year cycle join the 1,000 year cycle as it terminates. Every fifth cycle of the 100-year pattern which coincides with the 500-year cycle is exceptionally severe.

From Maxwell-Wheeler research of the 1950's we learn that we are presently experiencing the Cold-Dry phase of the 100-year cycle. This happens to be 'in phase' with the fifth and most severe cold spell of the 500-year cycle. Therefore, the droughts affecting much of the world will be the most distressing in 500 years – a fact acknowledged by the British government in 1976 with respect to a drought so intense that it dried up the River Thames and allowed Welsh householders only a few hours daily access to water.

Because of non-cyclic factors and unforeseen variations which enter every situation, these cycle patterns are never exactly 100% accurate, but they are an accurate *guide* within specific known limits.

According to author Steiger, the year 2,000 marks the end of the

67

present 100-year and 500-year phase of the Cold-Dry cycle and the beginning of the Warm-Wet one. Since events culminating with the 500-year cycle are the most intense, the cold temperature climax with its devastating droughts and great migrations and social revolutions is scheduled to be exceedingly rough.

Although the predicted transition to the new climatic and cultural Warm-Wet phase, scheduled around 2,000 AD, was calculated in the 1950's, it coincides exactly with prophetic and cyclic timetables mentioned from other sources throughout this book. In this respect, we are in the same relationship to the years 1475-1500 which presaged the birth of a new phase of consciousness, culture and world discovery known as the Renaissance.

As we have said the four climates of each cycle repeat themselves in periods of 100, 500 and 1,000 years. This series of cycles based on harmonic progression (to point zero, thence reversing its progression) accounts for the Ice Ages and great Geological divisions of time. In its broader capability and application, Wheeler calculated three such major historical time divisions into his overall weather computations, noting that an 'interval' occurred in 1928 where the harmonic progression of weather cycles reversed again. This he regarded as a 'step-up' of the evolutionary pulse, equivalent in magnitude to those of the past – the emergence of vertebrates, mammals and primates and man's social order. Wheeler said this latest reversal, falling as it does within a greater Cold-Dry cycle, will be 'difficult to live through', accompanied by an approximate transitional period of 25 years bringing about Earth movements equivalent to the last cataclysm responsible for the creation of new geological features, reversing mountains and oceans in many places. The year 1928 which indicated the beginning of this major reversal of weather-cycle frequency is also indicated in the prophetic chronology of the Great Pyramid as a major event in the unfolding of human history. The chapters ahead attempt to provide some insight into the magnitude of such an unfolding.

To summarise, then, the sun has been acting up in recent years, changing major wind tides and causing other related anomalies. The planet is definitely cooling off. It is also losing rotational velocity.

Research into natural weather cycles seems to indicate present chaotic weather change as normal to the scheme of things. But how catastrophic and unbalancing are the human attempts to set it to rights? Perhaps we should consider human tampering as a built-in and important game condition of the evolutionary plan. We sow the seeds of our own progression, whether on the crest of destruction or within 'the flow'.

Ice Balance The phenomenon of polar ice balance is a *key event* in the future location of the Earth's geographic poles. Many changes are coming which naturally and un-naturally augur to coax the poles into a new location. While Arctic regions increase their ice-mass, the National Science Foundation reports the vast West Antarctic ice sheet is deteriorating due to warm underground lakes, and huge areas are collapsing into the sea. Dr. Richard Cameron, NSF programme manager for glaciology, reports that something dramatic is happening and the study of the West Ice Sheet and Ross Ice Sheet Projects is urgent for it has been in only the last two or three years that scientists have begun to realise that the ice sheets which form the polar caps could break up rapidly. Physicists Amory Lovins and Peter Fong believe we may only have about 100 years of Antarctica left if city energy consumption continues to create 'hot islands' of increased temperature.[6] In the meantime, the USSR, with the worst weather in a century, plan on removal of the Arctic ice pack as one of their three major projects to improve Soviet weather. *Time* magazine reported that 'Changes in Earth's tilt and distance from the sun could significantly increase or decrease the amount of solar radiation falling on either hemisphere – thereby altering climate.' As we shall see in later chapters, the Earth's tilt *is* changing, quite radically.

Quite simply, the changing weather patterns are only the *symptoms* of a deeper process at work. Beyond all the physical manifestations is that other, invisible, stretch of the phenomenal spectrum; the place where effects are gestated, their source being generated in causes beyond our immediate perception. They set in motion forces which unfold to the dictates of principles as sure as mathematics. As our solar system approaches the Central Sun, moving deeper within its aura and into the lighter regions of the universe, it causes the solar spectrum to expand beyond the ultra violet end, with an attendant reduction of infra-red (thermal) rays in sunlight; the average temperature of the Earth is declining accordingly and increasing the Arctic ice cap. On the other hand, higher frequency radiation (non-thermal) is increasing due to the greenhouse effect which converts it into heat on Earth, resulting in massive breakup of the Antarctic ice sheet.

Meanwhile, in an attempt to study and understand these phenomena, the Global Atmospheric Research Programme of the World Meteorological Organization and the International Council of Scientific Unions have teamed up for observations, mobilizing ships, aircraft, land stations, weather satellites and ocean instrumentation buoys. Other national, international, government and meteorological agencies are studying the problem, and conferences and reports are proliferating on all levels to investigate the situation. To date, none of them has come up with an answer to the underlying cause of all the turmoil; namely, that the Earth is limbering up for a major reversal of her poles.

As Einstein once put it, 'Something's moving . . . . ' Well, yes it is, and most of us don't like it one bit!

References
1. *Mechanics Illustrated* (Oct. 1974).
2. *Science News*, August 14, 1971, p. 108.
3. *Scientific American*, 'Volcanoes and World Climate' (April 1952).
4. Lowell Ponte, *The Cooling* (Prentice-Hall, 1976).
5. Cyclomatic Engineering, PO Box 382, Glenview, Ill. 60025.
6. *Press Democrat,* November 14, 1976, 'Ice Age Theory is Foreboding'.

6. Shifting Poles

PART I Our home the Earth, that blue and green globe in space, is a living organism of great energy and beauty. Being a negatively charged planetary body, it was declared female, and because she generated and sustained all living things she was called Mother Earth. Through her oceans and flowing rivers she circulates her life force over seven tenths of her surface and the capillaries of the land. Her mighty digestive system enriches the soil, eventually returning all life forms and matter back to the receptive Earth. The Indians say, 'When the body grows old, the flesh begins to resemble the Earth.' Sometimes she rumbles deep inside and sometimes she excretes hot gasses and molten lava from the pinched up wrinkles of her rocky skin. With the passing of the ages her breathing has shifted whole continents and ocean beds, nudging them to new geography. The ancients knew and understood her nervous system and built temples of healing and worship in quiet places of the spirit; energy sources of such discreet and refined vibration that they became holy places, linked by paths of pilgrimage and trade. The human body contains this same network in the form of meridians, along which foci of energy can be specially photographed as points of light, and stimulated by needles or pressure to heal and regenerate. Through us the Earth becomes self-conscious.

The weather is but an outlet for her emotional nature, and if she cries and rages, floods and erupts, trembles or begins to flip out (or over) we should take notice and learn why. The Earth does have a tolerance flashpoint and is responsive to stress. Apparently there is a limit to how much land can be stripped of resources, coal, trees, vegetation and species and how much air and water can be polluted

71

The Indians say, "when the body grows old, the flesh begins to resemble the Earth."

to support the equation of 'progress, progress, progress = survival'. Apparently we don't know what that limit is, but the Earth does and she's trying to tell us. Now.

There have been many other civilizations which reached great techno-cultural peaks and dissolved into faded records on ancient papyri: thousands of years reduced to a reference, great upheavals retold as myth, folklore based on fact or fantasy. We've never really been sure about any of this, but research by the major Earth sciences in recent decades has placed at our disposal many missing pieces of the puzzle.

Legend, historical records and geological evidence reveal that during the approximate three and a half billion years of Earth's existence there have, in fact, been many reversals of the Earth's geographical poles. They caused cataclysmic upheavals which deluged entire continents, made mountains out of molehills and seabeds, and razed civilizations to rubble and humanity to recurrent grubbing around with stones.

As little as a decade ago, the theory of continental drift (the slow shifting of continents due to weakness in the suboceanic crust) was highly controversial. Today there is agreement on its validity. The theory of terrestrial pole reversal is a similar situation, but more serious in that it is not yet recognized as a controversy by the scientific community, even though the evidence and data are all around. Wandering of the magnetic poles, however, is a well established geophysical fact. Opinion is divided amongst adherents of terrestrial pole reversal theory as to how it happened in the past and whether it occurred simultaneously with magnetic reversals or independently. There seems to be evidence to support both conclusions. This theme is a crucial factor in terms of evolutionary progression. It is the outward change signifying profound inner transformation within the consciousness of life-evolvement. Important prophecies on the subject may mean more if we first discuss the physical basis of their probability.

It might be helpful to start off with a little 'third party credibility' in as much as the late Dr. Albert Einstein endorsed the theory of

73

geographic polar reversal and wrote a 'Foreword' to the first edition of *The Path of the Pole* by Charles H. Hapgood. This impressive work defines a phenomenon of polar shifting which occurs when the rigid outer crust of the Earth undergoes, periodically, extensive displacement over the viscous and possibly fluid inner layers. Einstein wrote in appraisal of Hapgood's treatise, 'Such displacements may take place as the consequence of comparatively slight forces exerted on the crust, derived from the earth's momentum of rotation, which in turn will tend to alter the axis of rotation of the earth's crust.'

In discussing the dynamics of the Earth as a living organism, we will explore reversal of the magnetic poles and how the magnetic field is generated, and the fact that over the years it appears to have weakened greatly. We will present several theories to account for this, but isolate no singular stimulus because all geophysical events are interrelated and of cumulative influence. We will also cite geographical and historical evidence to confirm our assertion that the terrestrial poles have also about-faced, and are likely to give an encore – within our own lifetime. The physical process involved in such a happening is outlined, together with future influences which could contribute to history repeating itself. We shall also touch upon a new theory of rotation.

Magnetic Poles The magnetic poles are not in quite the same place as the geographic poles. In 1975 the Magnetic North was at 76°N and 100°W (980 miles from the actual North Pole.) The South Magnetic Pole was at 66°S and 139°E – 1680 miles from the South Pole. I mention this because by the time you read this they may well be in quite different places. They like to wander around somewhat and during the 100 years between 1850-1950 their customary meandering averaged a mere two miles each year.[1] However, since 1950 (the time when Earth's cooling and increased volcanic activity began) the N. magnetic pole has moved 200 miles – a 400% increase of declination. We find that in 1960 the U.S. Navy's Hydrographic office issued a replacement of the 1955 isognic map because in those five years the magnetic poles had shifted 100 miles due North. The wandering of these poles is now so extreme that maps are updated each five years.

Physicist Arnold Zachow, electromagnetics consultant at Villanova and Drexel Universities, states that it is the locking of the Earth's core to the mantle which is the source of the geomagnetic field. As the Earth revolves it generates a magnetic field along the axis of rotation which both radiates and attracts energy and serves to deflect cosmic rays away from the planet. The strength and direction of the magnetic field are influenced by the speed of the Earth's rotation and also by sun cycles. The greatest perturbations of Earth's magnetism always accompany the appearance of large sunspots as they pass through the central meridian of the sun. This is one of several reasons for the recent slowing down of our rotation and appears related to the extreme wandering of the magnetic poles over the past two decades.

In all parts of the world, rock formations are found with reversed magnetic polarity. Iron oxides in lava or igneous rock are non-magnetic when liquified by extreme heat, but they acquire a magnetic orientation upon cooling which matches the Earth's own polarity at any given time. As they cool they become fossilized into permanent alignment. Archeologists have excavated pottery and shards from ancient kilns the world over which show reversed magnetic directions peculiar to moist clay before firing.

Pioneering efforts to measure this planet's magnetic field at sea began around 1935 and each of the oceans has revealed the same sequence of 171 magnetic reversals, extending back 76 million years. Continuous ranges of undersea mountains wind throughout the depths of the world's oceans. Along the ridges of these submarine ranges there is a spreading of the Earth's crust where molten rock over the ages has gradually extruded, becoming magnetized in the direction of the Earth's prevailing magnetic field as it cooled, leaving multiple layers of sandwiched and alternately magnetized rock. It estabishes a detailed time-scale for past magnetic reversals and accounts for the direction and rate of continental drift, and, possibly, the origin of many earthquakes. [3]

It is confusing to scientists that the great majority of rocks with inverted magnetic polarity are charged up to 100 times more strongly than could have been produced by terrestrial magnetism. [4]

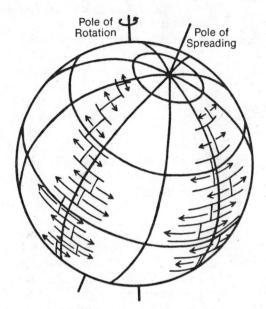

Pole of Rotation

Pole of Spreading

The greatest and fastest areas of ridge spreading occur in most ocean beds closest to the equator, rather as if the globe were splitting like a huge squashed orange, the rate decreasing regularly with distance from it.
This can be attributed to the fact that the Earth is very slightly pear-shaped, being about 30 miles fatter in diameter just below the equator, and flatter at the poles, due to the greater centrifugal force of rotation there. As the Earth expands this way it slows down.[2]

Certainly there is speculation as to the nature of the forces which could involve such massive magnetic exaggeration. Is this evidence that the Earth at one time revolved faster and thereby generated a stronger protective magnetic field? During the past 1800 years the strength of this field is estimated to have fallen to less than two-thirds of what it was.[5] We know that reversals in the magnetic field were accompanied by declines in the intensity of the field, which may have persisted, and that in the last 100 years alone its strength has decreased by at least 10%.[6]

Weakening Magnetosphere This data indicates an increase in the amount of radiation now reaching the Earth's surface from space, because the strength of the protective magnetic shield is proportionate to the speed of Earth's rotation. This is probably all right if we are to mutate and evolve at a satisfactory pre-determined pace, but how dangerous is this trend combined with depletion of the delicate ozone layer of our atmosphere which protects all life from lethal ultra-violet radiation? Supersonic transports, nuclear testing, aerosol use and the clearcut-

76

ting of tropical forests, all foreshadow the conversion of this protective belt to ordinary oxygen. The extinction of whole species (especially marine) has been linked to magnetic reversals. One theory is that the reduction or cessation of the geomagnetic field, which probably accompanied the reversals, allowed lethal amounts of solar radiation to penetrate the Earth and exterminate certain life-forms, or that the resultant weather patterns became inhospitable. Another theory, and one which we personally endorse, suspects irregularities in the Earth's rotation, whereby the glacial ages were sponsored by changes in the tilt of the Earth's axis. As a result, great earthquakes occurred. There can be little doubt that the radical weather changes to which we are all having to adjust, and the increase of earthquakes since 1976, are related to the fact that the Earth's rotation is slowing.

Time-loss The Paris Observatory, which keeps time for the whole world, has been delaying the New Year since 1971. The U. S. National Bureau of Standards has publicly stated, 'The Earth is slowing down enough that extra time is needed to keep atomic clocks synchronized to the spin of the Earth.'

With magnetic shielding greater in the past than at present, Carbon 14 levels would have been much lower. This may indicate that deduced historical dates that are crucial to many of the sciences may contain a degree of error.

Magnetic Pole Reversal Theory The next question is, what exactly causes reversals of the magnetic poles? Scientists still do not know how or why the magnetic poles reversed, only that they did. Polarity within an electromagnetic device can be achieved by reversing the current instead of turning the core over, and a thunderbolt striking a magnet can theoretically effect the same result. The planet *is* a huge magnet, so a short circuit between it and another celestial body transiting the Earth could result in the magnetic poles exchanging places. For instance, we know that tremendously powerful arcs of electrical charges are continually sparking between Jupiter and one of its moons, Io. In the case of the Earth, if the passing sphere were a comet, dense clouds of magnetic debris from its tail could have been electrically charged, the strength of its magnetic field depending upon its charge.[7] This would theoretically account for the increased intensity of discovered incidences of magnetic pole reversal, as well as the mystery of rocks with reversed magnetic polarity up to 100 times stronger than normal.

Michael Papagiannis, an astronomer at Boston University, postulates that the constant stream of energized solar particles which produces the solar wind thrusts on Earthward, causing a torque which can influence the magnetic poles and their meanderings.[8] Dr. Immanuel Velikowsky in his monumental works, *Worlds in Collision* and *Earth in Upheaval*, has a wealth of information and historical documentation on the subject. He provides fascinating evidence to account for a number of these events, which very probably accompanied actual transposition of the terrestrial poles as well: Venus, originally a comet from Jupiter, struck the Earth and the planet Mars several times, causing aerial phenomena and global terror, which are alluded to in the lore of most ancient peoples. These convergent phenomena resulted in Venus' orbital stability as a planet. Mars also encroached upon our planet's gravitational field several times, and triggered exactly the kind of apocalyptic havoc outlined in the Bible's *Book of Revelation*.

The more recent of these occurrences, Dr. Velikovsky links to the plagues at the time of the Exodus at the end of Egypt's Middle Kingdom, around 2,500 BC, again in 1500 BC, and even as recently as 687 BC. In fact, he has researched the most convincing array of cultural documentation to support his assertion that during the 700 years between the last two reversals the year contained only 360 days, and that changes in the Earth's rotation brought the present five additional days into the solar year.

Meteorite Showers and Falling Stars

A report in the *New York Times*, April 12, '59 described the discovery of a layer of ash along the Pacific Ocean floor covering an expanse of 1575 miles, several hundred miles from the coast of Central and South America. Scientific evaluation of the discovery embraced the possibility of falling debris 'from a collision of heavenly bodies in outer space'.

In this connection scientists have discovered that the Earth's geomagnetic reversals were often accompanied by rains of meteorites and tektites. This fact is immensely important to the overall theory of geographic pole reversal as historical accounts of cataclysm, as well as prophecies about the future, include mention of hail from heaven or stars falling upon the Earth like a plague. At least four such occasions have been intensively documented. One particle shower, around 700,000 years ago, left a litter of tektites strewn over an area 6,000 by 4,000 miles.[9] Samplings from the ocean bottom indicate that at least a quarter of a billion tons of these fragments covered almost a tenth of the Earth's surface at the time of the last reversal of magnetic polarity. Scientists also acknowledge that cosmic debris in the form of falling meteors and tektites not only slows the Earth's rotation, but can influence its actual orbit. Don't miss that! This indicates that magnetic and geographical poles probably shifted at the same time. Pioneering marine geologists Billy Glass and the late Bruce Heezen have studied the occurrence extensively, attributing meteoric tektite rains to the impact of a cosmic body entering Earth's atmosphere periodically and at the time of the last reversal of the Earth's dipole magnetic field. It has been established that the rate of magnetic reversal has increased over the decades. Occasionally, the interval has been no more than 10,000 years. Scientific opinion is unanimous that the next reversal would seem to be due. [10] *Time* magazine even went so far as to say that 'another switch is now long overdue.'[11] This 'overdueness' is very likely related to the extreme pole wandering of the last few years.

The surreal or weird events of that book of prophecy, *Revelation*, may become quite plausible when viewed in the correct perspective. For instance, tektite falls and polar reversals appear as 'And the stars of heaven fell unto the earth, even as a fig tree casteth her untimely figs when she is shaken of a mighty wind. And the heaven departed as a scroll when it was rolled together; and every mountain and island were moved out of their places' (Revelation 6:13-14) or 'And there fell upon men a great hail out of heaven, every stone about the weight of a talent ... for the plague thereof was exceeding great' (*Revelation* 16:21) and 'Immediately after the tribulation of those days ... the stars shall fall from heaven and the powers of the heavens shall be shaken' (*Matthew* 24:29).

79

Even minor changes in the Earth's axis of rotation or 'wobble' can affect 'to a surprising extent both the climate at the surface of the Earth and the forces and stresses within it,' says physicist Heirtzler.[12] There seems to be no set linear progression to the Earth's changing dynamics, but rather an interaction and synergistic fusion of geophysical events such as earthquakes, volcanic eruptions, weather changes, solar activity and rotation changes. For instance, within the last few years it has been established that earthquakes of 7.5 magnitude on the Richter scale are either the cause or the effect (we maintain it is the latter) of an irregular wobble described by the North pole of rotation. Since 1900 this rotational irregularity has been measured by astronomers who say that it reaches a maximum every seven years – a period of activity which exactly correlates with peaks of earthquake activity. [13]

We do not know for sure whether radical changes in the Earth's axial spin and the magnetic dipole reversals were simultaneous, but judging by the evidence available it seems very likely. One has to bear in mind that the existence of flying saucers is not officially acknowledged in spite of the now overwhelming evidence that they exist; a decade ago the theory of continental drift was not acknowledged either; nor was acupuncture, or ESP. Venus was

Earthquake energy and mean daily shift of the polar wobble: 'A definite correlation.'

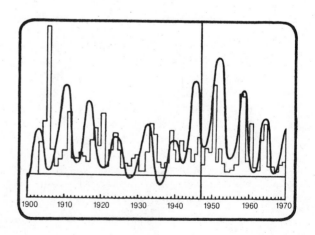

doggedly declared to have a surface of swirling gas, yet Russian satellite pictures have established a solid rocky one. Examples are numerous and a warning to us to keep an open mind.

Geographic Poles

If it is true that the planet's poles have periodically and radically swung around, producing immediate displacement of geological features and climates, the upheaval must have been of gargantuan proportions. We can assume abrupt extinction of countless species and life forms as they were swept up in the folding of ocean beds, ice-sheets and forest cover, bombarded by molten detritus or swallowed by rupturing land masses. Evidence comes from various sources.

Evidence of Pole-Shifts

One would normally expect the great deserts to be in the hottest equatorial regions of the world, but they're located instead considerably North and South of the equator. The ice-ages, contrary to traditional belief in millenially creeping ice-sheets which gradually enveloped continents, are now thought to have taken place much more suddenly; I would even say they were 'ready-made'. In as much as the planet rolled over, its ice-capped poles settled at the equator and evaporation quickly caused icy precipitation at the new terrestrial poles, forming new polar icecaps. Scientific publications contain no scarcity of relevant information about enigmatic discoveries such as the International Geophysical Year's (1957-58) data that oceans all over the world suddenly rose 200 feet 7,000 years ago – a period thought to have been the Biblical flood. Then there are the intactly preserved bodies of mammoth herds found in profusion with leaves and fircones, in the frozen tundras of Northeast Siberia;[14] shells and marine fossils discovered atop the Himalayas and other mountain groupings; fossil trees and coral reefs within the Arctic circle, only 8°15′ from the North pole;[15] quadruped species from both arctic and tropical regions, found buried together in caves and excavations in the United Kingdom and Europe;[16] and literally millions of animals: mastodon, bison, horse, etc. mangled and mingled with uprooted trees which were mined out of miles of excavations along stream valleys near Fairbanks, Alaska.[17] Whales, too, have been found beached several hundred feet above sea level hundreds of miles inland in various parts of North America.[18] The inventory is practically endless.

Historical records also lend an interesting and supportive perspective to this subject and most ancient cultures have something to contribute from their annals. For instance, the Egyptian priests, in relating the history of their people to Herodotus told him (*Enterpe 142*) that the sun had 'four times risen out of his usual quarter', and that he had 'twice risen where he now sets and twice set where he now rises'. Records of the Earth's great cycles were probably preserved exclusively by a hierarchy of initiates, just as profound knowledge of astronomy and astrology was contained within the religious 'mysteries' of that time and embodying those principles of concealed knowledge in which humanity and the cosmos are related (see Chapter 8, *The Great Pyramid*). In the tomb of Senmut, architect to the Egyptian Queen Hatshepsut, the night sky with constellations and zodiac is shown in complete reverse along the Eastern ceiling.[19] Other Egyptian documents are consistent with this theme. Papyrus Anastasi IV, Magical Papyrus Harris and Papyyrus Ipuwer refer to the Earth being turned upside down, the seasons reversed, time disordered and that the sun failed to rise.[20] And in Breasted's *Ancient Records of Egypt* III, Sec. 18, the reference, 'Horakhte, he riseth in the West' appears. Horakhte was the name given to Horus, the sun-God, when he rose in the morning sky.

Sura LV of the Koran speaks of the 'Lord of two Easts and of two Wests'. The Talmud says 'Seven days before the deluge the Holy One changed the primeval order and the sun rose in the West and set in the East (Tractate Sanhedrin), and another rabbinical source says that in the time of Moses 'The course of the heavenly bodies became confounded.'[21] In the ancient Finnish epic poem *Kalevala* we read that 'dreaded shades' enveloped the Earth and 'the sun occasionally steps from his accustomed path.' It also tells of a time when iron hailstones fell (ancient descriptions of the meteorites and tektites scientists have associated with geomagnetic reversals, and similar to Biblical descriptions of hail and falling stars during events which allude to the planet rolling around) and the sun and moon were stolen from the sky, but that after a period of darkness they were replaced by a new sun and moon. The beautiful and intricate creation myth of the Hopi tells of twin beings stationed by the creator at the North and South Poles, jointly to keep the world rotating and ensure stability of land and gentleness of air movement. At the end of the first three worlds they were instructed to leave their positions, and with no one to control it the world plunged into chaos 'and rolled over twice', after which a new world was born.

These references are not entirely restricted to historical data, either. Persons of vision have always been attuned to reality beyond the range of the ordinary senses. Shortly before his death in a San Francisco hospital, in 1971, Murchid Samuel L. Lewis, spiritual leader of the Chisti Order of Sufis, said that the 'sheep had been separated from the goats' and that the world would very soon know about it. This was a Biblical reference to the sorting out of people at the Last Judgement. His grave marker, located in the rolling foothills of the Sangre de Cristo Mountains in Northern New Mexico, bears this simple inscription:

'And on that day, the sun will rise in the West
And all men, seeing, will believe.'

Edgar Cayce the 'sleeping prophet' said in one of his 1932 readings that 'The extreme Northern portions of the Earth were then the Southern portions – or the polar regions were then turned to where they occupied more of the tropical and semi-tropical regions.'

Perhaps such accounts as that of Joshua commanding the sun and moon to stand still (Joshua 10:12-13) are not so far-fetched after all, when viewed in the light of these findings. If the Earth's axis tilted in the presence of a strong magnetic influence, and its rotation continued undisturbed, the sun could appear to lose its diurnal movement for an equivalent number of hours.

Just how relevant all this information is to the planet today remains to be seen. We know that when any resilient object, a planet for instance, spins, it tends to flatten at the poles and acquire an equatorial bulge, becoming increasingly disc-like. When its orbital momentum causes enough torque to transcend its reduced stability forces, polar shifts occur. [22] Combine those ingredients with some unusual planetary alignments and rapid changes in polar ice cover and you have the makings of a very precarious axis!

83

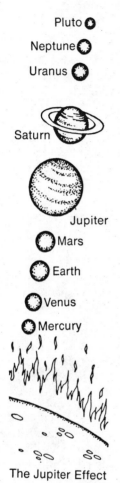

Pluto

Neptune

Uranus

Saturn

Jupiter

Mars

Earth

Venus

Mercury

The Jupiter Effect

1982 Configuration

The process of acquired shape and spin, combined with weight of polar ice coverage and external astronomical influences, *is* thought to cause sporadic shifts in the Earth's axis of rotation. The late Hugh Auchincloss Brown, engineer and author of *Cataclysms of the Earth*, and Chan Thomas, researcher and instructor at the University of California in Los Angeles, have both independently studied the subject for decades and maintain that every few millenia the polar ice caps reach a weight which, aggravated by the Earth's wobble, spins the poles around, causing the shell to slide around its molten layers. Other events, such as the forthcoming 1982 astronomical alignment, would contribute to this tendency. Outer equatorial layers of the rotating globe move at a higher linear velocity than points on the inner layers, but at the same angular speed. If the Earth were suddenly to decelerate because of external celestial influences, the inner layers would slow down or come to rest, while the outer layers would tend to continue rotating, causing friction between the various liquid and semi-liquid layers, and producing heat. The outermost solid layers would be torn apart, causing mountains, and even continents, to rise and fall. [23]

Between the turn of the century and 1970, the South magnetic pole has meandered in a path of 4°30′ in latitude and 17°30′ in longitude *away* from the South terrestrial pole. Meanwhile, the North magnetic pole is moving due North *toward* the geophysical pole – a 25°30′ longitudinal difference and 9° in latitude. According to researcher George Van Tassel, editor of a journal for religious and scientific research, [24] if this accelerated wandering continues at its present rate, the North magnetic pole will arrive at the North geophysical pole in approximately 1992-95. If and when these two poles merge, the South magnetic pole will also be further removed from the South geographic pole, indicating a polar imbalance, based on the laws of gyroscopics, causing the Earth to oscillate. (Any wobble in the Earth's rotation reacts like a top when it slows down.) The weight of the polar ice caps will then create torque, being impelled to the periphery of the spin, or the new equator, perpendicular to the elliptic.

The external astronomical influence most likely to affect the stability of terra firma in the near future is a configuration which occurs

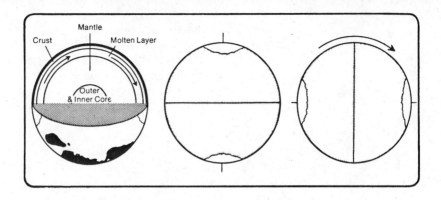

once every 179 years. Around 1982 the nine planets of the solar system will be observed on the same side of the sun. They will not be in *exact* alignment at that time, but close enough to create intense influence. The combined gravitational pull will actuate strong tides and induce great magnetic storm flares on the sun, which will already be at the peak of its 11-year cycle. Again, we stress that sunspot cycles are motivators in human consciousness and affairs, having profound and little-understood psychological influence upon the group mind. Increased solar behaviour during that time will surely affect global weather and could act to reduce the high altitude West-to-East winds, the circumpolar vortex. If this happens it will drastically change the direction of the Earth's surface winds, further decelerate its rotation and precipitate earthquakes. This vortex has already undergone changes which have brought disastrous weather changes to many parts of the world. It doubled speed after the last and largest-ever burst of solar storms which arrived, out of phase and unexpectedly, in 1972 and 1978. Solar anomalies are likely to increase in intensity in the coming years.

The recent publication, *The Jupiter Effect* (Walker & Co., NY) by astronomers Gribbin and Plagemann, confirmed information already known to metaphysicians for decades. They state that the aforementioned stresses will produce severe geostrophic strain on the world's weak or unstable areas. Changes in the position of the geographic poles have been recorded at least four times during this century after major earthquakes. The scientists tell us that the 1982 alignment phenomenon will cause the planet to wobble on its axis, slowing the rotation and generating a jolt likely to trigger massive earthquakes and even a change in pole position.

There is special concern for California, situated on the San Andreas and other fault systems and already overdue for seismic relief. Each of the eight large earthquakes in the San Francisco area since 1836 has occurred within the two years following a period of intense sunspotting. [25] It is the present increasing combination of anomalies, internal and external to the Earth, which conspire to make this particular occurrence of the nine-planet configuration so potentially cataclysmic. Nostradamus, the sixteenth century French visionary predicted a great earthquake before the end of this century. In 1940 Edgar Cayce prophesied a catastrophic California quake for the same period. Paramahansa Yogananda also alluded to the subject, 'You have no idea what a terrible cataclysm is coming.' [26] And Jeanne Dixon has spoken of a big catastrophe for 1983 'more disastrous than anything we have ever known.' She believes it marks the end of an era and expects a messianic figure to emerge at that time. For reasons which will become clear later in the text, a major pole shift is not likely to occur at this time.

Seismic and volcanic activity appear to be inter-related and linked to stress which originates outside the Earth. At a conference on the subject of Atlantis, physicist Arnold Zachow confirmed that energies emanating from the sun produce the solar wind which activates energy currents. They precipitate through the Earth's surface crust, carrying intense electrical charges which filter down into the core. He speculates that when sunspot performance is especially intense there is a jerking of the mantle and core which is, theoretically, powerful enough to sink an entire continent. This is what the authors of *The Jupiter Effect* are saying, too.

There follows some dramatic graphic evidence of existing polar disturbances. At the beginning of this century, the North geographic pole (designated by the intersection of x and y in the following chart) was contained within the centre of the Earth's axial wobble. Since around 1960, however, it has become erratic, rolling back upon itself, creating earthquakes and a decrease in the stability necessary to give momentum about its axis. The North pole is no longer centred within the axial spin, but off to the extreme right of the chart, and the path of the pole is no longer as circular as it was. Correspondingly, the whole pattern of climactic zones in the Northern hemisphere is shifting South at a time when the North magnetic pole is also undergoing extreme wandering – all of which indicates that the Earth's rotation is disturbed and is decreasing, preparatory to a major axial relocation. We now know that the relationship between changes in the Earth's tilt, wobble and the path of its orbit around the sun and previous ice ages are all related to the geometry of Earth's orbit. Serbian geophysicist M. Milankovitch in 1930 said as much, but it was not until recently that there was any evidence to validate his theory.

A New Theory Since 1950 the 400% increase in magnetic polar wandering has helped support the theory that the Earth spins not, as held by traditional science, upon its South polar axis, but upon its magnetically active axis. Let us be quite clear that national boundaries and the lines of latitude and longitude are man-made designations found on globe models only. As the late Captain Scott would attest, it is not possible to pinpoint terrestrial North; we go by our computation of it only. Now, the magnetic dipole is a physical fact with no basis in theory; it actually exists.

Five primary international monitoring stations compile observations on polar motion variations. However, they are each located upon identical geographic latitudes only, so their data is at variance with what is actually happening. In *Voices in Stone* Bernard Pietsch suggests that if stations (necessarily mobile) were also situated at latitudes of identical magnetic dip, more accurate graphs could be obtained. The gyroscopic effect of Earth's equatorial bulge appears to confirm that our planet does spin upon its geographic

87

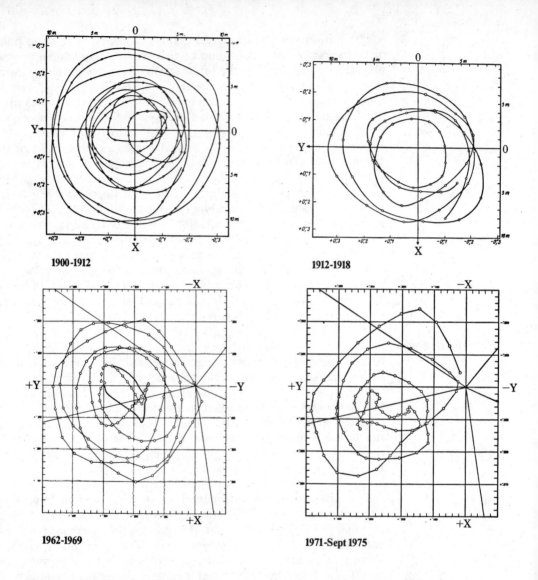

1900-1912

1912-1918

1962-1969

1971-Sept 1975

Graphs of the International Polar Motion Service, indicating deterioration of stabilizing forces which affect the Earth's axial spin, and displacement of geographical North (intersection x and y) to right of centre.

South polar axis, but it is suggested that this very bulge accounts for the wobbling of the geographic North pole when the axis of the magnetic dipole wanders. Advanced translations of geometry from the Great Pyramid appear to substantiate this hypothesis. [27]

PART II The subject of the polar switch lends itself to factual definition, philosophical consideration, and that area of abstraction which lies beyond the vanishing point: the place where logic and intuition briefly merge before translation into the subtler energies of a different reality. In the final analysis, things never happen to us; they happen *from* us.

You may believe the cataclysmic events covered in this chapter to be part of a coincident epic, unrelated to any of the discernable patterns which historical perspective finds most comfortable. But humanity, responding freely within the law of cycles, bore responsibility for events of the past, and will do so again. That's how it is. The first section of this book dealt with the thought-word-action chain, and how, when natural laws are ignored chaos always results. The story continues: all energy contrary to the evolutionary life-force is negatively polarized. It eventually transmigrates to lower and more destructive life and energy forms. The collective negative energy (of thoughts, words and actions) in its varying forms and degrees, descends to the appropriate vibratory frequency of less evolved forms. It can animate and energize bacteria or vermin, for instance, causing epidemics; weather, in the form of storms, floods, and hurricanes; geographical upheavals within the Earth itself, and disturbances from the outer environment of space – all vehicles of negative karmic feedback. This is what Edgar Cayce meant when he said that many a land could be kept intact by the consciousness of its inhabitants. This is also why tampering with nature to modify and eradicate undesirable weather is so useless and dangerous. It's like dispensing drugs to treat symptoms which may or may not disappear, and creating serious side effects in the process. The negative energy will simply manifest more powerfully in another place at another time.

Physical effects are, we acknowledge, generated by physical means. That is all we can directly observe. But these causes are only the visible extensions of a longer line of causation through the subtler realms which have their root source in the consciousness and energy-field of individuals and groups of people.

The world's daily crises of failing food supplies and economies, energy scarcity, expanding populations and dwindling resources, are not the 'acts of God' conveniently ignored by insurance corporations. Ignorance and fear were the culprits, along with their companions, greed, dishonesty and just plain stupidity – a conspiracy of unconsciousness in which we have all held membership. The negative attributes of individuals seemed to become an asset when power and profits got involved and the industrial revolution served as the excuse that was needed to succeed and get ahead at any cost: that was free enterprise. Many have begun to see technology as a usurer delivering convenience, efficiency and profits in exchange for the exorbitant dues of ecocide and human suffering, estrangement from all that is natural. On a diet of natural resources the industrial revolution's technological offspring gave birth to corporations, conglomerates and fiscal networks so powerful that they soon transformed the face of the Earth. Its computerized nervous system crackling with superhuman intelligence it now demands more and more of the failing resources that spawned its genesis. It even inspires aggressive gambling for oil and nuclear addictions.

Perhaps the most threatening of all ideas at the moment is the belief that the right politics or technology can solve our problems. Under the misguided directions of society, they have not only failed at the task so far, but have compounded the problems. As the appropriate model for this culture, the failsafe ways of nature have been regarded as irrelevant and ignored. Physical effects always have their source in spiritual causes. How can a bunch of 'effects' be successfully juggled to correct a 'cause'? When the fire alarm sounds so urgently why are we repeatedly disconnecting it instead of locating the fire?

Those people aware of the crises facing civilization cannot

possibly change them as quickly as is necessary, because the karma
of generations of self-interest and ignorance has begun to shake
loose the foundations of the planet. For the vast and hungry
majority of world citizens, it's time for a change, and it's getting
late. But people *can* change themselves. That's one vital truth we
cannot afford to overlook. Each person can accept responsibility for
him/herself, can become involved in the process of social action,
peaceful change and innovation. Together we can reshape our lives
and our world. It will take all the concerted effort that can be
mustered because there are so many of us now and because it was so
late when we finally woke up. But that's the nature of our sojourn
on this twirling green globe – to learn and evolve, under that
effective and radical teacher, hardship. It's not necessary, of course,
but that's the way its coming down, because the 'Master Plan' for
paradise on Earth has been ignored. Let's find out once again the
laws it comprises and see if we can do it right this time round.

If the cataclysms of the Earth and solar system are, as we assert,
cyclical and according to cosmic and divine rhythms, responsibility
for the present mess still rests with the human race. We alone are
responsible for the degree of potential catastrophe as the Earth's
poles become transposed.

To the extent that people can begin living their best basic values
(irrespective of what others may be doing), break out of the old
non-serving habit-patterns and realign themselves with natural law
and human values to the best of their ability, *the future can be
improved*. We are creating it now, minute by minute. 'If not now,
when? If not you, who else?'

> And by that destiny, to perform an act,
> Whereof what's past is prologue;
> What to come, in yours and my discharge.
>   William Shakespeare
>   *The Tempest*
>   Act II, Scene I

PART III

How Could It Happen?

There are other potential sources which could contribute to our planets's terpsichorean tendency; some are physical, some metaphysical. They include the possible migration of the retrograde Venus, and liberation of the satellite Phobos (meaning 'terror') from its orbit around Mars, since it revolves centrifugally, straining at the leash, as it were. As Phobos is a relatively dense body it would gravitate towards the centre of the system, passing close to Earth or even colliding with it, rather than hurtling off into space. Its direction of travel would be crucial. If it should happen to be in the same direction as Earth's revolution, cataclysm would probably be averted (although you'd probably want to be sitting down when it happened!) However, if it contacted this planet or our magnetic field from a course counter to Earth's spin, all hell would be let loose. Nostradamus, the prophet and physician of France, wrote in one of his quatrains:

> The year 1999, seventh month,
> A great king of terror will descend from the skies
> To resuscitate the great king of Angolmois,
> Around this time Mars will reign for the good cause.

The 'great king of terror' could well be its namesake, Phobos, especially since it is linked in the verse to Mars. Angolmois is a province in central France and this connection is unclear except that it may refer to the point of impact. The last line is a reference which is explored in Chapter 13 (*Astrological Predictions*).

Riley Hansard Crabb, UFO authority and director of the Borderland Sciences Research Foundation, also has information that Mars' satellite will escape, encroaching within the Earth's atmosphere and surprising our planet into a reluctant orbit, out between Mars and Jupiter, and that Pluto may be lost from the solar system. In his remarkable book, *My Contact with Flying Saucers*, Dino Kraspedon describes a similar possibility, according to a conversation on the subject with the captain of a visiting craft from Io, one of Jupiter's moons. Some scientists today believe that this Jupiterian satellite could, conceivably, support life.

Meanwhile, the Hopi prophecies state that the last and final war will be preceded by the appearance of a blue star, far off and yet invisible, which is soon to make its appearance. (Blue stars are even hotter than the sun and extremely rare. Astronomers at Ohio State University have theorized that the 1978 'rediscovery' of SS-433 in the constellation of Aquila is in fact a luminous blue star.) The event is foretold in a song which was sung at the major ceremony in their annual cycle in the winters of 1914 and 1940 preceding the two world wars and again in 1961, just prior to U.S. involvement in the Vietnam conflict. When the 'Blue Star' ceremonial Kachina dancer next dances in the plaza, it will come, they say.

Around 1964, Ramatis, the famed Brazilian spiritualist, predicted the approach of an immense celestial body from deep space close to our solar system. Ramatis divined the name of the ominous visitor as Hercolobus — a name which does not tell us much. But if the phonetics are adjusted slightly to Arcolobus it makes much more sense. 'Arco' means force. 'Lobus' means lodestone — a mineral having magnetic attraction for iron.[28] It was Sir Harold Spencer Jones, the British Astronomer Royal, who first established the magnetic properties of over 100 stars in 1952. The number of magnetic stars discovered since then has increased. Although this body was not destined to intersect any of our planets' orbits, Ramatis declared that it will create serious disturbances in our planetary system during the 1980's and that by the 1990's its overpowering gravitational pull would draw the Earth to a vertical position with respect to its elliptic.

A decade later, on Oct. 18, 1974, the *Times* in London picked up a report from the British scientific journal *Nature*. It describes the discovery of 'the largest object yet discovered in the universe.' Dutch radio astronomers reported a contour-map photograph of an object in deep space out beyond the constellation of Leo Minor, three times larger than anything previously identified in the universe. English astronomers at Cambridge and Leicester Universities have discovered a vast source of X-ray emissions in deep space indicating the possible presence of 'the greatest concentration of mass yet known in the universe [which is] inexorably pulling Earth and the rest of the galaxy toward it.' Our galaxy's orbital drift, moving at 600 kilometers a second, could be due to the gravitational pull of this mass, estimated to be 100 million times greater than our galaxy, says the 1979 *Christian Science Monitor* News Service release which reported the discovery. It remains to be seen whether this object and that of the Hopis' and Ramatis' prediction have anything in common.

Even in the 1940's, the Sanctilian University of California was concerned with the subject and, drawing upon cosmic knowledge, foretold that by 'the latter years of the century' it would be the gravitational force of the Central Sun which would be the mundanely unidentified cause of distortion in the orbits of our solar system's planets, rendering somewhat inaccurate the mathematical computations previously made by astronomers with respect to eclipses. English astronomers at Cambridge and Leicester Universities have discovered a vast source of X-ray emissions in deep space indicating the possible presence of 'the greatest concentration of mass yet known in the universe [which is] inexorably pulling Earth and the rest of the galaxy toward it.' Our galaxy's orbital drift, moving at 600 kilometers a second, could be due to the gravitational pull of this mass, estimated to be 100 million times greater than our galaxy, says the 1979 *Christian Science Monitor* News Service release which reported the discovery. Details differ but the orbital disturbance of our solar system is a consistent theme. The Bible says that disturbances in the heavens are a sign of the 'last days' — but don't let that disturb you. Read on.

Solar Evolution Our sun is the point of emergence through which light and life, mundane and divine, is channelled through the Central Sun from the other intra-dimensional suns beyond. Yugas, the great cycles of cosmic time, are related to the revolution of our sun around the Central Sun. With each complete revolution our sun increases its vibratory frequency, passing the increased energy on to its planets. We are on the verge of an ascending spiral, and this transmission of energy has already begun. We have also noted that magnetic pole reversals are becoming more frequent as time goes by, and that the decreased intensity of the Earth's magnetic field contributed at these times to the increase of cosmic and ultra-violet radiation reaching life on Earth from the sun. This is how evolution is fostered and prospers, through the resultant mutation and survival of the fittest, both physically and spiritually.

Within the evolutionary scheme of things, major moons become major planets, generating moons of their own. There will eventually be a general displacement of all the bodies belonging to our solar system, including the establishment of our present moon as a planet and the arrival of a new moon. This macrocosmic process is analogous to the microcosmic spectrum lines which represent certain jumps of electrons into closer orbits to the nucleus of the atom – a phenomenon as little understood as the evolution of a solar system or the shifting of the poles. It's all to do with transmutation. 'Transmutation' is the science of naturally occurring changes within the atom's nucleus and therefore provides the missing link between matter and spirit. [29] According to the rhythmic pulsations of evolution, each element is not fixed and immutable, but transmutes in its appointed time and way into the next and more complex one. From hydrogen, the simplest element, on up the spiral to the human organism, the most complete and complex, the process unfolds. According to the same Law, the planet itself is like an atom in the body of the universe and is transformed physically by the evolution of its elements and spiritually by the consciousness level of the beings which inhabit it.

Major planets eventually become suns, which in time become super suns. When the Central Sun was a physical plane sun, our sun was one of its planets. In discussing the fact that Earth may be subject to forces which can bring about its displacement into a new orbit, promote our moon to planetary status, bring about a new moon, and leave Pluto to fret somewhere in distant space, the following explanation may help.

In talking of the birth of a new moon, we should point out that areas of seismic activity are located primarily along the edges of the Earth's tectonic plates (loose pieces of crust) which slowly

95

heave against each other until pressure and slippage cause relief via volcanic eruptions or earthquakes.

The Ring of Fire is a circle of volcanic and seismic activity around the Pacific rim which contains about 80% of the world's volcanoes. It coincides precisely with the outline of the central Pacific plate which is slowly edging Northwest against the stubborn thrust of the Eurasian plate. Emerging from the centre of this Ring are the Hawaiian Islands which, measured from the ocean's bottom, represent the highest points on the Earth's crust—500 feet taller than Everest.[30]

A New Moon   The new moon of planet Earth, when the time is cosmically ripe and sufficiently cataclysmic, will undoubtedly be sucked, hurtling molten, into space from that area now defined as the Ring of Fire. The myth of Venus originated in a similar way. She was born, fully mature, from the head of Jupiter, father of the Gods. This can be regarded as a metaphor for the birth of Venus as an errant comet from the celestial body of Jupiter, the largest planet of our system. The enigmatic 'red spot' on Jupiter is the scar of that cataclysmic separation. (Venus subsequently caused terror on Earth and havoc in the solar system until stabilized into orbit as a planet.)[30] Scientists have concluded that Venus was formed in an entirely different manner, or from different material, than the rest of the solar system because concentrations of Argon 36 (an inert gas) a hundred times greater than on Earth or Mars were discovered by the 1979 Venus Mission. We are reminded of the 'Many and various "internal combustions" breaking loose' forecast while Uranus is in Capricorn during 1992-95 (see Chapter 13, *Astrological Predictions*). It is almost too coincidental to mention that this is the same date computed (in *Proceedings* No. 9 of the College of Universal Wisdom in California) for the merging of the geographical and magnetic North poles if magnetic North continues to migrate at its present rate. Should that happen, we're told, polar displacement and associated phenomena would be the result.

A later section of this book dealing with *Earth* discusses the subject of the planetary grid, a network of magnetic force lines similar to the acupuncture meridians of the body. Where the lines

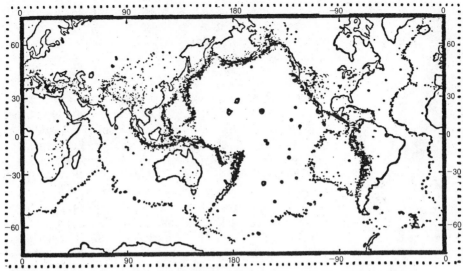
Worldwide distribution of Shallow Earthquakes and Tektonic Plates. The Pacific 'Ring of Fire'.

Tektonic Plate Map

intersect each other there are energy vortexes analogous to the power points along these meridians where needles can be inserted for healing. Well, the Academy for Future Science in Los Gatos, California, through revelation,[31] states that the Earth's magnetic fields are aligned through 'aerials' of magnetic energy marking the points where energies from deep space pour into the Earth's surface. These aerials are balanced on the Earth by the magnetic North and South poles and in the future when solar flare radiations bombard the magnetic points of the Earth, its magnetic fields will be thrown into imbalance, causing a spinning of the shell to new meridians.

The magnetic fields are *already* in a severe state of imbalance, according to Australian researcher Bruce Cathie. In his works *Harmonic 66* and *Harmonic 695* (A.H. & A.W. Reed, London) he lends scientific amplification to the subject by asserting that atomic bomb detonations have occurred at key nodes of the planetary grid, disrupting it with alien energy and creating a massive effect akin

97

to static in the circuits. Many of the aerials mentioned above (whose function it is to keep in alignment the terrestrial and celestial magnetic fields associated with Earth and to channel specific cosmic frequencies into the grid network) have been obliterated.

There is a strong correlation here between the celestial grid associated with Earth and the etheric body which interpenetrates and energizes the human physical body. Psychics see this etheric sheath as a web of fine light fibers. Serious mental and emotional problems are sometimes the result of these two bodies becoming misaligned with each other. When this is the case, and on occasions when electroshock therapy *is* successfully applied, it is thought by some to be due to the shocking of the etheric and physical bodies back into correct juxtaposition. The planet appears to have a similar problem with its physical and etheric fields out of synchronization. UFOs apparently utilize the celestial grid to negotiate interstellar space and it is Cathie's view that one of their main missions regarding our planet is to assist in realignment of the planetary and celestial grids—for their own ends as well as ours.

The strange and sudden reactions of nature, geophysical and climatic problems already covered in this text may be symptomatic of this little-understood imbalance. Perhaps an eventual pole shift will be the 'electroshock' necessary to restore cosmological and biospherical harmony. Information is accumulating, however, that suggests such an event may represent an evolutionary quantum leap *far* beyond the conceptual understanding of a 'mere' field alignment.

A New Time-Space Continuum

We cannot state categorically when these events will occur, but only that they are cosmically scheduled within the great plan of evolutionary unfolding and that they can be logically accounted for right now within our own lifetime.

The Society for the Investigation of the Unexplained, in Columbia, New Jersey, believes the Bermuda Triangle to be one of ten magnetic anomalies spaced equally above and below the equator, which form the major nodes of the grid. Russian scientists, researching magnetic maps of their own, agree but believe the North and South poles should be included to make twelve key 'nodes'.[32] This is valuable backup data for the esoteric information that shifting of the Earth's geographic poles will act to realign these twelve major magnetic vortex 'nodes' with a higher vibrational frequency of existence. In this sense they act like valves to a new time-space continuum; like time-warp locks to the next evolutionary level. The *Book of Revelation* (21:12) describes the New Jerusalem descending from the heavens after the Battle of Armageddon, prepared for residence by the righteous. It has twelve gates, complemental to the twelve power points of the grid which will realign the Earth at its polar shifting with the twelve points of the new dimension, as we ascend into the new reality that descends upon us.

Axial Alignment

Only when all planets of the solar system have their axes aligned with that of the sun, and the sun has its own axis pointing toward the Central Sun (of which it is a satellite) can the sun increase its own vibratory rate and progress towards Central Sun status. This cannot be accomplished, however, until all life on each or any of the planets has cultivated the capacity to sustain that higher frequency, or until life unsuited to it has been removed. This is the nature of today's accelerated changes, the consciousness revolution and the distress which will result from not understanding the process which is at work. The purpose of the Earth's repositioning is more closely to align its axis with that of the sun, and its life with that of the appropriate vibrational frequency for its expanding consciousness. The New Jerusalem, the new heaven and new Earth, are invisibly present. They await us as the new Reality, a world in which we are about to be reborn when we have created our new bodies of light.

Earth as Sun?

'God will call out of the nations of the world a chosen people who will generate a new race to inherit a new Earth that will grow out of the old. It will be a planet of Light, like the Sun, brilliant and fiery, under the direct rulership of God. Man will save himself by generating a new body of Light.'[33]

'For them which shall remain . . . shall be made whole, and they shall be as new. The Earth shall be purified and it shall give forth a *new Light* from the place which is appointed Her within the firmaments. There shall be a new Moon – and She shall have a new Sun, and in turn She shall be a Sun unto lesser worlds – for that is She being prepared.' [34]

Do not then think of the future as 'the end of the world' in the negative sense, but remember that its destructive aspect is but a healing crisis within the natural order of cosmic progression. It is an occasion for the advancement of humanity as spiritual beings, renewal for the planet and evolution for the solar system. A new beginning is stirring even now and all you have to do to be a part of it is to get it together in the best way you know how!

References
1. Emil Sepic, *The Imminent Shift in the Earth's Axis* (125 14th Street, Eureka, CA 95501).
2. *Nature,* March 5, 1960, p. 677.
3. *Scientific American,* 'Sea Floor Spreading', Dec. 1968.
4. *Science News,* 'Paleomagnetism', July 1949.
5. *Science Digest,* 'The Mysterious Earth', Dec 1960.
6. Emil Sepic, *Op. Cit.*
7. Immanual Velikovsky, *Worlds in Collision* (Dell Publishing, 1967).
8. *Science News,* Jan. 5, 1974.
9. *Scientific American,* 'Tektites and Geomagnetic Reversals', July 1967.
10. Ibid.
11. *Time,* 'Magnetic Havoc', Nov. 30, 1970.
12. *Scientific American,* 'Sea Floor Spreading', Dec. 1968.
13. *Science News,* Aug. 14, 1971, p. 108.
14. *Journal of the Philosophical Society of Great Britain XII* (1910), p. 49.
15. Archibald Geikie, *Textbook of Geology,* 1882, p. 869.
16. James Geikie, *Prehistoric Europe,* 1881, p. 137.
17. *American Antiquity V,* 'Archeological Investigation in Central Alaska', 1940, p. 305.
18. Dunbar, *Historical Geology,* p. 453.
19. A. Pogo, *The Astronomical Ceiling Decoration in the Tomb of Senmut (XVIIIth Dynasty),* p. 306 (Isis Press, 1930).
20. E. Erman, *Egyptian Literature,* 1927, p. 309.

H.O. Lange, *Magical Papyrus Harris*, 1927 (K. Danske Videnskabernes Selskab), p. 58.

21. Pirkei, Rabbi Elieser 8, Leket Midrashin 2A, Ginzburg, *Legends VI*, p. 24.
22. Dunbar, *Op. Cit.*
23. *American Antiquity, Op. Cit.*
24. *Proceedings*, PO Box 458, Yucca Valley, CA 92284, Summer 1975 No. 9.
25. *Newsweek*, Oct. 7, 1974, p. 57.
26. Swami Kriyananda, *The Road Ahead* (Ananda Publishing), Alleghany Star Route, Nevada City, CA 95959.
27. Bernard I. Pietsch, *Voices in Stone*, PO Box 1217, Rohnert Park, CA 94928.
28. Rodolfo Benavides, *Dramatic Prophecies of the Great Pyramid* (Editores Mexicanos Unitos, SA, Luis Gonzalez Obregon 5B, Mexico I, D. F. 1968. English edition, Neville Spearman).
29. Louis C. Kervran, *Biological Transmutations* (Swan House, 1972).
30. Immanuel Velikovsky, *Worlds in Collision* (Dell Publishing, 1967).
31. Academy for Future Science, *The Keys of Enoch*, PO Box FE, Los Gatos, CA.
32. *New Age Journal*, No. 5.
33. Gene Savoy, *The Child Christ Codex* (International Community of Christ, 100 N. Arlington Ave., Reno, Nevada 89505, 1973).
34. Association of Sananda and Sanat Kumara, *The Sibors Portions*, Part 1, Box 35, Mr. Shasta, CA 96067.

Part Three
Timetable and Guidebook

7.   Prophecy and Pragmatism

Prediction and prophecy have fallen into disrepute in this century largely because science, with its own built-in aspect of predictability, has replaced the need within the human psyche. Then, too, prophecies in general have had a notorious reputation for not coming true, or for simply fulfilling themselves at the wrong time, in the wrong place and under different circumstances. Sometimes they appear to be plain irrelevant. This did not seem to bother primitive people, with their unreasoning belief in omens; the Gods had simply changed their minds. Even amongst cultures and societies only slightly less sophisticated than our own, prophecy still has its place of respect as an extension of the religious impulse. But, for those brave souls caught up in the age of saran wrap and printed circuits, there seems to be no place or need for the message of such a medium.

The rapid changes of fast-paced urban living and 'nine-to-fiveing' snatch most of us into the freneticism of a Keystone Cops scenario at least several times a week. As the Red Queen said to Alice, 'It takes all the running you can do to keep in the same place. If you want to get somewhere else, you must run at least twice as fast as that!' Is it any wonder that predicting the future has been making a slight comeback amongst those practitioners of 'escapism' who still have enough of that ancient instinctual reliance upon providence? Escapism to some means faster linear progress, as they rush to meet the future with its technological magnificence. To others, it can mean a change of perspective, another kind of reconnaissance through the looking glass.

The trouble with prophecy has always been that the laws of prediction have not generally been understood – even by the prophets themselves. If a stone age tribe (better described as an isolated group of people simply doing their own thing in their own way) came upon a discarded transistor radio and their shaman said it was a talking box and that a certain man would speak through it at the next full moon, he could be right. However, if the batteries were run down or the programme had been pre-empted, the tribe would believe him to have been mistaken. Then, if a neighbouring tribe were to report that a foraging party had come upon an abandoned automobile and their medicine-man had declared it to be a horseless chariot, capable of carrying persons at great speeds, they could think it mighty suspicious if it did not move in spite of his best efforts and incantations. As the tribe moved into closer peripheral contact with civilization and found more artifacts, their soothsayer could soon be in big trouble, even if his divination of the objects were correct.

This analogy holds good for modern prophecy too. Many times the prophetic vision, when received, has simply been too advanced to fit into the cultural matrix of the times. As a result, the description of the vision was couched in such limited vocabulary as to be unintelligible, even to the contemporaries of the times predicted. The story of Ezekiel's wheel in the Bible may have been an account of some subjective weirdness which Ezekiel underwent after a breakfast of wild mushrooms, or it may have represented an encounter with beings from space who were transported from the heavens in a circular craft.

In 1891 E. Curtis Hopkins mused that 'faith is only confidence in the actions of a principle as sure as mathematics'. Knowing the principle or law governing a phenomenon allows a greater margin of certainty when faced with a seeming paradox or lack of substantive detail. For instance, when a prediction fails to materialize, there's a natural tendency to refute its validity. It could well be a dumb divination, but one should also consider that the seer was seeing the future correctly but not understanding it, or interpreting it wrongly. How can a no-show prophecy be true and correct? To a linear way of thinking, this is indeed a contradiction, but understanding certain principles can reveal how, from a different vantage point, the apparent dilemma is resolved.

Free Will and Karma   A prophecy can be averted because of the interaction of the karma and/or free-will of those involved in the chain of events leading to its fulfillment. This is seldom done consciously (unfortunately), but when there's a non-event this is sometimes the reason. Let's say an event was presaged in the year 1910, due to materialize in 1925. That is to say, if circumstances were to unfold as a logical chain of events, 1925 would see the fruition of the prediction. However, the future contains not only that which will be, but also everything else that may be. For instance, it would be logical for the humblest or dimmest of oracles to forecast that a blind man walking in a straight line toward the edge of a cliff will very shortly disappear, over the edge to his death. That is the prediction. However, the blind man could suddenly change his mind and alter his direction, based on nothing more than his personal whim. The prediction would then prove 'false', due exclusively to operating the element of free-will. Taking this same circumstance again, the blind man could avert the prophecy if it wasn't his karmic destiny to 'go' at that time. He might unexpectedly remember that he'd left his dinner on the stove and turn back just as he reached the edge. If it *were* his fate to fall off the cliff, an example of the saving grace of good karma might be that he stepped over the edge as predicted, but landed on a ledge, where he was discovered by a passing sheep herder who led him to safety!

Humanity has the facility of free-will, but is still subject to those whims of fortune known as destiny or fate. The Greek translation for destiny is 'Moira' which also means 'the sum total of one's experience'. Two thousand years ago Heraclitus said it, 'A man's character is his destiny.' From a psychological viewpoint, character could be defined as a combination of heredity and environment, tempered by desires, fears, attitudes and all the learning and acquired marks of personality which make each of us so interesting and individual. These subtly motivate actions and steer our course through life, guiding our destiny within certain flexible bounds. But it is the faculty of free-will, governed by the elements intrinsic to our nature, which enables us to soar beyond these limits and to triumph, in spite of adversity, over our circumstances.

Fate, returning bad karma, the events of destiny, can only be

Grace cancelled by divine dispensation. This is known as the Law of Grace.... A merchant was told by the oracle that he would meet with death in Bhagdad. Not wishing to meet with his fate so soon, and planning to avert the encounter, he travelled instead to a far distant city. And he entered in by the North gate and mingled a while in the market place. Quite suddenly, there, in the crowd he saw Death staring at him with pale eyes, and he was afraid. And death said unto him, 'Boy! Am I ever surprised to see you here; I was just on my way to Bhagdad to meet you!' Apparently the Law of Grace did not come through for our merchant, if it had all would have been well.

If prophecies have any useful function at all it is to reveal a glimpse of the future for examination, now. In life, if we don't like a sneak preview we don't have to see the film. If we don't understand it, we can still attend or wait for it to go away. With a prophecy it's not that simple, but in the case of a particularly fearful augury we can ignore it or try to understand its practical implications. These would be, a) to warn, b) to prepare, and c) to provide an opportunity in the present for changing the future.

The destiny of a nation can be modified by the collective free will of its people, and the fate of a planet can be changed by the collective free will of its nations. And that's what the following prophecies all have in common. Each of them originated at different times from different cultural backgrounds – Egypt, Israel, Japan, the America of the Red Indian and the America of today. What emerges, though, is a single prophecy, a single theme. Different descriptions of the same picture are presented, but the message is clear and the conclusion unmistakable. Earlier chapters have already provided physical/scientific explanations of how these prophecies can actually manifest and why they are likely.

Let us then be warned. Let us also be prepared; and above all, let us realize this opportunity now to work together and influence destiny.

8. The Great Pyramid

'In that day shall there be an altar to the
Lord in the midst of the land of Egypt,
and a pillar at the border thereof to the
Lord. And it shall be for a sign and for a
witness unto the Lord.'
                                    (Isaiah 19: 19-20)

From the most ancient times one structure above all others has inspired and intrigued scientists, archaeologists, metaphysicians and researchers alike. It is the Great Pyramid of Gizeh. As one of the Seven Wonders of the World it is a master work of mathematical precision and engineering excellence. Its inscrutable mystery remains. Like the smile of the Sphinx, it is only partially understood.

The Great Pyramid (named Khufu or Cheops) covers 13 acres on the Gizeh Plateau, three miles southwest of Cairo on the bank of the Nile. It is companion to two others, Khafra and Mankara, and the Sphinx. Authorities differ as to the exact date of its construction, but anyone reading the comprehensive research on the subject in Jalandris' *The Hall of Records* could be left with little doubt that it was built prior to the Flood and/or last pole shift, circa 12,000 BC.[1]

This pyramid was not intended for interment, but was initially used by one of the twelve ancient mystery schools as a centre for initiation into the 'mysteries' of higher knowledge. Each of the chambers and passageways has a specific significance within these rites, which are frequently referred to in the *Egyptian Book of the Dead*. In the long term, the Pyramid was intended as a monument of records and prophecy (4,000 BC to 2,001 AD); a gift to future generations from the masterminds who conceived and built it. Dave Davidson, a structural engineer, was the first to perceive the message of this monolith, in 1924. It took him 24 years to decipher the code.[2] Its records and predictions are written in the language of mathematics, geometry and astronomy, as well as the types of stone used, their colour, layering and the direction in which the passages turn. The numerical chronology carved within its passages does not provide *details* of the events, only the mathematically deducible dates. You don't see the dates themselves carved into the masonry, but dates implied by a time-scale. The events themselves provide the details and the course of history has confirmed their significance and importance. The builders' knowledge was, without doubt, more advanced than our own. Many of the Earth's exact dimensions, which are disclosed by the Pyramid, were not verified by modern science until the International Geophysical Year (1957-58) when the first satellite was launched.

Remarkable facts, unparalleled for accuracy, are presented by the Pyramid's architecture. The pyramidal inch was engraved at the entrance of the structure by those ancient workers to advise posterity of the basic unit with which they worked. Multiplied by 25 we have the correct measurement for the sacred cubit of the Bible. This number, multiplied by 10 million, gives the longitude of the Earth's polar radius. 100 million pyramidal inches is the distance travelled by the Earth during its 24-hour revolution – data now confirmed by modern astronomy. Being a sub-multiple of such figures makes it more of an immutable measurement than the metre or standard inch.

Here are a few of the impressive statistics found within the Pyramid:

1. The sum of the diagonals is 25,825″ mirroring the precession of the equinoxes – 25,826 years.

2. The pyramid represents the solar quadrant, indicating precise dates of the summer and winter solstices, and spring and autumn equinoxes.

3. Although the pyramid's builders antedated Archimedes, the mathematician, by several thousand years, they already understood the Pi formula. The circuit of the base, divided by twice the height produces Pi, which is the ratio of the circumference of a circle to its diameter (3.1416).

4. The height of the pyramid, multiplied by one million, gives 148,208,000 kilometres – their calculated distance of the Earth to the sun, agreed upon by our scientists.

Perfect 'Imperfection' The Pyramid has some apparent inconsistencies and measurements which seem to lack precision. Sceptics tend to isolate them as proof that the Great Pyramid's statistics are contrived generalities and not specifics. However, with the help of a little math or a small calculator the serious student of mysteries *can* reconcile them.

One glaring instance is the widely circulating myth that the Pyramid stands in the exact centre of the Earth's dry land area. If this were true the Pyramid would be located at 30° x 30°. Instead, it is found at a latitude of 29° 58′ 51″N or 01′ 9″ less than the 30th parallel. Its longitude is 31° 09′ 00″E. It is particularly interesting to note that the sine of its North geographic latitude is .4997139. The sine of the 'perfect' centred location of 30° is .500000. Subtracting the former sine figure from the latter gives .0002861. (Again, we would mention that in esoteric numerology it is acceptable to shift decimals and drop zeros.) The result is 286.1 – the factor of displacement.[3]

Precisely described, the 286.1 factor of displacement represents the proportion of a geometrical figure, such that the smaller dimension is to the greater as the greater is to the whole. It is often referred to as the golden proportion or the golden section. Its function is to facilitate advancement or development to higher levels. It is a factor intrinsic to phenomena of the natural world – the helical strands of the DNA, the measured chambers of the nautilus shell, the mathematical precision of pine-cone formation and the delicate spacing of plant leaves as they curl around the stem toward the light. It is the factor of displacement which allows for the possibility of continued development. Without it there is only a closed system and evolution cannot occur. Thus, the Pyramid itself was built at that precise location 'just short of perfection'. It stands as a giant metaphor and tribute to cosmic principle. In Lemesurier's *The Great Pyramid Decoded* (Avon) the 286.1 golden proportion appears repeatedly throughout the Pyramid.

The foregoing is but a token sampling of the kind of information embodied in this magnificent structure which shows how intriguing and profound the Pyramid's message is. It implies that other data contained within its geometry and measurements are also accurate, including the dates of major historical events over the centuries.

The symbolism of the chambers and passageways, with their varying heights, widths and levels, was of implicit significance to the individual initiates of the mysteries in those ancient times. The references, both esoteric and exoteric, are consistent also with the development of the planet. In other words, humanity as a whole must experience and overcome the same trials of life as the individual as he or she personally evolves towards perfection. Being a mathematical model of the microcosm and the macrocosm, we learn many things from researching the Pyramid. There are indications of cosmic harmonics in the heart-beat; human biorhythmic cycles of intellect, intuition, emotion and function appear directly to correlate to the varying depths of each of the corner-stones.[4] The scope of this chapter does not allow a list of them all.

Throughout the *Egyptian Book of the Dead* we find frequent references to the symbolic significance of the Pyramid. Made up of a collection of ancient papyri, this book fulfills the same purpose as the *Tibetan Book of the Dead*, except that it is a manual for the living. More correctly entitled, *The Coming Forth From Day*, it refers to the sacred Egyptian art of 'the coming forth from this life into another'. It is known to the Hindus as 'soul travel'. The initiate's consciousness leaves the body to travel, at will, the

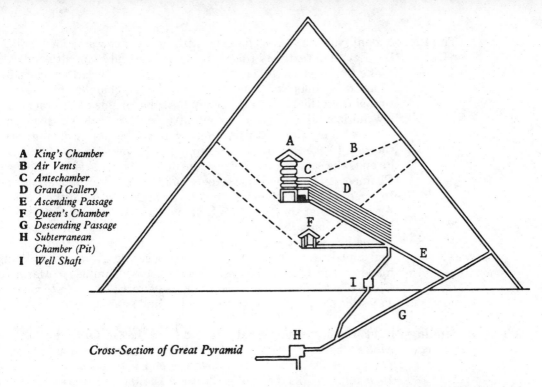

A King's Chamber
B Air Vents
C Antechamber
D Grand Gallery
E Ascending Passage
F Queen's Chamber
G Descending Passage
H Subterranean
   Chamber (Pit)
I Well Shaft

Cross-Section of Great Pyramid

spiritual realms as it normally would after death. (St. Paul the apostle was also acquainted with this facility: 1 *Corinthians* 15:31)

The Descending Passage: Representative of the materialistic life, in ignorance of the higher principles, it passes the ascending passage and steadily leads downward to a state of degeneration and chaos. The chronology of dates shows 2622 BC at the Pyramid's entrance. This is the date of Cheops' death, after whom the Pyramid was named. During this millenium the pole star was Alpha Draconis (Draco the Dragon, see chart p. 48) which ruled over the maxium darkness at the height of the age of night, the midpoint of cosmic wintertime. During this period it actually shone through the Pyramid's entrance and directly down the Descending Passage to the Pit, thus confirming the symbolism of the world in spiritual and intellectual darkness.

113

The Pit or Room of Chaos: A dank subterranean chamber with rocky floor and low ceiling. The Egyptian texts say this room signifies a mad humanity and call it The Chamber of Ordeal. In the floor of the pit is a deep shaft, by which it is thought the initiates entered the chamber by a secret tunnel from the Nile via the Sphinx. At the far side of this room is a low horizontal passage of about fifty feet. It leads nowhere and comes to a dead end. A point of no return. The time-scale indicates the date 1939 at the passage beginning and shows August 20, 1953 at its end (the same date which is indicated at the far side of the King's Chamber). The period spans the second World War and, according to some schools of thought, ends with the transition of the Piscean Age into that of Aquarius.[5] It implies a time during which humanity embarked upon an irrevocable course. The planetary karma had apparently been set by that time. Also, on that date we find bloody revolution gripping Iran, gigantic atomic tests being made by the USSR, the beginning of the Mohammedan war, and China consolidated as a communist country. Jews returned to Palestine after battles with the English and Arabs.

Ascending Passage: Leads to the Queen's Chamber and from the Grand Gallery to the King's Chamber, at the same gradient as the descending passage. It's just as easy to regress as it is to ascend, it tells us. The Egyptian texts refer to it as the Hall of Truth in Darkness. The passage starts with the year 1486 BC, the date when Moses is said to have brought the Law. In this sense it represents the opportunity for humanity symbolically to choose the ascending or descending path. It ends with the date 4 BC which is a slight surprise as one might expect to find the birth of Christ recorded here. In this regard, research has uncovered some rather interesting data – namely, that Jesus *was* born in 4 BC. In 533 AD Dionysius Exigus proposed that the calendar years be counted from the birth of Christ instead of from the founding of Rome. His researches indicated that Christ had been born during the 28th year of the reign of Augustus Caesar. He failed, however, to take into account the fact that Augustus reigned for four years under his own name of Octavian before he was proclaimed Augustus by the Roman Senate.

114

Queen's Chamber:	An opportunity for 'redemption'. It's also called the Room of the New Birth. Many astrological references are implicit in the measurements and geometry of this chamber. The year 1844 marking the founding of the Bahai faith in Persia is one of the more obvious dates here.
Grand Gallery:	Leading to the ante-chamber and King's Chamber. According to the *Egyptian Book of the Dead,* the initiate had to justify his courage and integrity before being admitted to the Grand Gallery, called the Hall of Truth in Light, and referred to as the 'crossing of the waters of life'. Researchers have identified the Gallery as representative of the Christian era, since it begins with the date 30-1/4 AD on one side (representing the time of the Crucifixion which is consistent with the time difference noted in relation to Christ's date of birth) and by emphasizing the year 1776 on the other side, predicted the American War of Independence. The Gallery ends with the date of the First World War in 1914. Possibly signifying the expansion of consciousness which Christ's teachings brought, the Gallery walls are corbelled with seven courses of stone, representing the seven spiritual lokas or planes. There is also geometrical evidence that each side of the Gallery represents 180° and that the two walls with their seven stone layers are symbolic of the 360° of space and the seven planets of the solar system as they existed at the time of the Pyramid's construction.[6]
The Ante-Chamber:	Leads to the King's Chamber. The Egyptian writings call this the Room of the Passage of the Veils, where understanding the mysteries which obscure truth precedes initiation and 'going before the Great Judge'. Immediately prior to this ante-chamber is a perfect stone cube, the Great Step. Here the chronology changes from inch/year to inch/month. With the date 1909 the ceiling of the Gallery drops to about three feet and one can but speculate upon the significance of this date. The Luminous Lodge, a European occult society (of which Hitler was an initiate) believed this year to be a critical turning point between a contractive and expansive cycle of cosmic rhythm affecting world history.[7] It certainly marked the onset of the scientific era. It must be remembered that no thorough research has been done so far on the significance of the

Pyramid's chronology. The indicated dates could range from births of key historical figures, to world events, small trigger-events or turning points in cosmic history, or the intricate workings of the universe as they relate to and influence Earth's destiny.

Each side of the ante-chamber is a small passage, low enough to oblige the initiate to crawl in and out of the chamber. The dates connoted at each end of the first low passage indicate times when civilization was 'brought low' or debased: August 4-5, 1914 and November 11, 1918. These dates cover the duration of World War I. January 31, 1917 is also shown in sequence and is the exact date of the United States' entry into that war on behalf of the allies.

The space within the ante-chamber itself spans a ten-year pause between hard times; the 'period of intermission': from the date on which the armistice was signed to end World War I on November 11, 1918, to the commencement of the great economic depression on May 29, 1928, (the year which also marked the beginning of a major reversal of weather-cycle frequency). Cemented between the walls of this chamber is a prominent stone referred to as the Granite Leaf. Its centre bears the chronological date of September 17, 2001 AD. This is the final date offered within the chronology and the only way to deduce what may be expected on that day is by astrological prediction. (Interpretation of a computerized natal chart ends this chapter.) The second low passage, after the ante-chamber, barely a metre in height but double the length of the first, bridges the years from the end of the Depression to 1936. These were years of intense preparation for the second World War, in which failing economies depended upon armaments manufacture. Nazis, Fascists and Communists came into heavy conflict and revolution in Spain erupted. Stalin began his purging activities and Hitler stomped into the Rheinland. The Egyptian texts describe this passage as a time of chaos and confusion in which spiritual values disappear.

The King's Chamber: This is the topmost chamber of the Pyramid and the system of rooms and passages ends here. The room represents the conquering of death by life; the victory of wisdom over ignorance. The Egyptian sources refer to it as The Room of the Mystery of the Open Tomb and Room of Judgement and the Purification of the Nations. This latter name is an important and accurate description, and one which we are already experiencing. It was here that the initiate came before the Great Judge in a spiritual sense. A red granite coffer, without a lid, is found in the chamber and one source quotes it as being the one-time repository of the Biblical Ark of the Covenant.[8] This is certainly an interesting possibility as the measurements of both are consistent with such a fit. The King's Chamber bears the date of 1936 at its entry and ends with August 19-20, 1953 at the far wall. The date is the same as the blind passage leading from the subterranean pit. As above, so below: whether a person ascends toward the light or regresses into darkness and ignorance, they are affected by the same deadline. Also of chronological significance is the date of March 4-5, 1945, which marks the mid-point of the chamber. On these dates successful laboratory experiments were conducted with the atomic bomb, serving as the basis for the first experimental detonation at Almagordo in July of that year. The first atomic bomb was subsequently manufactured and exploded over Hiroshima in August, 1945. This is a particularly interesting prophecy because the Biblical and Hopi predictions of following chapters both identify this event as the beginning of the 'last days' or 'time of great purification'. This is a key event of major significance.

The King's Chamber is where the actual initiation took place, and the events and times prophesied within the stone chronology there address themselves to the time of the awakening of humanity. From this time on we see the limitation of the Piscean influence declining and the awakened expansiveness of the Age of Aquarius permeating human consciousness.

Pyramid Power and the Initiate At this point it is useful to ask ourselves just what is the mystical nature of four triangles joined at their apex? The function is implicit in the very name: Pyra, from the Greek for fire or flame; Mid, meaning middle or centre – hence, 'the flame in the middle'. This is clearly illustrated in a recent Kirlian photograph showing plumes of light energy being drawn through the pyramids' apexes. By virtue of its shape and ability to draw and radiate energy, the

117

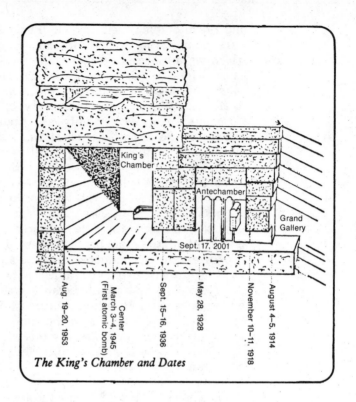

The King's Chamber and Dates

Pyramid helped the initiate to 'pyramid', i.e. to 'peer amid' (look within), and to contact that force of universal energy which was the catalyst in transforming his or her consciousness.

This ancient symbol, used by many esoteric traditions, is basically representative of the Trinity and the spark of life within. Less obviously, it shows the true function of the Pyramid and the transforming power of the 'flame within' as experienced by the apostles on the day of Pentecost, and the mind when aligned with the higher forces.

We know from recent scientific experiments with 'pyramid power' that organic cells placed within a pyramid facsimile will undergo a certain change so that dead cells, as in the case of meat or mummies, will not putrify but become dehydrated instead. This can be done with food also. Meditators experience phenomena such as sensations of heat, colour and time-distortion when sitting within a pyramid structure. Steel molecules will realign if a razor blade is placed North-South within a pyramid, keeping it sharp for 'hundreds of shaves'. Within the Great Pyramid, the coffer itself is placed in a North-South direction, which leads one to seek some correlation between experimental phenomena and the effects upon a person aligned with the magnetic flow during an initiation rite.

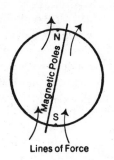

Lines of Force

An Experiment

There is one additional fact to notice in making comparisons, and that is that the King's Chamber and the coffer are off-centre to the axis of the Pyramid. They are located in the same ratio as the heart is to the body. This may be because the magnetic pole of the Earth itself is just off-centre.

According to Reshad Feild, the English geomancy expert, we can experiment with this phenomenon for ourselves: take a glass, half filled with water and run your hand over the top of the glass, about two inches away from it. Move it up and down and from side to side until you begin to detect some kind of subtle reaction after a little while (possibly a tingling of the palm, temperature change, etc). It is the forcefield surrounding the glass which you will feel. If you do this again with your eyes closed you'll find that it is slightly off-centre. Again, this could be related to the Earth's magnetic pole being off-centre. If you repeat the experiment, but decide that when your hand stops the glass will be directly beneath it, in most cases you'll find this to be so when you open your eyes. Now, what exactly is happening? The first time you were totally subjected to the laws of gravity, but the third time, when the head or thinking centre was brought into play, you had the opportunity to adjust the magnetic force-field by will. This concept has most profound implications. As Feild sums it up, '.... Once man has been able to transform the energies of his lower being and surrender himself to the higher force, the lower energies moving through the different spheres activate the latent brain cells which can then redirect the transformed energies.'[9]

We have looked at a pyramid but have not grasped its true function. We've heard its name but not understood its meaning in relation to its form, nor have we known its origin, although it has always been with us. It was Benjamin Franklin who initiated the symbolism of the Great Pyramid onto the Great Seal of the United States. We glance at it daily on the reverse of our dollar bills. Both he and George Washington were associated with one of the twelve mystery schools referred to earlier. They continue to this day and are generally referred to as the 'Brotherhoods'. The inscription beneath the pyramid of the Great Seal bears the words 'Novus Ordo Seclorum' and translates appropriately as 'A New Order of the

Ages'. The eagle on the Seal's reverse side is an esoteric symbol of initiation. A type of cosmic alchemy is implied here. The founders of America understood that the initiation of the nation was at hand.

This ancient symbol, used by many esoteric traditions, is basically representative of the Trinity and the spark of life within. Less obviously, it shows the true function of the Pyramid and the transforming power of the 'flame within' as experienced by the apostles on the day of Pentecost, and the mind when aligned with the higher forces.

Sri Yantra Mantra

In *Rhythms of Vision* Lawrence Blair writes about the study of the interrelationship between wave-forms and matter called 'Cymatics'. The late Hans Jenny built a tonoscope to transform sounds into their visual representation and apparently the universal sound 'OM' produces a circle with the correct utterance of the 'O'. By the time the 'M' fades away the circle has become filled with concentric triangular shapes, identical to the centre of the Sri Yantra Mantra, meditation upon which is said to produce the visual after image of the Central Sun.

From 17th century
Alchemical Treatise

There is a way of manipulating matter and energy so as to produce a 'field of force'. This field acts upon the observer and puts him in a privileged position vis-á-vis the universe. From this position he has access to the realities which are ordinarily hidden from us by time and space, matter and energy.[11]

'The manipulation of fire,' say the alchemists, 'makes possible not only the transmutation of metals, but the transformation of the experimenter himself. The latter, under the influence of the forces emitted by the crucible, i.e. radiations emitted by nuclei undergoing changes in structure (as within Pyramid initiations) enters himself into a new state. Mutations take place within him. His intelligence and his powers of perception are raised to a higher level. He passes to another stage of being, attains a higher degree of consciousness.'[10] The elements, instead of being manipulated *by* the practitioner, as in alchemy, act *upon* and *within* the initiate to the same effect. Humanity is currently undergoing an identical but slower process to the experience of the initiate or alchemist. The spirit of fire, embodied by the light of the Central Sun, is becoming stronger with every day. Those who are ready have felt its quickening warmth within already as their inner being responds involuntarily to the impulse of increasing light.

Contemporary pyramid research has revealed some exceedingly promising implications for the future in areas which pose a threat to civilization:

Food Scarcity – through seed germination, increased plant growth and food preservation.

Pollution – early tests show that pyramid space can purify water, air and soil.

Energy Sources – through generation or enhancement of known and unknown energy fields.

War – peace is dependent upon humanity's greater understanding and elevation of consciousness. The Pyramid shows promise of serving as an initiator of higher levels of awareness. [12]

The Capstone There are many theories regarding the missing capstone of the Pyramid, including that it was solid gold and ripped-off long ago, or that it was the triangular 'stone of truth' cemented into the passage roof behind the granite plug which originally blocked the first ascending passageway. Others postulate that it was used as a time capsule for records from the ancient civilization of its builders and is buried in the Gizeh vicinity awaiting discovery. Physicist Arnold Zachow suggests that if the capstone were made of crystalline copper sheeting, containing a multi-faceted group of crystals, then it could have functioned as a gigantic dialectrical energy capacitor or accumulator.

However, in keeping with the universal law exemplified by this incredible monument to the ages, it is exceedingly unlikely that a capstone ever existed because the base is not an exact square and therefore the apex of the converging triangular sides could not have ended in the perfect point expected of the equilateral sides of a pyramid. This irregularity was built in to the structure in order that its sides might convey certain information.

123

Speaking philosophically of the flat apex, Dimitry Merezhkovsky, in *The Secret of the West*, [13] says, 'if we could contact that eternal reality which lies above and beyond the material object, and of which that object is but a symbol, the material object must disappear in the vanishing point which the apex of the Pyramid represents; and it is only as we thus cause it to vanish that we can pass in consciousness through that point into the illimitable experience of the reality which transcends time and space.'

1953-2001 AD After 1953 the Great Pyramid falls finally silent – with the exception of one more date – September 17, 2001, by which time the mystery will have been revealed and the cycle completed. No retreat or compensation for error is possible after 1953 and one can only assume that an evolutionary deadline has been passed. If the planet's destiny was set by that date, the task now remains of adjusting to the challenge of the intervening years until 2001. Just how we meet that challenge is crucial to the future of civilization. If the architects of the Great Pyramid were as perceptive as we believe, they left to us the assignment of steering the course of the planet through the trying times ahead.

There is complete wisdom, cosmic principle and experiential promise embodied in this structure to provide the answers for survival. We have not been left, bereft, with a handful of dates and symbols. What we have is '. . . an altar to the Lord in the midst of the land of Egypt' – a model of WoMan. They are one and the same.

It is significant that in spite of the Pyramid's real potential for limitless energy, increased food production, and combating pollution, it is not the government who is giving any attention to researching these possibilities. It is ordinary individuals and groups with a shared vision and consciousness who are bringing to light a profound body of knowledge which will make all the difference in the world to the unfolding years between now and 2001 and to humanity's unfolding between now and planetary initiation. We shall write our own destiny; it cannot be written for us.

Legend and prophecy persist that a repository known as The Hall of Records and containing 'the wisdom of the ages' exists beneath the Giza Plateau and within the Pyramid itself. It is predicted that this compilation of records, artifacts and inventions from all previous world civilizations will not be discovered until humanity has become conscious enough to use the information correctly and for the benefit of all. The implications are that the discovery will occur toward the end of our planetary purification at the end of the century so that surviving humanity will have the right knowledge, tools and resources with which to rapidly rebuild and restructure the civilization of the New Age in the wake of the old.

A Natal Chart
Sept. 17, 2001 AD

In order accurately to chart the motion of the cosmic tides prevailing on September 17, 2001 AD, the last predictive date of the Great Pyramid, a computerized natal chart was drawn up for 12:00 noon on that day, according to the tropical placidian system.[14] Three themes emerged from the chart: implications that this date is the time set for planetary initiation, magnetic changes and the final stages of karmic retribution.

The most outstanding feature of this incredible chart is the conjunction of the sun and new moon in the midheaven (symbolizing a new beginning). If you employ siderial astrology (or where the planets are in the sky astronomically rather than symbolically) the sun/moon then conjunct on the Leo/Virgo cusp.

In alchemical texts the sun is depicted as the heart and the moon as the pineal gland or 'third eye'. Sun and moon, correctly oriented in the sky symbolize the 'Grail' which is the holy symbol of transcendental consciousness. In this case, they both conjunct in the sky exactly above the Sphinx which is the image of the Lion of Leo, representing the urge of the creative force. Occultists have attributed the head of the Sphinx to Virgo, the Virgin Priestess, symbol of purification and initiation. The paws have long been regarded as the four fixed elements of Libra, sponsor of harmony and balance. Virgo appears immediately before the second and indrawing half of the zodiacal cycle (as does humanity as the sixth kingdom of creation — see Involution/Evolution chart, p. 53). Libra, represented by the image of the setting sun, shows that the essence of being is projected into the world of spirit, the higher self, suggesting the balance of the subjective and objective consciousness

125

of the initiate. Therefore, both astrological systems allow for a similar interpretation in this case.

Planetary Initiation With reference to initiation, another outstanding feature of the chart shows a grand trine between Mercury, Saturn and Uranus, in air – a configuration which Theosophical co-founder Alice Bailey associated with specific energies affecting the three higher chakras at the time of initiation.[15] It also represents individuation in the Jungian sense, with the help of the Masters. However, such attainment appears hampered by certain emotional Martian energy which has not been spiritualized – possibly in the form of war and/or the complete purging of all back-karma. The soul lesson to be learned here is: 'I and my Father are One.'

A 6-year process culminating in 2001 AD suggests a transformation of our relationship to the sun in areas of magnetism. This is indicated by Venus, reflecting the polarity of Uranus, the planet of magnetism. The opposites of sun and moon, quincunx Uranus, brings about radical change and transformation and indicates a possible adjustment of the Earth's position with respect to the sun, whereby the magnetosphere and magnetic poles would also be changed in direction and intensity. Mercury is conjunct 23° to Arcturus which represents calamities and physical catastrophes. As Edgar Cayce has prophesied that in the year 2000 or 2001 the poles would shift, this event would certainly 'transform our relationship to the sun' which would then begin rising in a non-East location.

The Rainbow Bridge When the poles do shift, it is philosophically reasonable to suppose that the evolutionary upgrading of the planetary vibration will see the Earth's heart chakra (located at the etheric retreat of Shamballa, over the Gobi Desert of E. Central Asia) roll over to take up new residence at the North Pole, thus becoming the planet's new Crown Chakra. The equivalent within human consciousness is consistent with the configuration of Venus in 26° of Leo which epitomizes the law of 'As Above, So Below'. Rudhyar's *An Astrological Mandala* fittingly describes this degree and sign with the image, 'After the heavy storm a rainbow' and relates the linking of heaven and Earth to the covenant with one's divine nature and promise of immortality. (We are reminded that in the Bible the rainbow was given as the sign of God's covenant with Noah after the flood at the end of the last cataclysmic cycle of history.) Hinduism also speaks of the *Antakarana* which is the 'rainbow bridge' whereby awareness is transferred from the heart to the crown chakra of the initiate. It represents the complete uniting of the human and divine aspects of consciousness which enables the harmony of cosmic law to manifest in perfection upon the Earth and within humanity. We have here an astrological configuration which encompasses this complete process, above and below, for the planet and for us.

Realignment of Magnetic Field   Another reference to magnetism as it relates to radiation appears with Neptune placed between six and seven degrees of Aquarius. At 6° people are seen assuming individual responsibility for helping to draw into the mass consciousness releases of transpersonal energy in order to make the hitherto instinctual aspects of consciousness fully accessible. This faculty is the necessary preparation to the 'emergence of new mutations according to the great rhythms of the cosmos'. We're referring to the beginnings of the sixth root race which will populate the New Age when it stabilizes. The *Astrological Mandala*, which can be likened to an astrological *I Ching*, shows the 7° symbolized by a child being born out of an egg - in other words, the cosmic egg out of which the universe is born, and the appearance in the Earth of new beings free of ancestral karma and the inertia of humanity's past patterns. It describes the new being as a product of evolution, a mutant, expressing a fresh projection of the creative spirit of the cosmic whole and free of traditional beliefs and cultural or racial influence. In the chapter on Shifting Poles we discussed the possibilities for genetic mutation from the increased radiation reaching Earth via the weakened ozonasphere and the slowing of the Earth's rotation. And although this appears most frightening, we are divinely assured (see chapter on Survival) that changes in radiation will only attune those who are His to that which He is: divinely improved mutants or high frequency beings who are the product of Revelation and Transformation!

The *Astrological Mandala* reveals that in spite of the intense

127

karmic retribution which the chart indicates, Pluto in 13° of Sagittarius shows that 'it is possible to joyously herald the dawn from high above the actual stresses of existence' but that the New Age will have to deal with a residual of unfinished business from the world of today and the shadows of the past.

Jupiter in exact quintile (72°) to the Sun and Moon, shows that people who undergo severe trials in the name of purification as preliminaries to 'dropping the veil' before initiation, and who experience the energy of their higher consciousness with day-to-day consistency, will be protected and transformed by the intensity of the energies at work.

It is also noteworthy that it is America (whose Sun at 13° Cancer is conjunct Jupiter in this chart) where transformation of the creative forces will begin at the close of the old world order. The 'New Order of the Ages' will first take root on what is now known as the North American continent, and may be known in the future as the New Atlantis.

References

1. Jalandris, *The Hall of Records*, c/o A.U.R.A., 1548 Grace St., Lincoln, NE 68503.
2. Dave Davidson, *The Great Pyramid, Its Divine Message* (W. Rider & Son, London, 1924).
3. Bernard I. Pietsch, *Voices in Stone* (5353 Gates Rd, Santa Rosa, CA 95404).
4. Ibid.
5. Eklal Kueshana, *The Ultimate Frontier* (Stelle Group, PO Box 5900, Chicago, IL 60680, 1963).
6. Pietsch, *Op Cit.*
7. Trevor Ravenscroft, *The Spear of Destiny* (Putnam, 1973).
8. Kueshana, *Op Cit.*
9. *East West Journal*, July 1974, p.6.
10. Pauwels & Bergier, *Op Cit.*
11. Ibid.
12. Schul and Pettit, *The Secret of Pyramid Power* (Fawcett, 1975).
13. Dimitry Merezhkovsky, *The Secret of the West* (Jonathan Cape, London, 1933), p.326.
14. Astro Numeric Service, Box 512, El Cerrito, CA 94530.
15. Alice Bailey, *Esoteric Healing* (Theosophical Society).

9. Meishu Sama and Johrei

In the frozen heart of winter when the snowflakes swirl and settle in the bare branches of the plum tree, the sleeping centre of all natural things stirs with an inner knowing. At that moment in time, nature's unseen finger is turning the Earth around in her elliptical journey, reminding her of cherry blossoms and butterflies, and she allows herself to be drawn once again back to that eternal source of green things, warmth and light.

On such a day, in 1882, Mokichi Okada was born in a Tokyo slum. It was December 23rd; the first day after the winter solstice when the daylight lingers to incubate the summer.

The importance and relevance of this very process in our lives is what Mokichi Okada (later known by his spiritual name of Meishu Sama) came to reveal through his life's work and teachings. Just as winter gives way to summer at the time of the solstice, the frequency at which matter vibrates is increasing as the Earth now enters again the aura of the Central Sun, becoming transformed by its special energies and passing from the old age of darkness into the New Age of light and harmony. 'God created the universe in perfect harmony,' Meishu Sama said, 'with law and order pervading it. Discord of any kind is man-made, and its cause is to be found in the violation of the laws of creation, of nature. If man will only discover and obey these laws which actually govern our existence, will learn to live in harmony with them, everything in this world will go well.' And it was at dawn on the summit of Mt. Nokogiri near Tokyo that Meishu Sama received the revelation that that very day, June 15, 1931, was the actual beginning, within the spiritual realm, of the New Age of light.

Meishu Sama had apparently been purified and prepared for his life's work by working off intense amounts of negative karma in his early life. He experienced a long history of chronic ill health, personal bereavements and fiscal disasters (he was the inventor of the artificial 'morning sun' diamond) so crushing that a man possessed of less endurance and character would have been totally overwhelmed by them. It was not until the death of his wife and third child that he turned from atheism and began his spiritual quest for the meaning behind the extreme hardships in his life. He spent a number of years in intense religious enquiry and finally became affiliated with a Shinto sect, but was never fully satisfied.

Cataclysm as Purification

In 1926, at the age of 45, he entered a state of receptiveness to divine revelation which lasted three months and in which was disclosed to him God's divine plan for the New Age. He was told how he would be used as an instrument for the releasing of divine light, to dispel negative conditions, and for the full revelation of truth in order to prepare humanity for the New Age. 'Seeing truth means to penetrate into the very core of matter . . . To see truth is, as it were, to climb to the top of the pyramid. The higher we climb, the wider our field of vision becomes and the more we can see.' [1] Meishu Sama learned in his revelation that the Earth is going to have to face 'a mighty upheaval, the greatest cataclysm in all history'. He declared that at the event considered as the Biblical 'last judgement' a great cataclysmic action will take place in the spiritual realm followed by a similar counter-event in the physical world which will karmically rectify the mistakes of civilization throughout the centuries. It was revealed to him that humanity is standing at the threshold of a great transitional period, a turning point from the old age of darkness to the New Age of light. (See chart, p. 48.) Divine light is now being released, the tremendous spiritual vibration of which is overwhelming to the negative state that exists in the world today. He was told that only as a person becomes attuned to this higher vibration will s/he change his or her attitudes and be able better to pass through that period of flux. However, to accomplish this, people must be purified both spiritually and physically. It is for this purpose that divine light is being released at this time, so that as many as possible may be awakened to higher knowledge and truth.

'Not only the purification of the human body, but a worldwide purification in every field is impending' said Meishu Sama. 'This means a general house-cleaning of the whole world and the obliteration of the clouds of negativity accumulated during thousands of years.' In his first volume of *Teachings* Meishu Sama declared that 'Extreme changes of climate and weather are all man-made'. He explained that human actions and speech of a violent, destructive or negative nature create clouds in the spiritual realms which gather near their source until (like rain) they are finally dissipated by natural law in the form of turbulent weather or disasters.

Survival through Service

Only individuals with fewer clouds of negative karma who perform greater services in the establishment of the coming 'New Order of the Ages' will be spared in the upheavals. He said this purification is coming to pass according to natural and divine law in order to rid the world of discord, disease and poverty and turn it into a paradise where the old conditions of life will be eclipsed by health, prosperity and peace. And that's what Meishu Sama set out to do – establish a prototype of paradise on Earth.

So, from this foundation of one man's vision has emerged a movement which today is one of the strongest spiritual forces on the planet: The Church of World Messianity. The three cornerstone principles of its approach to spiritual, mental and physical purification are, 1) Johrei – a method of spiritual cleansing, 2) a consciousness and appreciation of beauty, and 3) Nature Farming.

Purifying the Spiritual Body

Meishu Sama taught that every individual has a certain amount of accumulated clouds of negative karma on the spiritual body, created through thoughts and actions contrary to universal law. Normally they are only eliminated when some major purification occurs according to the natural course of events such as sickness, accidents and various problems. Since these clouds are of a spiritual nature, they can only be removed by a spiritual power: the power of the Light. And this is the power released through Meishu Sama. It is called 'Johrei', which means 'purification of the spiritual body'. When directed by one person to another, divine light permeates the spiritual body, dispelling the negative clouds and further awakening

131

the inner being to truth so that the errors which caused the accumulations may not be repeated. The objective of Johrei is not the healing of the physical body (although healings do occur as a fringe benefit). According to Meishu Sama, a person's mental attitude and health improve because the blood, which is a materialized form of spirit is purified. After a person has received Johrei a few times, physical purification begins, usually in the form of elimination of toxins in some manner.

Nature Farming Johrei is also used on seeds and plants. This is the Nature Farming aspect of Meishu Sama's teachings. The basic purpose of this farming method is to bring out the natural energy of the Earth and to utilize the soil itself to its fullest potential. The products of Nature Farming are superior in quality and taste and stay fresh longer. Experimental farms were established throughout Japan in 1953 and today over 15,000 farmers and gardeners contribute nature farmed produce to the growing demand for this kind of food in Japan. Robert Rodale, organic farming expert, and author and editor of *Organic Gardening and Farming*, wrote this after his visit to Japan in 1972:

> Another strong force for improvement in growing methods in Japan is a remarkable religion [non-denominational] known as the Church of World Messianity, which recommends that its million members eat food produced on what it calls 'nature farms'. No fertilizers or pesticides of any kind are used – even compost is frowned upon, but leaders of the church are very sympathetic to the organic gardening and farming idea and say that organic food is preferable to chemically-grown produce. Although the idea of a religious approach to farming might seem strange to some Americans, the ... program is very popular in Japan and also in Brazil, Hawaii and California... Worship centers and shrines [at Atami and Hakone] are an exhilarating experience – they are fantastically beautiful and modern, but also combine the best of traditional Japanese landscape design and appreciation of nature. A new institute operated by the church in Kyoto includes a natural food restaurant and store, a well-equipped laboratory to study the nutritional value of nature-derived foods, and a clinic emphasizing natural healing,

and many other departments seeking to help people find health and happiness. It is a remarkable place.

Actually, World Messianity is an environmentally oriented concept, with particular pertinence to problems that are faced by the people of any highly industrialized society. The fact that this religion is thriving in Japan is an interesting commentary on the resourcefulness of the Japanese in seeking new and different ways to solve their most difficult environmental problems.[2]

Consciousness of Beauty A consciousness of beauty in nature, through art appreciation, environmental improvement, landscaping and floral arrangement was encouraged by Meishu Sama. The magnificent art museum he established in Hakone is one of the finest in the world, and there is a school for flower arrangement – the ancient art of ikebana. Today the members seek to develop their awareness of the countless beautiful things in everyday living, for every phase of beauty contributes to the expansion of spiritual understanding and upliftment.

Meishu Sama died in 1955. He did not live to see the establishment of paradise on Earth completed but he lived long enough to accomplish his goal of creating its prototype.

Is changing the world the impossible dream? The Utopian myth? Well, Meishu Sama looked at it this way, 'God's plan is very interesting for it is just like the seed of a fruit ... the fruit is the world and the seed becomes the center ... and at the center of the seed itself is its essence. Because of this, in order to change the world the smallest seed only need be changed. It is just like throwing a rock into a pond – it creates ripples. In this way, making this world into heaven, the very centre of the centre, the tiniest point – that's where the various changes are made. Make these changes and you create a paradise on earth.'

And those transforming ripples continue – the beautiful sacred grounds of the Mother Church at Atami and Hakone in Japan are the heritage and spiritual focus for hundreds of thousands who practice the techniques he brought for purification, and share his vision. The process of transformation has begun. . . .

133

Meishu-Sama in His Garden
The Sacred Grounds in Atami, Japan

References
1. Meishu Sama, *The Door of the Mystery Opened* (Church of World Messianity, 3068 San Marino Street, Los Angeles, CA 90006).
2. *Organic Gardening and Farming* (Rodale Press, March 1973).

10. The Hopi

The Hopi are a proud and peaceful nation. Since ancient times they have farmed the land and cared for the Earth with diligence and love. Their forefathers knew the Great Spirit and lived in harmony with His laws. The Earth Mother and the Hopi were as one, and the land was productive in response to the care it received. Water, trees and rocks were understood and alive in a special way for these 'peaceful ones', as they called themselves, and to them the Great Spirit entrusted a particular area of land for safekeeping, and for posterity. The Great Spirit said it was the spiritual centre of the continent, and the land was called Tukunavi - Black Mesa.

It was a primal trust which was bestowed, for the Mesa must be tended by its stewards with prayer, ritual and fasting in order that the balance of nature be preserved for the whole world. It was intended to be a holy place, remaining undefiled until the time of the Great Purification, when all the good people would be protected there and the Great Spirit would return to His people once more.

In Northern Arizona, atop the sacred mountain of the Hopis and Navajos, lies Black Mesa, an island in the sky of over two million acres which rises 3300 feet from the desert floor. Today the traditional Indians of these tribes continue to live as their ancestors did, tending their land and growing crops of corn, beans and squash, and grazing sheep and goats. It's a hard life and planting is followed by prayer and hauling water. Only the Indian has learned to cultivate and harmonize with this arid land; mostly rock and sand, hardly any trees. Using a minimum of technology and the intuitive flow with nature bestowed by their culture, they alone have

135

understood the way of that land and come into creative agreement with its harshness.

Tracing the history of these quiet people and the mystery of their lore reveals that the living core of their existence and purpose is identification with their myth. It is lived by the traditional Hopis with fidelity and is preserved intact. The Hopi myth embraces the complete cycle of creation from the beginning of their nation until the time of the Great Purification when the Great Spirit will return. It is very similar to the Christian expectation of the 'tribulation', and subsequent return of Christ.

The Fourth World   We are told that in the beginning the Great Spirit laid out ears of corn before the people who had just emerged into this new world from underground ant caverns where they had been protected during the destruction of the third created world, and while the poles changed places. The leaders of the various groups were invited to select some ears of the corn for the long journey ahead. Because the Hopi waited until last and took the smallest ears they became the chosen ones. The leader of all the survivors (those who had not lost the use of their spiritual eye by wrong living) from the previous world had two sons. The elder was light-skinned and a great inventor. The younger was endowed with an innate understanding of nature's ways and had skin 'the colour of the Earth'. The Great Spirit gave the life-plan for harmony and balance to these two brothers, and the instructions were carved on stone tablets. He told the gathering that in the future, when the elder, white, brother travelled back to the country of the younger, it could be the beginning of the Great Purification leading to the end of the new fourth world, if the life plan were not carried out faithfully.

The various groups were then given instructions about their different languages and foods and their particular form of worship and directed to travel to all parts of the world and to live according to their instructions. The Hopi journeyed to the place where the Great Spirit had lived at the spiritual centre of the continent and in this sacred area they were to pray for balance and harmony and to live within the life-plan which had been taught to them.

The Petroglyph Prophecy Carved on a rock in the vicinity of Oraibi village's garbage dump is a petroglyph that conveys the prophecy of the Great One. It concerns the coming great purification which will mark the end of the Age. The Hopi have always been preparing for this time in their rituals, and fast for three days before their ceremonies. The prophecy tells of the gradual devastation of the Earth's natural processes because of humanity's interference. The Hopis are today concerned for the whole planet and fear that every living thing might be destroyed. They are especially anxious for the spiritual centre and for all people to heed the instructions of the Great Spirit, 'otherwise everything will go down.' Says one Hopi elder, 'If the white man would stop trying to teach us Christianity and begin to listen to what the Great Spirit taught the Hopis, then everything would get back in harmony with nature. As it is the white man is destroying this country.' The tribe pray that their system of ethics and vision will be utilized by the white man in time to avert the complete breakdown in the energy systems which hold the Earth Mother together. The Hopi regard the conditions of their life as a reflection of the rest of the world and the world as a mirror of their life.

This symbol, given the Hopi nation by the Great Spirit, means, 'Together with all nations we protect both land and life, and hold the world in balance.'

The Hopi inhabited Black Mesa 'since the beginning' many ages before the Mesa became known as the 'Four Corners Area' where the white man later designated the borders of Utah, Colorado, New Mexico and Arizona. This symbol also represents the convergence of these states, at the spiritual centre of the continent.

The Great Spirit, in the beginning, told the Hopi that when the white brother eventually returned to the red brother's land he should be welcomed home if he came bearing the sacred symbol, the cross within the circle. If he should come with only the cross the red brother should beware and know that the Great Purification was not far off. The missionaries brought only the cross when they came, and the white brothers who followed brought only oppression.

The Hopi Shield Symbol They knew nothing of the sacred circle.

137

Carved on a rock not too far from Oraibi village is a petroglyph that conveys the prophecy of the Great Spirit. Starting in the lower left hand corner and moving to the right; the petroglyph means roughly the following: The Bow and Arrow are the tools which the Great Spirit (to the right) gave to the Hopi. He is pointing to the spiritual path of the Great Spirit. The upper path is the White Man's path, with two white men and one Hopi to represent the Hopi who adopted white man's ways. The verticle line joining the two paths (just to the left of the first man and circle) represents the first contact between the Hopi and the White Man since the emergence from the lower world.

The lower path is the spiritual path of the Hopi. The first circle is World War I, the second World War II – and the third is the Great Purification, which the Hopi feel we are now approaching, after which corn and water will be abundant, the Great Spirit will return, and all will be well. Notice how the White Man's path eventually becomes very erratic and finally just fades away. The quartered circle in the lower right corner is the symbol for the Spiritual Center of the Continent, which for the Hopi is the Southwest.

The Hopi Life Plan

Prophetic Symbols The knowledge of world events has been handed down in secret religious societies of the Hopi. The leaders throughout each generation have especially watched for a series of three world-shaking events, each accompanied by a particular symbol. These symbols, the swastika, sun, and the colour red, are inscribed upon a rock and on the sacred gourd rattle used in Hopi rituals. Microcosmically, they represent primordial forces which govern all life and are presented to individuals during initiation rites. Macrocosmically, they are symbols used by three 'world purifiers' who bring about circumstances that shake the world and release negative planetary karma. The ceremonial shaking of the gourd rattle, therefore, signifies the stirring of life forces as well as the shaking of the Earth itself. On the rattle, the swastika stands for the spirals of force emanating in the four directions from the sprouting seed. The swastika is surrounded by a ring of red fire – the sun, which encircles with its deep warmth to germinate the seed.

From their sacred teachings the Hopi knew that out of the violence and destruction of each world-shaking and purifying experience, the strongest elements would re-emerge with a greater force to produce the next event. World War II, therefore, championed by Germany and its swastika, merged later with Japan, 'land of the rising sun'. (Naziism, again on the rise, seeks to recreate a greater Reich, including not only the German lands now occupied by the Communists, but also Austria and Italy. According to the *Observer* in London there are strong affiliations within the United States and England. Nazi activity and anti-semitism are again stirring.) When these symbols appeared on the international scene, it was very clear to the Hopi that a major and final phase of world prophecy was being fulfilled and they then released for humanity many of their secret teachings in order to help offset the third and final 'great purification' which, on the petroglyph, is portrayed by a red hat and cloak.

According to the Hopi elders, 'The red hat and cloak people will have a huge population.' They will bring ancient wisdom and sacred texts from the East. Buddhist 'Red Hat' sects have established centers in the U.S. and we are reminded of the prophecy by Padma Sambhava, the great Vajarayana master of the original Red Hat sect in the eighth century: 'When the iron bird flies, and horses run on wheels, the Tibetan people will be scattered like ants across the world. And the Dharma will come to the land of the Red Man.' In its positive aspect this cross-reference of the two prophecies represents an important means of assisting the West's transformation to the higher state of consciousness necessary to avert disaster. If the knowledge is rejected, say the Hopi, the negative aspects of the color red will manifest from the East in the form of an aerial invasion by men who will darken the sky 'like a locust swarm'. This sounds similar to the Biblical Revelation's reference to the great Red Dragon (Communism?) which threatens the nations, and the invasion by 'the Kings of the East' and 200 million soldiers (*Revelation* 9:16).

The forces of swastika, sun, and third force energized by the colour red will culminate in total rebirth or annihilation of all life, say the prophecies.

The Hopi play a central role in the survival of the human race and this delicate sphere upon which it lives, through their vital communion with the unseen forces that hold nature in balance. If they are able to maintain their tradition in accordance with their ancient religious knowledge and instructions, natural forces for the entire planet can be strengthened and sustained since their land on the Mesa is the spiritual centre, the point of energy-balance. Their burden is now heavy as this ability becomes increasingly difficult to maintain. The impediments are enormous. All land and life is threatened, everywhere; the concern of the Hopi is well founded.

Tearing the Land Since 1970 their land on the Mesa has been torn apart and devastated by coal strip mining, and digging for oil and uranium. Many of the Hopi shrines, the sacred foci of their prayer and rituals, have been desecrated. The delicate network of power paths (ley lines, like the body's acupuncture meridians) which radiates out over the Mesa land to keep the energies of the planet harmoniously stabilized have been interrupted and irreparably damaged.

The Heartland Gouging the land for uranium and strip mining is, the Hopi say, tearing at the very heart of the Earth Mother. When this happens nothing can prevent her death throes and the ensuing 'great purification.' This may sound like quaint superstition or a primitive metaphor but there is interesting corroboration. In *Magnetic Fields of the Human Body* [1] Dr. David Cohen reports that the strongest electromagnetic frequencies emanate from the heart and lungs of the human body. Considering the notion that the Hopi land is the heart of the Earth Mother, we read in *Earth Vibrating* [2] that the Four Corners area supports the highest concentration of lightning phenomenon on the North American continent. Dr. Elizabeth Rauscher of the Stanford Research Institute has also informed the author that magnetometer research in that area has detected intense geomagnetic anomalies. Certainly, the author's brief experience of camping in the area was interesting, illuminated as it was throughout the July night by the lightning and thunder of an electrical storm so violent it resembled a Hollywood soundstage.

Atom Heart Mother It is there, at the Four Corners, that the largest energy generating power grid in the entire world is being built to provide electrical power for urban centres such as Los Angeles, Las Vegas, Phoenix, Tucson and the Central Arizona Project. A consortium of 23 power companies and several government agencies has been formed to ensure energy for the development of those areas. The construction of 6 major and 50 smaller power plants is having a staggering impact upon the Southwestern wilderness, upon the Hopi and their Navajo neighbours. Standing there amidst the incredible din which seems to vibrate the very ground one stands on, with the black fly ash raining down on you, it is not hard to equate this power grid to a massive organ, pumping vital electrical life-force over its arterial power-lines to nerve centres in distant cities – a physical manifestation of malevolent subversion.

Strip mining, of course, irreversibly damages the terrain, and pollution controls for coal-fired generating plants are still unsophisticated. Air pollution is now so critical in the area that Shiprock, a spectacular outcropping which was originally visible for 125 miles across the desert before the power plants came, is now visible for less than a mile when the wind prevails from the Four Corners area. Under such conditions the Hopi contine to strive to maintain their simple life style. It is a losing battle.

Cultural Erosion Many of the non-traditional Hopi, particularly the young people who have been educated away from their traditional roots in the white man's schools, were hopeful that the mining would bring financial prosperity to their people. But the older folks said, 'How can we sell this land to accumulate money to buy more land? It is already our land. We cannot buy it again with the very thing that comes out of it. To buy and sell land is not right in the sight of the Great Spirit.' Be that as it may, Peabody Coal Co. (a subsidiary of Kennecott Copper Co.) leased the land for 35 years. Promises of high Indian employment did not materialize and none of the Indians has prospered from the deal. It is economically cheap to use water from the Colorado watershed and from deep wells in the Mesa to cool the power plants and to transport coal in the form of slurry to Nevada, 275 miles away. But water is ecologically valuable in this dry region and the huge amounts required by the plants will have far-reaching environmental effects. The Hopis and Navajos fear, because of the strip mine blasting, that their wells may be damaged and drain out into the lower wells of the power companies. Natural springs are drying up; the water tables are becoming rapidly depleted; rainfall is sparse and access to some traditional watering spots has been cut off by the mining operations.

The Hopi knew long ago from their prophecies that the Mesa was rich in resources, but the Great Spirit had specifically instructed that they not be removed until after the Great Purification. He said the Earth's wealth would otherwise be used for selfish gain and evil purposes. And it has. Today, the Hopi see the Earth Mother's heart being torn open. She is being raped and plundered and they are powerless to protect her according to their trust.

'If the land belongs to the Hopi, why is it being used this way?' you might ask. The Hopi's own Tribal Council was responsible. The traditional Hopi themselves do not recognize the 'democratic' Tribal Council Superimposed upon them by the U.S. government under undemocratic conditions. It serves the interests of government and an estimated 15% (non traditionals) of the Hopi nation. It is the Kikmongwi (hereditary chieftains and spiritual leaders) who are their chosen and traditional leaders. Who really owns the land, and did the Tribal Council have the authority to lease it? The traditionalists feel the land belongs to the Great Spirit and that they are simply its stewards. They would never, under any circumstances sell it. Yet that, in essence, is exactly what they have been duped and forced into.

Leases for the strip mining were covertly signed in 1964 – six years before operations began. John Lansa, Hopi Leader, asserts 'The Tribal Council does this for money. What he (the chairman of the council) did was illegal. The Hopi people did not even know about the contract for a long time. And then the Peabody Coal Company was already on Black Mesa.' Certainly, there were probably errors in translation and gaps in understanding. According to the *Airzona Republic,* 'People were told the coal would be used to produce

142

electricity and understood it to mean they would be getting Johnny Carson at the hogan.' It didn't work that way.

Conflict of Interest

Perhaps the real crux of the matter lies with the Federal Government. The Department of Interior is committed to the development of the Southwest. However, the Bureau of Reclamation and the Bureau of Indian Affairs are also branches of the Dept. of the Interior and were established for the protection of American Indian interests. But we note that the Bureau of Reclamation had partnership arrangements with the Navajo Plant (one of the six major plants mentioned earlier) for 24% of the funds of the plant and needed 60% of the coal from Black Mesa to fire that plant and produce electricity for pumping water for its own Central Arizona Project. Thus, the Department of the Interior is a buyer of the coal and water from Black Mesa. It is also trustee of the lands which it advised the Indians to lease, and of the very resources it buys! Considering the disruption and suffering caused to the Indians, one may well ask if the Bureau lived up to its obligations to protect their interests.

There are no government agencies which actually protect the interests of Native Americans. Cash settlements are sometimes awarded for lands illegally taken by the United States. Land is never returned. On certain rare occasions it may be 'held in trust' by the government for the use of the Indians and for a specific time period. The Hopi have been culturally undermined by this process. In 1951, without the knowledge or consent of the majority of Hopi people or religious leaders, the U.S.-imposed Tribal Council filed a cash settlement claim against the U. S. government for lands and resources taken in violation of a treaty. When the case reached its final stages in 1977 the Indian Claims Commission ignored the petition of the Hopi majority who opposed the idea of receiving money for the ripped-off lands. It bestowed a five million dollar settlement on the Tribal Council anyway. The terms of the illegal settlement barred the Hopi from asserting any ' . . . rights, claims or demands against the U.S. in any future action.' It also extinguished their aboriginal claim to the land as an indigenous people, and, by implication, the use of the lands for religious worship and ceremonial practices.

143

Prayer Routes   In speaking of the ceremonies, which reflect the teachings of the Great Spirit, an old Hopi man says, 'There is a seeing of things that can't be explained. There are shrines out there in the spiritual centre which are markers for spiritual routes which extend in all four directions to the edge of the continent. Through our ceremonies it is possible to keep the natural forces together. From here ... our prayers go to all parts of the Earth. They are the balance that keeps all things well and healthy. This is the sacred place; it must not have anything wrong in it.'

Energy Crisis   Only a few years previously, in the early 1970's, Black Mesa became the cause celèbre of the environmental movement and the public's indignation was thoroughly aroused. But by 1975 the demand for power had increased so much that the utility companies insisted they needed more plants to meet the growing demand (much of which it paid the media to create for them) for urban sprawl, the neon glitter of Vegas, a high level of luxury and unrestricted consumption. Our culture has embraced the philosophy of the cancer cell – growth without limit. Within the concrete stomach of corporate America, the Southwest is being digested with a cold intensity to maintain credence in America's productivity on world markets (in lieu of faith in the dollar) and the obsolete pioneer ethic of expansion and progress. The Black Mesa issue, like yesterday's news, has been assigned to that place where shadows flicker and fade but make no sound – the trash can of the mind. The energy-crisis syndrome has totally swept this issue under the rug: to hell with the Indians' rights, their way of life and sacred land – we need energy. We need profits.

Legal counsel for the Indians is no longer optimistic in spite of the fact that 'the noise, dirt and general devastation of the mining area is incredible!' The Hopi are prepared to hold on bravely although the day-to-day trials of their way of life have become increasingly difficult and legal fees must be spent on taking care of the immediate problems of survival.

Correspondence with the Hopi's attornies reveals that the operations to date have substantiated the fears of the strip mining's early opponents: families have been forced from their homes and grazing

144

lands without any real efforts being made to relocate them. Procedures to compensate individuals for their losses have been established but have never become operational and violations of the lease contract terms by Peabody are numerous. The appropriate federal agencies have not exercised the supervision of the mining company's operations that is necessary to minimize the destruction of Black Mesa and its residents. In addition, the Owen Bill of 1974 deprived the Hopi and Navajo peoples of the right to settle their own disputes over an area of sacred land on the Mesa.

Health hazards to local folk and their livestock are legion.

Exposed coal is igniting, giving off smoke ten times stronger than any city air pollution. Where water, oil and gas are not fenced, livestock have drunk the polluted water and died while more are endangered by contaminated trash and litter being dumped into the mine pits. Blasting noise and dust destroys property and nerves and scatters huge amounts of debris. The movement of personnel vehicles and mine equipment also creates dust pollution which has destroyed vegetation in the area. Accidents and at least one death have resulted from the unsafe conditon of the mining company's road from the Mesa trading post which was constructed without compensation or permission through private Hopi land and interferes with crop growing and grazing. Juniper and pinion trees which took hundreds of years to grow (and are valuable to the ecology of the area) have been destroyed in minutes, together with native vegetation for feeding livestock. Burial sites have also been bulldozed.

Now you know the story of Black Mesa and the spiritual, human and ecological values that are threatened by the desecration of that torn land. In an interview with Jack Loeffler of the (now defunct) Black Mesa Defense Fund, Hopi leader John Lansa spoke these words:

The Prophecies   The Hopi prophecies are drawn on a rock in Black Mesa. The prophecy says there will come a time of much destruction. This is the time. The prophecy says there will be paths in the sky. The paths are airplanes [vapour trails and air lanes]. There will be cobwebs in the air. These are the power lines [giant transmission

145

lines span the desert from Black Mesa to LA and Vegas].

According to the prophecies, 'A gourd of ashes' would be invented which, if dropped from the sky, would boil the oceans and burn the land, causing nothing to grow for many years. This allusion to the atomic bomb would be the signal for certain teachings to be released to warn the world that the third and final event could bring an end to all life unless people correct themselves and their leaders in time. As you will later read, Jesus himself made an identical prediction, and the chronology of the Great Pyramid is very clear about it also. John Lansa continues:

The prophecy says men will travel to the moon and stars and this will cause disruption and the time of the great purification will be very near. It is bad that spacemen brought things back from the moon [Lunar bacteria from an Apollo II core-tube soil sample from the moon killed three types of Earth bacteria in NASA experiments and this is the reason for the now mandatory quarantine procedures for astronauts.][3] The Great Spirit says in the prophecy that man will not go any further when he builds a city in the sky. People are planning to build a space station. When that happens the great purification will come next.

The Great Spirit says that the Hopis will be the only ones left who will remember the truth and even they will be confused. But if they live according to Nature here at the spiritual center of the continent they will survive the great purification. The Hopis are to try and tell people how to live and then each person will decide if he will be a good person or a bad person. The bad people will all be destroyed. Many of them will just die of fright. That is why the Hopi bathe in cold water every morning – to keep their hearts strong. It will really be very bad at the time of the great purification. ['And men's hearts will fail them for fear and for looking after those things which are coming on the Earth.' *Luke* 21:26.]

The Hopis know that you can't treat Nature the way Peabody is or something will happen. There will be a time of many earthquakes or droughts or floods. Many people will get sick and die. The Hopis know this because the Great Spirit told them.

The Great Spirit said, 'I was the first – I will be the last.' ['I am Alpha and Omega, the first and the last.' The prophet John was then instructed to write what he saw in a vision regarding the 'great tribulation'. *Revelation* 1:11.]

So the Great Spirit foresaw it all – the corporate rip-off and its illegal overtones, government's self interest, the disruption of a people, glossed over and diminished by a nation's panic for energy.

Sympathizers are now few, for people wish to justify these travesties in exchange for the illusion of security to placate the spectre of scarcity. The needs of the white power structure leave no margin for individual, cultural or religious respect. The Black Mesa issue is perhaps the supreme example of how far we have come in our delusion, confusion and lack of planning.

The following thoughts, written by friend and working associate, Penfield Jensen, strike at the core of our collective error and mismanagement of the Earth. I quote them here because they sum up the situation with an eloquence hard to duplicate:

Black Mesa is the symbol of all that is terrible and intolerable about our world. The extraction of coal from the flesh of one of the world's last traditonal lands...is criminal when viewed against the backdrop of our global destruction of everything and anything which preaches harmony and integration with the land. What Peabody, the Bureau of Reclamation and Southwest Edison perpetrate against the Hopi, all our technology perpetrates against the species: the destruction of a landscape and a culture in order to create profits (and waste). The Masai, the Indios of Brazil, the Trobriand Islanders, the Bushmen – aren't they telling us something too? What they say is simple. The Earth is our Mother. Start with that. From this common sense of what is sacred can grow what must become the means of our survival: a sense of ourselves as totally integrated with the processes and necessities of the land.

References
1. *Physics Today*, Aug. 1975.
2. Joan Price, *Earth Vibrating* (PO Box 4577, Aspen, Colorado 81611).
3. *Science News*, July 3, 1970.

11. Edgar Cayce

Edgar Cayce (1877-1945) was a modern American mystic. He has been referred to affectionately as 'the sleeping prophet' and as a prophet of the New Age. Today his many readings constitute a massive cross-indexed source of psychic records and associated data which have been compiled for the use of psychologists, students, researchers and anyone who wishes to investigate them.

The Association for Research and Enlightenment in Virginia Beach, Virginia, was founded in 1932 to preserve these records, conduct investigations and experiments, promote conferences and seminars. Information continues to be catalogued and indexed under the thousands of subject-headings as trends and events in the world today confirm and reflect the prophecies of Edgar Cayce. Quotations in this chapter are taken from those indexed readings.

This remarkable man was born on a farm near Hopkinsville, Kentucky, and as a child his talents went pretty much unrecognized, being dismissed as overactive imagination. He did impress his parents, however, by developing a degree of photographic memory when he slept with his head on his school books. Much later, as a young stationery salesman, his voice was threatened by a gradual paralysis of the throat muscles. Doctors had failed to discover the cause of the problem, and hypnosis had given but temporary relief. Edgar recalled his childhood sleep-learning ability and asked a friend to give him hypnotic suggestion, by which he was able to enter a self-induced trance. Much to his own surprise he knew exactly what medication and therapy to prescribe for himself – and was very soon cured.

A group of local doctors heard about his unusual ability and before long Edgar Cayce was diagnosing their patients for them. His trance abilities developed so rapidly that he was even able to prescribe and diagnose for a patient 'in absentia' by purely telepathic means, their name and address being all that he needed. News of Mr. Cayce's skill soon spread, and after the *New York Times* carried a prominent story on him, people from all over the country began to seek his help.

Edgar Cayce was a devoted family man, Sunday school teacher and gifted professional photographer, yet over a period of forty-three years he managed to give over fourteen thousand telepathic/clairvoyant readings.

The changes which Edgar Cayce foresaw in the course of his many consultations were to come on all levels – science and international affairs, social conditions, future-shock, humanity's spiritual growth and understanding of inner reality. All of them are especially relevant today, for it is now that the more important changes of which he spoke are unfolding.

Land and Food The echoes are reaching us that a world food shortage is very close. Changing weather patterns and crop failures within the United States have amplified this possibility to the extent that it has become a daily news item. In 1943, a Norfolk, Virginia, resident asked Cayce if the purchase of a farm was still advisable. The reply was yes, 'because of hardships which have not begun yet in this country, so far as the supply and demand for food is concerned.' At another time he said, 'Anyone who can buy a farm is fortunate, and buy it, if you don't want to grow hungry in some days to come.' Another person was advised in a reading to hold his farm acreage, 'for that may be the basis for the extreme periods through which all portions of the country must pass. . . .'

Other references include advice for returning to the land. In a 1938 interview he stated, 'All that is for the sustenance of life *is* produced from the soil. Then there must be a return to the soil. Every man must be in that position that he at least creates, by his activities, that which will sustain the body – from the soil; or where he is supplying same to those activities that bring such experiences into the lives of all.'

Earth Changes A tremendous amount of information was given by him about future land changes before the end of the century. This would add to the problems of food scarcity, he said, and predicted that the Great Lakes would empty into the Gulf of Mexico in the future. This would appear to be by way of the Mississippi Valley, if the warning comes true. If it does, an important food producing region of the United States will be lost. He said, 'Saskatchewan, the Pampas areas of the Argentine ... portions of South Africa ... these rich areas, with some portions of Montana and Nevada, must feed the world!'

Cayce predicted that new lands will appear in the Atlantic and the Pacific; amongst them, Poseidon, which was one of the five residual islands from submerged Atlantis. (In 1974 archaeological researchers discovered part of this island off the coast of one of the Bimini Islandss in the Bahamas – exactly where Cayce had predicted.) Other lands, he said, will sink.

First Signs During a reading in 1932 somebody asked the sleeping prophet how soon the changes in the Earth's activity would begin to be apparent. His reply was, 'When there is the first breaking up of some conditions in the South Sea [South Pacific] and those as apparent in the sinking or rising of that that's almost opposite same, or in the Mediterranean, and the Etna area, then we may know it has begun.'

The most probable area 'almost' opposite Etna, marked by 'the breaking up of conditions' in the South Pacific is where the Western boundary of the Pacific plate itself breaks up to form the Southwestern curve of the Ring of Fire. Here, approximately between the Fiji and Tonga Island groupings deep sea trenches busily intersect isolated island bases on spearate sections of the Earth's sub-marine crust. The moving sea floor turns down at the trenches rimming the Pacific and deep earthquake epicentres line that downward path where floor material moves under land masses. The Tonga Trench is particularly abundant with these epicentres. It appears to be located on a major node of the planetary grid.

151

Research shows the process of which Cayce spoke is indeed under way with plenty of action in both the Tonga and Etna areas:

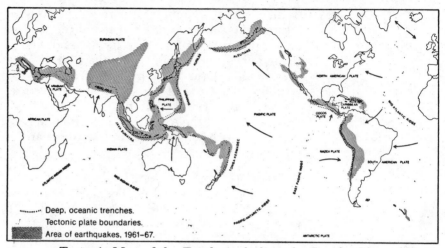

.... Deep, oceanic trenches.
Tectonic plate boundaries.
Area of earthquakes, 1961–67.

Tectonic Map of the Earth, including the Pacific 'Ring of Fire'.

The Tonga/Fiji region is one of the most seismically active locations in the Ring of Fire. In 1967 the Smithsonian Institute reported that a new island thrust up for three months adjacent to Tonga. In June 1977 there was a quake at Nukualofa in Tonga which registered 7.2 on the Richter scale. The Tonga Trench extends in a Southwesterly direction into the Kermadec Trench and here, in 1968, massive seismic activity registered in the Kermadec Islands and was felt as far as Australia and New Zealand. In the Fall of 1975 a series of strong earthquakes was reported in the S.W. Pacific and Bouganville Island, while the adjacent Solomon Islands quaked three times in the Spring of 1977 to the tune of 7.4. During 1978 a temporary island was thrust up near the Solomons and all of the other areas recorded multiple quakes above 7.0 on the Richter scale.

Meanwhile, there has been corresponding activity on the other side of the globe. Mount Etna itself erupted in early 1975, forming a fissure and lava channels on its North face. More violent activity followed in July of 1977 causing a new crater to explode on the Northeast side. As far back as 1959 a Reuters dispatch from Athens reported water levels in several Greek harbours had dropped, exposing the sea bed in places and beaching craft in mud.[1] A more recent materialization of Cayce's warning about this area concerns the water level of the Caspian Sea. It has been sinking, leaving villages and port facilities high and dry. By 1975 half the fish catch had been lost and there is now anxiety that atomic blasting begun by the Soviets (to cut a canal through to the Pechora River, reverse its flow and compensate for continuing water loss) will cause major climatological repercussions. Scientists fear that the reduction of warm water from the river's northward flow could reduce the Arctic Ocean temperature and cause the icecap to expand further (and, we would restate, further imbalance the poles and all the havoc that implies).

Once the chain of geographical changes began, Cayce said, they would be followed by many others. He predicted that the greater portion of Japan (where the Pacific and Eurasian plates thrust together) would go into the sea, and that the upper portion of Europe would 'be changed as in the twinkling of an eye.' He declared that many of the battlefields of that time (1941) 'will become ocean, bays and lands over which the new order will carry on their trade one with another.' He also foresaw that the Earth would be broken up in many places. 'There will be open waters appearing in the northern portions of Greenland, and South America will be shaken up from the uppermost portion to the end.'

Of the United States, he said, 'The greater change will be in the North Atlantic Seaboard. Watch New York, Connecticut and the like. Many portions of the East Coast will be disturbed, as well as many portions of the West Coast, as well as the central portion of the United States. Los Angeles and San Francisco, most of all these will be among those that will be destroyed before New York, even. Portions of the now East Coast of New York or New York City itself, will in the main disappear.'

There was also a timely warning for West Coast residents and one

153

which presages many of the other major land changes. 'If there are the greater activities in the Vesuvius, of Pelee, then the South Coast of California – and the areas between Salt Lake and the Southern portions of Nevada – may expect within the three months following same, an inundation by the earthquakes. But these, as we find, are to be more in the Southern than in the Northern Hemisphere.' Stress along the San Andreas fault (formed by the North American Plate edged by San Francisco, and the Pacific Plate, supporting Los Angeles and areas South) is expected to be released any time by what scientists fear to be another massive and overdue quake. Although there has been no stirring yet of Vesuvius or Mt. Pelee volcanoes, there has been a *very* close call. La Soufriere volcano on the Caribbean Island of Guadeloupe erupted with 'atomic bomb intensity' in August 1976. Mt. Pelee on the northern rim of Martinique is but a scant 80 miles South. Meanwhile, at almost identical latitude on the opposite side of the globe, an earthquake of the same magnitude (Richter scale 0.7) simultaneously hit the Philippines.

In relation to the subject of earthquakes, it is, perhaps, useful to know that the position of Uranus within 15° of the meridian at the time of the large quakes is significant. The stresses within the Earth's crust appear to be seismically triggered by the position of Uranus which is the only planet with an axis of rotation coinciding with the plane of its orbital revolution. (A possible magnetic field would have a different influence on the solar plasma than would the other planets).

Pole-Shift In answer to some questions on historical perspective, Edgar Cayce tapped into the universal consciousness again to confirm that 'The extreme North portions (of the world) were then the Southern portions – or the polar regions were then turned to where they occupied more of the tropical and semi-tropical regions.' While discoursing on the phenomenon of the poles' displacement, we find that when he was speaking of the future of the Arctic and Antarctic regions, this information surfaced. 'There will be upheavals ... that will make for the eruptions of volcanoes in the torrid areas, and there will be the shifting then of the poles.' Cayce said this would occur around the year 2,000-2,001. This is the same year as the last date indicated within the Great Pyramid, so we know an important event is in store for that time.

Safety Areas　Fortunately, some far-sighted people questioned Cayce about which areas would be exempt from the upheavals he was announcing: 'Safety lands will be in the area around Norfolk, Virginia Beach, parts of Ohio, Indiana and Illinois and much of the Southern portion of Canada and the East portion of Canada.' None of these locations has been free of earthquakes in the past. It would seem that we should be prepared to accept the unexpected in these matters, for another person was also told, 'Norfolk is to be a mighty good place, and a safe place when turmoils are to arise, though it may appear that it may be in the line of those areas to rise, while many a higher land will sink. This is a good area to stick to.'

Meishu Sama, the Japanese master, had pronounced in June 1931 that the New Age of Light had officially begun in that month. Although the two men were unknown to each other, their perceptual acuity must have been very similar, as Cayce, in a 1932 reading, said that the New Age had just officially begun.

Naturally, the people who consulted him on these subjects were anxious to know how they should regard the changes that were to come about. He gave a variety of responses on the subject, and a warning, 'What is needed most in the Earth today? That the sons of men be warned that the day of the Lord is near at hand, and that those who have been, and are, unfaithful must meet themselves in those things which come to pass in their experience.' When pressed to explain what he meant by 'the day of the Lord', he responded, 'That as has been promised through the prophets and the sages of old, the time and a half time (a Biblical reference to the time approaching the tribulation) has been and is being fulfilled in this day and generation, and that soon there will again appear in the Earth that One through whom many will be called to meet those that are preparing the way for His day in the Earth. The Lord, then, will come "even as ye have seen Him go." ' When asked how soon all this would be, he goes on record as answering, 'When those that are His have made the way clear, passable, for Him to come.' He was

155

speaking, of course, of those who understand the 'master plan', consciously or unconsciously, and are working for change within themselves and society and on all levels, to make the imminent transitional period as smooth as possible.

'There are those conditions that in the activity of individuals, in line of thought and endeavour, oft keep many a city and many a land intact, through their application of the spiritual laws. . . .' (It is fully apparent to many that California, one of the major hubs of consciousness and overdue for seismic relief, may be just such a case.)

The prophet spoke of 'tendencies in the hearts and souls of men' as being such that upheavals may be brought about in the Earth. These physical traumas will be due, he said, to the 'desires, the purposes and aims' of us all.

When things finally settle down, Cayce foresaw that emphasis will no longer be upon pure biological evolution, but sociological progress in the form of developing human mental attributes. Telepathic communication and full consciousness of the Creative Forces will enable future humanity to use them as an addition to established science, in order to improve the quality of life. A 'new comprehension' and a 'new vision' will emerge from the hectic passage through the remaining years of the century.

'When there has been in the Earth those groups that have sufficiently desired and sought peace, peace will begin. It must be within self.' Mr. Cayce's biographer, Mary Ellen Carter, points out that destiny is influenced by man's will, but there is a time when it is rendered irreversible, by his will.

References
1.   *St. Louis Globe-Democrat,* June 5, 1959.

12. The Bible

'For no prophecy of scriptures ever
originated in the mind of man, but holy
men of God spake as they were moved by
the Holy Ghost.'

(II *Peter* 1:21)

The Bible contains many prophecies and references to 'the fullness
of time', 'the harvest', the 'latter' or 'last days', the 'purification of
the nations' and the battle of Armageddon. God spoke clearly of
these times (and sometimes not so clearly) through his prophets of
the Old Testament, through the disciples who recorded the life and
teachings of Jesus in the Gospels, and through John's vision of the
Revelation. The various Biblical prophecies present warnings to the
reader of the signs to watch for before the finale, so that all who
receive the message might prepare themselves, and be awakened to
their spiritual identity and divine heritage. Again, we stress that it is
not the end of the world, per se, that is predicted, but the end of the
Piscean age and present world system. Preparation is needed to
achieve sufficient faith, strength, understanding and purity to make
the transition to that promised land of a highly evolved and truly
righteous society of the Aquarian, Golden, or New Age. It will usher
in the final stage of the Yuga, the 26,000-year equinoctial cycle and
culminate in bringing humanity into the fourth dimensional or
spiritual state of consciousness. Jesus said that once the signs of the
end began they would all be fulfilled within one generation. We are
that generation.

The Bible records that it has always been God's way to provide
ample time and forewarning before catastrophes or judgements. A
renewal of religious interest and spiritual revival are important
signs of the predicted times, and this is also happening today.

157

The Prophets   In the ancient world of the Hebrew prophets, villages and centres of trade and commerce were scattered over an arid landscape of relentless sunlight and hazy barren hills. The prophets who emerged to stir the pulse of conscience were a remarkable breed of men. Many times wandering between communities and royal cities, they would appear out of the wilderness areas to warn or admonish, help or advise. They were probably a thorn in the flesh of the populace, feared yet revered, as they spoke out against kings, corruption and unGodliness. Through His prophets, God spoke directly in those days to people who would hear and dealt just retribution upon those who would not, or so it seemed. It was a simple affair, uncomplicated by the intricacies of technology and media.

In the visions of the various prophets concerning the last days we see again and again events quite similar, if not identical, to those recorded in the annals of many ancient peoples, several of which are discussed in the chapter on Shifting Poles.

Joel
c. 820 BC   The Earth shall quake before them; the heavens shall tremble; the sun and moon shall be dark, and the stars shall withdraw their shining. (Ch 2:10)

And I will show wonders in the heavens and in the Earth, blood, and fire and pillars of smoke. The sun shall be turned into darkness and the moon into blood, before the great and terrible day of the Lord come. (Ch 2:30-32)

The sun and the moon shall be darkened, and the stars shall withdraw their shining. The Lord also shall roar out of Zion, and utter his voice from Jerusalem; and the heavens and the Earth shall shake; but the Lord will be the hope of his people and the strength of the children of Israel. (Ch 3:15-16)

Isaiah
c. 775 BC   For the stars of heaven and the constellations thereof shall not give their light: the sun shall be darkened in his going forth, and the moon shall not cause her light to shine. Therefore will I shake the heavens, and the Earth shall remove out of her place, in the wrath of the Lord of hosts, and in the day of His fierce anger. (Ch 13:10 and 13)

Habakkuk c. 628 BC He stood and measured the Earth: He beheld, and drove asunder the nations; and the everlasting mountains were scattered, the perpetual hills did bow. (Ch 3:6)

Nebuchadnezzar's dream of an image made of various metals and symbolizing the different 'ages' was recorded in the chapter on Cosmic Cycles. But several years later, in the first year of the reign of Belshazzar, (Nebuchadnezzar's successor as King of Babylon) Daniel the prophet was called upon once again to interpret a similar royal dream (*Daniel* Ch 7):

Four great beasts arose from the sea. The first was like a lion with eagle's wings and turned into a man. The second creature had the appearance of a bear, and the third was a four-headed leopard with the four wings of a fowl. Although there was no specific description for the fourth beast, we read that it had great iron teeth, nails of brass and ten horns. Apparently, it was 'exceedingly terrible and strong' and, like the dream of Nebuchadnezzar, this one also represented the four earthly kingdoms which arose after Babylon – Medo-Persia, Greece and Rome. Daniel said this fourth kingdom, the present era (it passed from military Rome to Papal Rome, and still continues, symbolically) will 'devour the whole Earth and shall tread it down and break it in pieces'. Perfectly logical.

The present civil(?)ization has been responsible for military and ecological destruction on a scale unequalled in the entire span of history. The ten horns of this strange monster were declared by Daniel to be ten kingdoms. Later, this same beast rears its ugly head many times in the *Book of Revelation,* with some modifications, but always with the ten horns. The important role played by this symbolism in our future should not be overlooked, then, since it is emphasized so strongly. These ten kingdoms represent the ten-country limit set by the European Common Market – there are nine members so far.* During the course of the king's dream the ten horns

*In January, 1981, Greece officially became the tenth and final member of this confederacy.

159

were joined by another which had eyes like a man and spoke great things. We are told it/he made war with the saints. Here is the anti-Christ spoken of later in *Revelation*. He will be a world leader who will arise and govern as the personification of evil. Daniel declared he 'will change times and laws' and all authority will be given into his hands, but that ultimately he'll be supplanted by the powers of heaven.

At the time of the end Daniel said there will be a period of trouble 'such as never was since there was a nation!' but that God's people shall be delivered, every one that shall be found written in the Book [of Life]. Yom Kippur, the Jewish Day of Attonement, is celebrated for this reason, so that names may be renewed for another year in the Book of Life.

The Gospels   Several hundred years later, the Gospels were written. They are the nearest to a contemporary Biblical account of the life and teachings of Jesus. The writers of the Gospels, Matthew, Mark, Luke and John also recorded in a first-hand and informal way very interesting information about the people and customs of two thousand years ago. Jerusalem then was the hub of the civilized world where trade routes by land and sea met. The culture was still predominantly Greek with Roman politics and Jewish religion. The political, social and moral attitudes of that time were quite corrupt and not so very different from our own (barring, perhaps, the sexual revolution), and the disciples themselves were originally just plain folk from all walks of life. Matthew was a former tax-collector, and Mark a scholar from a wealthy family. Luke had been a physician and John (who also later wrote the *Revelation*) was a fisherman.

One day, on the Mount of Olives in the Judean Hills, the disciples asked Jesus privately when the end would be, and what would be the signs of His second coming. He was ready to share his knowledge with them and spoke of wars and rumours of wars, of famines, pestilence and earthquakes and that they would be but the beginning of troubles. He warned of religious persecution; false prophets and impostors claiming to be Christ himself, and performing such heavy miracles that even the wisest might be deceived. He said that unless God intervened, humanity would be wiped out entirely, but that for the sake of the 'elect' the time of trouble would be shortened.

Advent of the Atom In his discussion, Jesus also confirmed the visions of the Hebrew prophets, 'Immediately after the tribulation of those days shall the sun be darkened, and the moon shall not give her light, and the stars shall fall from heaven, (tektite showers?) and then shall appear the sign of the son of man in heaven. The powers of heaven shall be shaken' (*Matthew* 24:29). In this passage, the original Greek word for 'heavens' is 'Ouranos' which is the root word for uranium. One could read instead, 'The powers of uranium shall be shaken, and then shall appear the sign of the Son of man in heaven.' Uranium is shaken to produce atomic power. It is a matter of record and certainly a curious coincidence that the first nuclear experiments were known as 'Project Trinity' while the result of that dynamic fusion was code-christened 'Baby Jesus'. This interpretation concurs exactly with the data from the King's Chamber in the Great Pyramid – for exactly in the centre (as the penultimate date before the chronology ends) March 3-4, 1945 is indicated. This was when the first atomic bomb experiments were conducted. Also, the Hopi prophecies say the same thing. In a letter of appeal over the Black Mesa issue, the Hopi elders wrote to President Nixon, 'The Great Spirit said that if a gourd of ashes is dropped upon the Earth, many men will die and that the end of this way of life is near at hand.' Matthew, Mark and Luke each report Jesus as saying right after this, 'Verily, I say unto you, this generation shall not pass away until all be fulfilled.' And it looks verily possible.

'Watch ye, therefore, and pray always, that ye may be accounted worthy to escape all these things that shall come to pass, and to stand before the Son of man.' (*Luke* 21:36). This was His last advice to the disciples on the subject, for He was speaking also of the events concerning the destruction of the Temple of Jerusalem, which came about in 70 AD, and which would have been witnessed by disciples still living at that time.

'And what I say unto you, I say unto all, Watch.' (*Mark* 13:37)

The Revelation   St. John the Divine was the youngest and most beloved disciple of Jesus. He had sat at Christ's side during the last supper, and it was to him that Jesus entrusted the care of His mother, Mary, during the crucifixion. We know that Jesus was aware that John had been chosen to receive the prophetic vision of the close of the Age, because John records at the end of his own gospel that, 'The saying spread abroad among the bretheren that this disciple [John] was not to die; yet Jesus did not say to him that he was not to die, but "If it is my will that he remain until I come, what is that to you?!"' (*John* 21:23). After Christ's ascension, the Roman authorities put the finger on John. His preaching activities concerning the new Christian doctrine posed a threat to the establishment religion and the government arranged for him to be forcibly exiled for apostasy. John was banished to the island of Patmos in the Mediterranean, and it was during his later life that he had the vision recorded in the last book of the Bible as 'The Revelation'.

The *Book of Revelation* is an obvious account of some very real future-shock, detailing signs of Christ's second coming and the events which presage the final judgement of humanity. Although interpretation has always been difficult and unsatisfactory, the veils of mystery are slowly fading, as world events today shed light on much of the allegory. Many volumes would be necessary to explore fully all the aspects of John's amazing preview, but there are a few highly relevant trends forming today which can be related to it.

The Seven Seals   The *Revelation* involves a series of happenings which take place in the spiritual world of the heavens. In the first part of the account, John sees a scroll with seven seals, each of which represents an aspect of retribution that must come to pass before the 'harvest is gathered', i.e. the last judgement when the 'sheep will be separated from the goats'. The seals are opened one at a time and the first four release that famous quartet, the four horsemen of the apocalypse, bringing pestilence, war, famine and death upon the Earth. It is important to know that the seven seals are allegorical to each of the seven chakras of the human body. Chakras are energy centers, valves between the etheric and physical bodies. The opening of each seal also means the opportunity to be transformed and purified by the particular energies released. The fourth seal representing death, for instance, signifies the death of the lower nature as it is transformed by the heart center (4th chakra) to become reborn as the higher self. This is the esoteric meaning of Jesus' statement that in order to enter into the Kingdom of Heaven one must be reborn. The more successful each person is in handling and transmuting within themselves (i.e. within each chakra) the intense surge of purifying energy released by the opening of each seal, the less necessary it is for these releases to manifest in the external world as catastrophe and chaos. The four horsemen are followed by a now familiar scenario, '. . . a great earthquake: and the sun became black as sackcloth of hair, and the moon became as blood, and the stars of heaven fell unto the Earth, even as a fig tree casteth her untimely figs, when she is shaken of a mighty wind. And the heavens departed as a scroll when it is rolled together: and every mountain and island were moved out of their places.' (Ch 6:13-14) and people from all strata of society are panicking and running frantically to the hills and mountains for protection. This would appear to be yet another vision of the reversal of the Earth's poles, accompanied by meteor showers or the tektites which have been scientifically recorded during past geomagnetic reversals. It is possible that pole reversal might be accomplished in two phases, because later in the *Revelation* (16:18-21) when the kings of the Earth are gathered together to do battle at a place called Armageddon, we read, 'And there were voices and thunders and lightnings: and there was a great earthquake such as was not since men were upon the Earth . . . and every island fled away and the mountains were not found . . . and the cities of the nations fell. . . . There fell upon men a great hail out of heaven, every stone about the weight of a talent, and the plague thereof was exceeding great.' (Pole shift meteor showers again.) The 1982 planetary alignment could, in fact, be the physical stimulus to fulfil the former Biblical account of the events described by polar shifting. However, the final phase of shift is likely to come much later (possibly around 1992-95 with Uranus in Capricorn) as the result of something really Earth-shaking, such as a collision with a celestial body, a chain-reaction triggered by atomic war, or the birth of a new moon torn from seismic upheaval in the Pacific depths. Any of these could be the Earthly counterpart of the conflict originating in the spiritual

163

realms as the 'Battle of Armageddon'. Meishu Sama also referred to this final conflict as the necessary culmination of negative karma before the New Age can really be established on the Earth plane.

Before the seventh seal is opened, an angel commands with a loud voice, 'Hurt not the Earth, neither the sea, nor the trees, till we have sealed the servants of our God in their foreheads' (Ch 7:3). This 'seal of the living God' is represented by development of the spiritual or third eye governed by the pineal gland—the sixth 'Ajna' chakra. Once God-awareness has begun, this gland is activated and the spiritual eye begins to open to the light. (Jesus said, 'If thine eye be single, thy whole body shall be full of light' *Matthew* 6:22). It is important to remember that those with this 'seal' will be under divine protection in the future. And from *Revelation* 3:16 we understand that it is necessary for one to make a stand in the matter: 'So then, because thou are lukewarm, and neither cold nor hot, I will spue you out of my mouth.' A commitment is necessary, because a person is either 'on the path' or in the mass consciousness.

As the seventh seal is removed, John reports silence in heaven for half an hour before seven more tribulations are poured out, as a warning from God, to destroy a third of the Earth and its inhabitants: hail and fire mingled with blood burn up the vegetation, and 'a great mountain, burning with fire, was cast into the sea' so that a third of the sea and its creatures were turned to blood. Later when this plague returns again in full force, everything in the sea dies and the rivers and fountains become blood. There are a few historical records extant of the rivers and seas turning to blood. The phenomenon appears to have been associated with the fall of ferruginous particles or other soluble pigment from meteorite dust when an errant meteor or comet neared the Earth. The Hopi prophecies state, 'The whole world will shake and turn red...' Manuscript Quiché of the Mayas has recorded that the rivers turned to blood in the days of a great cataclysm when the Earth quaked and the sun's path was disturbed. The Egyptian Papyrus Ipuwer, which contained an account of the sun failing to rise, also mentions that the rivers were blood.[1] Babylonians also recorded red rain falling from the sky.[2] Nostradamus predicted 'reddened water' after 1999 when the 'great King of Terror descends from the skies'. This would tend to corroborate that a cyclical phenomenon is being foreseen by John, one which has actually happened before in historical times. He may even have been clairvoyantly viewing the closing events of a previous world epoch (the Akashic records). Meanwhile, back in the 20th century, red mud has been floating offshore along the Tuscan coast.[3]

'And the third angel sounded and there fell a great star from heaven, burning as it were a lamp, and it fell upon the third part of the rivers . . .' (Ch 8:10). As the fourth angel sounded, '. . . the third part of the sun was smitten and the third part of the moon, and the third part of the stars; so as the third part of them was darkened, and the day shone not for a third part of it, and the night likewise.' (Ch 8:12).

Seal of Protection   Later, as the fifth angel sounds, 'I saw a star fall from heaven unto the Earth; and to him was given the key of the bottomless pit . . . And there arose a smoke out of the pit, as the smoke of a great furnace; and the sun and the air were darkened by reason of the smoke of the pit.' Locusts swarmed out of this pit and tormented for five months all who did not have God's seal of protection in their foreheads. Although scholars put different interpretations upon this scenario, we are personally reminded of the Hopi prophecy concerning the people symbolized by the color red who invade 'like a swarm of locusts', darkening the sky with their numbers. The national flag of Red China sports a huge 'master' star with its four satellites against a red background. Could this be the time of a celestial body's collision with the Earth? Perhaps an immense nuclear detonation and/or Communist invasion is what the Prophet beheld. Nostradamus refers to a yellow race sweeping across Europe around the end of the century.

John says the pain inflicted by the tails of the locusts was far worse than a scorpion sting; the torment would be so severe that many would try to commit suicide. We read that the shapes of the locusts were like horses prepared for battle, that they had men's faces and the hair of women. Their breastplates were iron and the

165

noise of their wings was like many chariots running in battle. Modern interpreters compare this description and noise to Scorpion or Cobra helicopters and the means of torment to a form of germ warfare or nerve gas. A new era of chemical weaponry is even now being planned as the Pentagon seeks financing for its new 'binary' nerve gas weapon. The Soviets are, apparently, equally prepared. The Defense Intelligence Agency recently divulged that about half of the stockpiled Russian missiles and bombs carry mustard gas and 'V' gas which affects humans as DDT does insects.[4]

Ionized Winds and Insects

Alternatively, if we go along with the premise that most of the catastrophic conditions prophesied are related to the Earth's imbalance and axial change, the reference to locusts or an insect pestilence could be quite literal. (Drought in Africa has already caused one of history's worst locust plagues.) Atmospheric changes are the source of rapid proliferation of bacteria and insects. During the first few days of an electrically-charged wind[5] moving toward a low pressure centre there are outbreaks of vermin and insect eruptions. Scotland's Findhorn Community was advised by Paul Solomon (a respected teacher known for his ability to contact universal consciousness in much the same way as Edgar Cayce) to make friends with the local seagulls in order to receive their help in coping with severe insect infestations in the future. Massive electrical winds would be generated by shock waves from a celestial body colliding with, or passing close to, the Earth, which could account for an unusual and deadly insect plague. Insects, you will recall, are even now assuming plague proportions because of increasing immunity to pesticides.

The first seven trials just mentioned are a taste of even more intense ones which follow later, and are a preview of what is to come if humanity continues along its same course, ignoring natural law and divine will. For God says, 'As many as I love, I rebuke and chasten: be zealous therefore, and repent. Behold I stand at the door and knock. If any man hear my voice and open the door, I will come in to him, and will sup with him and he with me.' (Ch 3:19-20).

Then, later, '... There fell a noisome and grievous sore upon the men which had the mark of the Beast...' (Ch 16:2) and again, in verses 8 and 11 when the sun is 'totally smitten' scorching men with fire and sores. This could well be related to the prediction by scientists of an increase in skin cancer if the ozonasphere is allowed to continue deteriorating through man-made causes. Also, with the Earth's rotation slowing down, more intense ultra-violet will filter through the magnetosphere, with the same result.

Common Market At the beginning of the thirteenth chapter, John is standing on the shore by the sea as a beast with seven heads and ten crowned horns rears its ugly heads from the depths. It is a composite of the same monsters recorded by Daniel 2500 years earlier in his translations of the Babylonian Kings' dreams. Partly leopard, with feet of a bear and the mouth of a lion, it receives authority and power from Satan. As before, the parts of this beast symbolize the succession of worldly empires. Its ten horns represent the 10 nations of the confederacy over which the Beast will rule during the tribulation. The great red dragon of chapter 12:3 and the scarlet beast of 17:3 also have seven heads and ten horns and represent the modern 'Babylon' or worldly power, epitomized, as it probably will be, by the future full-blown functioning of the European Economic Community or Common Market. The horny beast will be represented by a powerful political leader, the Anti-Christ, identified as Beast 666. He is the mature growth of the serpent in the Garden of Eden—the instigator of humanity's fall from grace. He was fed by human acceptance and grew accordingly. He will temporarily solve many desperate world problems and gain tremendous popularity. However, he'll be a vehicle of the negative force—a man of deceptive charisma and hidden demonic power. Under his auspices the Jews will be enabled to rebuild their Temple. John tells us this anti-Christ will affiliate with an equally powerful false prophet or religious figurehead. Like the wolf in sheep's clothing, he will be exceedingly cunning, and brilliant, and attain enthusiastic acceptance by the masses when he begins to perform incredible miracles in public. Displaying elaborate siddhis or powers, such as invoking fire down from the heavens, will lead many to the erroneous belief that he is the long awaited Jewish Messiah. Around this time, the

167

gospels warn us not to be deceived by any claiming to be Christ (i.e. Jesus reincarnated). At the instigation of this so-called prophet, an image (referred to as 'the abomination of desolation') will be made of the anti-Christ, to be worshipped in the new Jewish Temple. This will be the basis of a new and compulsory world religion.

Big Brother   Right now a climate of acceptance is being prepared by religious leaders as the World Council of Churches works to accomplish religious amalgamation. If conditons are right, this will hasten world unity; if not, it will aid dictatorship. 'And he had the power to give life unto the image of the Beast that it should both speak and cause that as many as would not worship the image of the Beast should be killed.' (Ch 13:15). Surely George Orwell must have had this in mind when he wrote *1984* depicting Big Brother on television screens everywhere as the all-seeing eye to be worshipped and revered. Under his suppressive world government, the anti-Christ, Beast 666, will set things up for every person to bear his mark, his name or his number in their forehead or right hand, in order to buy or sell anything, including *food* and *oil*. With weather anomalies destroying world crops and the current oil/energy dilemma this is not so far fetched.

World Government   There will be a religious persecution and execution of those who will not comply. (We're told in Ch 20:4 that those who resist in the name of Christ will live and reign with Him 1,000 years at the end of the Age). Together, the dynamic duo of dictator and religious figurehead will rule with maniacal strength and charisma. Hitler and Himmler were amateurs compared to what we are told about these two!

Economic relief and a politically united Europe before the end of the decade is also the goal of the European Common Market. [6] Chapter 17:12 tells us that the ten horns are ten kings without a kingdom; that they have one mind, and give their power and strength to Beast 666. Once the membership of ten nations has been accomplished, a suitable leader will be sought to unite and seed the growth of a world-government.

One way or another, present conditions and leaders look to a world government as a solution to increasingly serious global problems. Under a world government, it is easy to see that everyone would have to receive some kind of personal identification, such as the social security number which is used in the U.S. right now. You can well imagine the problems involved with people in under-developed nations dealing with social security, ID or credit cards. Doug Clark of the Amazing Prophecy Center in Santa Ana, California, was in Brussels during 1974 and says, 'I did check that they [The Common Market Headquarters] had a very large computer and were thinking and discussing how they could computerize each individual of the world for equitable distribution of food, etc. . . .' Rumors exist (which the author has been unable to verify) that Common Market administrators refer to this computer as 'the beast'.[6a] Chapter 14:9-10 gives specific warning in this respect, saying that anyone who worships the image of Beast 666 or the man himself, or receives his mark, either on the forehead or hand, shall lose God's protection and wind up amongst the torments. A computerized move in this direction already exists in the U.S. called the Electronic Funds Transfer System. (See Economy chapter.)

Armageddon Seven more plagues, more terrible and intense than the first, are unleashed upon those who worship the image of the Beast or bear his mark. An angel pours out a vial over the Euphrates to dry up the river so that the way of Kings of the East might be prepared for the Battle of Armegeddon. 'And the number of the army of the horsemen were two hundred thousand thousand.' (Ch 9:16). It may seem stranger than fiction but in fulfillment of this prophecy the Russians have already built a dam near the headwaters of the Euphrates, and a road has been constructed from China through the Himalayas to Pakistan. India protested to the United Nations that this action was a threat to peace in Asia. Unfortunately, it may be more of a threat than anyone realizes. If the 'Kings of the East' refers to an Oriental invasion, the reader may be interested to learn how closely contemporary news events bring us to fulfillment of Bible prophecy: during a United Nations special session in 1976, the Soviet Union openly accused China of trying to take over the world. An Associated Press article by J. H. Hightower, datelined Washington DC, 28th April 1964, reported, 'The Red Chinese believe they cannot be defeated by long-range nuclear weapons... and if they were invaded they would rely upon their vast military power. One estimate is that in April, 1961, there were supposed to be 200 million armed and organized militiamen.'[7] Even the number of personnel quoted by the Bible and the press is identical.

John compared the heads of the horsemen to those of lions as they spewed smoke, fire and brimstone (sulphur). He says their tails were like serpents with heads which had wounding power (cannons? missile launchers?). By these means one third of humanity is killed.

The Book of Life   Finally, in the modern counterpart of the corrupt Babylon* we have the fall of the last world power. We are told again that only a third of the world's original population will survive. Once this has been accomplished, Satan is bound for 1,000 years. During this period all who overcame the horrors of the tribulation and the persecution by the establishment, will inherit the new heaven and the new Earth promised in *Revelation* 21:21. The dead are next resurrected and judged before the Throne of God, according to the Book of Life. Then, like the final curtain at a great cosmic drama, the New Jerusalem will descend from the sky, prepared for residence by the righteous, whose names were found written in the Book of Life. (The twelve gates of this celestial abode are related

*Interestingly, Nebuchadnezzar, King of Babylon (who dreamed of the image symbolizing the four great ages and Earthly kingdoms) was the builder of the Tower of Babel which attempted to reach heaven. According to the Bible, God struck confusion amongst its builders, making them speak in different languages, and the project was never completed. The Iraqi government is now financing the rebuilding of the tower on its original site South of Baghdad. This symbol of the corrupt ancient Babylon is materializing again as history repeats itself at the end of this Age. [8]

In a similar sense, reputable metaphysical writings and mystery-schools have commonly taught that prior to the disappearance of Atlantis scientific experiments were being conducted with life forces. Incidental to many genetic experiments, hybrid creatures of mixed human/animal origin were created and subsequently enslaved for a variety of base purposes. DNA recombinant experiments, gene splicing which creates new organisms through the transfer of genes between unrelated species of microbes, and the reported cloning of an actual human being are early stirrings of Atlantean history being repeated.

to the twelve major power-points of the planetary grid [described on page 229] acting as time-warp locks to raise physical existence to the new vibrational frequency of the next evolutionary phase.)

After the amazing and frightening implications of the above prophecies, it would seem appropriate to quote from Paul's gentle epistle to the *Romans* (Ch 8:28 and 15:4): 'We know that all things work together for good to those who love God, and to them who are the called according to His purpose.... For whatsoever things were written aforetime were written for our learning, that we, through patience and comfort of the scriptures, might have hope.'

The 'Rapture' Most Bible students are somewhat familiar with the concept of 'the rapture' which has its counterpart in the Hopi belief that all the good folks will be protected at Black Mesa, the spiritual centre of the continent, when things get really heavy. The modern parallel is the expectation of mass evacuations by UFO spacecraft at that time. A few words should be said about this, as the Biblical information on the subject is widely misunderstood.

A friend was discussing the future with a Christian woman who mentioned she did not intend to make any kind of physical preparation for hard times. When asked about this she said with assurance, 'Well, you see, we [the faithful Christians] shall be lifted up!' 'Lifted up?' my friend asked, not understanding her meaning. 'Yes,' she replied, 'You know, raised! lifted up!' She was apparently unable to explain exactly what she meant by her statement, but was confident that whatever its meaning she'd be a part of it, because it said so in the Bible. Hal Lindsay, in his book *There's a New World Coming* refers to this event as 'the big snatch' but makes the same error. The concept comes from a letter written from Athens by the apostle Paul to the early Christian group at Thessalonia. 'For the Lord himself shall descend from heaven with a shout, with the voice of an archangel, with the trump of God; and the dead in Christ shall rise first. Then we which are alive and remain shall be caught up together with them in the clouds, to meet the Lord in the air: and so shall we ever be with the Lord.' (1 *Thessalonians* 4:16-17). The passage relates to many other inferences in the gospels and *Revelation* about the *end* of the tribulation

171

not its beginning. Before anyone decides they won't be around for the heavy stuff, they ought to re-examine the source of their belief.

Christ Consciousness

There are many who believe that Christ (i.e. Jesus) will, quite literally, descend in glory from the clouds as foretold in the Bible, when He does come again. The Bible says that every eye shall see him, simultaneously, all over the world. It seems unlikely that media coverage will be functional by that time, so another explanation must be possible. By the time the Earth has been purified of all negative vibration and paid all karmic back-debt, those who survive will have attained much inner mastery ('The Kingdom of God is within' *Luke* 17:21). When this occurs, humanity will have begun to enter into a new vibration related to the next evolutionary phase, the fourth dimension. The real matter of the mater-real world will have become refined enough to be classified as that new subtle vibration, spirit. Christ's second coming will, therefore, be seen by every person in the world at the same time, but within an exalted state of consciousness, by all who have made the transition to that level.

The Christ consciousness will manifest as the consciousness of God through the Sun/Son and thence to all living things. Although there are many great beings who manifest the Christ consciousness, it was Jesus the teacher who held the *title* of Christ because He was the most perfect example in human form and made the sacrifice of assuming human karma by His death. Christ, let us not forget, is a *universal force* to be *experienced* . . . sooner or later by each one of us.

References

1. E. Erman, *Egyptian Literature*, 1927, p.309.
    H.O. Lange, *Magical Papyrus Harris,* 1927 (K. Danske Videskabernes Selskab).
2. F.X. Kugler, *Babylonische Zeirordnung*, Vol. 11 of *Sternkunde und sterndienst in bable*, 1909, p. 114.
3. *San Francisco Chronicle, Editorial Comment*, Feb. 22, 1976.
4. *Press Democrat*, Nov. 14, 1976/University of Pennsylvania bio-chemist, Dr. R.J. Rutman.
5. Such winds are the Khamsin, Sirocco, Sharav, Zonda, Foehn, Chinook, Mistral, Santa Ana, etc.
6. *European Community Magazine*, Dec. 1972. *Moody Monthly*, March 1974, p. 24.
6a. *The Gathering Storm*, Cosmic Awareness Communications, PO Box 115, Olympia, Washington 98507.
7. Hal Lindsey, *There's a New World Coming* (Vision House, 1974).
8. *World Magazine & San Francisco Chronicle*, Dec. 12, 1976.

13.   Astrological Predictions 1975-2001 AD

Perhaps the main stumbling block between astrology, the metaphysical abstraction, and astrology, the science, is the interpretive limitations of the astrologer. Astrology, like algebra, deals with symbolism rather than empiricism. As Michael Meyer states in his *Handbook for the Humanistic Astrologer*, 'Astrology is a functional application of the awareness of the active relationship existing between the microcosm and the macrocosm.'

Translating the forces and nuances of celestial influence into the specific and accurate situations of life is rather like defining aromas as they mingle and waft from a restaurant kitchen. It would require a good nose and culinary knowledge to be able to isolate from the many smells the specific foods a certain diner would ultimately be served, but it would take a much more subtle skill to predict what type of dish the patron could expect.

Our individual astrology is a map of ourselves within the cosmic scheme of things. Emanations from the various planets exert a variety of influences on the Earth and its inhabitants. These influences or forces predispose; they impel. Thus, the unfolding of planetary and individual circumstances is coaxed into existence by that infinitely delicate combination of freewill and unseen conduciveness.

We know from the daily climate of the news that some profound changes are needed if we are to survive the twentieth century. And we have seen from the preceding prophetic chapters that while certain changes are definitely needed, many others are absolutely unavoidable. Their severity may be reduced – if we are lucky and wise – but they cannot be cancelled. The final quarter of this century represents the transitional 'interface' between the old and new cycles. It's a repolarization point in the planet's history; on the human level it's a crisis of consciousness and ideology.

During the past three centuries Earth's inhabitants have been receiving preparation for the very times which lie immediately ahead. The three outermost planets, Uranus, Neptune and Pluto, are regarded as the three planets of transformation, and came into their present orbits in order to accelerate the growth of planetary consciousness. They were discovered at times appropriate to our evolution, bringing into conscious focus their specific offerings of celestial energy and metamorphosis. All discoveries occur when the consciousness is ready to expand. Dane Rudhyar, one of the foremost astrological philosophers of our times, sees this challenge of quickened evolution as an opportunity for global initiation *if* humanity as a whole is able to respond positively and courageously to this downpour of galactic and divine energies.[1] The Great Pyramid reflects the same message. These three planets played a very important role in shaping recent history and during the next few decades they will influence our collective destiny even more intensely.

If another planet spins silently out in space beyond Pluto, it will probably not be discovered until some time in the next century, serving as a symbol of the new birth. Astrologers feel sure that another planet does exist. Astronomers are open to the possibility. Dane Rudhyar has prechristened it Proserpine, after the goddess who emerged from the underworld (the unconscious) and Edgar Cayce predicted it would be called Arcturus (not to be confused with the star of that name).

Uranus   Uranus was discovered in 1781 coincident with the French and American revolutions, allowing timely and conscious cognition of its unique forces. The birth chart for the United States of America shows Uranus in the sign of Gemini, and whenever this combination occurs there is always tremendous upheaval, such as World War II. Uranus' particular energy is ruthlessly revolutionary, paring away all stultifying and limiting beliefs and behaviour. It is the first planet of transformation beyond Saturn, and therefore the first of spiritual awareness and attunement to the cosmos. It impatiently rips away the Saturnian mask of ego and limitation, saying 'Enough of this self-centred, timorous myopia. Look out, look out toward the cosmos!' It replaces the past with a new vision, releasing original and unique pro-evolutionary energies within us to help on our uncertain ascent. It nurtures genius. It nurtures fervent enthusiasms. The American revolutionaries two hundered years ago experienced the power of this kind of transformation, as do all who struggle against the hold of the past and against tyranny. However, it is really an externalization of the inner surge of renewal toward perfection which manifests. Uranus, of course, rules the sign of Aquarius which presides over the beginning of the New Age. The 'New Order of the Ages' seeded by America's independence as a nation, and celebrated on the Great Seal, was symbolized by the discovery of Uranus, which will oversee the preparatory events leading up to the actual establishment and anchoring of that new order over the entire planet Earth.

Uranus' energy is so radical, so transformational, that it eludes precise definition. Perhaps that first acid trip can best capture the kind of profoundly radical reality slippage which it brings. From a cosmic perspective, the sudden disruption of the familiar world and the preconceptions of other people's minds is actually the input of originality from the human soul. Towards the end of the century, Uranus will scintillate with an energy both magnificent and terrible in its force. Magnificent for those open and prepared for intense and transformational times, and terrible for those still savouring yesterday's hot-dog, the good old days and the evanescent recovery of 'the system'.

1981 AD At the time of writing Uranus is in Scorpio where it will remain until the end of 1981. In this sign and at this time there is abundant opportunity for the individual to breach the walls of the power structures which maintain society but alienate and subjugate individuals. Uranus rules the universal mind apsect of communications and Scorpio is subtle, unseen. A development in occult communication, making public many hitherto secret teachings, is one possibility, but attacks on the occult sciences and metaphysics is the other side of the coin which tries to suppress Truth. Carried to an extreme this could produce an atmosphere of the secret police state. The audacious Criminal Justice Codification Revision and Reform Act of 1975, formulated by the Nixon administration is a

175

good example. Colloquially known as Bill 1984, it sought to subdue categorically freedom of speech, freedom of the press, rights of assembly, the rights of criminal defendants and to exempt government officials from the penalty of illegal acts. Fortunately, that vehicle of State dictatorship was itself revised and reformed before enactment. Government surveillance of thousands of ordinary people has now come to light, and anyone can write to the FBI, CIA or IRS to receive a copy of any file that might be compiled about their private activities. It is perhaps significant to note that if there is *not* a file on you, the FBI will promptly open one. After all, if you had nothing to hide, why would you want to know what was on file about you in the first place? A large body of several hundred scientists and science writers have formed the Committee for the Scientific Investigation of Claims of the Paranormal and seek to restrict and invalidate the growing interest in unproven and mystic phenomena. We're seeing now the beginnings of legislation to strengthen and reinforce monopolies: corporate, medical and legal.

During the next few years the sexual revolution will continue to liberate and to shock, gender distinctions fading. Sex is the first area affected by the transformational process, and higher centres of awareness will gradually be awakened within humanity as it progresses. People's intuition and judgement will be increased markedly during January and February of 1983 when Jupiter *1983* AD conjuncts Uranus (a planetary conjunction brings an intensification of energies; the mating of two or more forms of influence and a new release of spontaneous activity). This short burst of acuity will especially affect government heads of all nations and is important because it allows a great deal of opportunity for constructive cooperative agreement and achievement to shape world affairs. If the economy fails to improve by 1983, today's problems affecting industry, labour unions and work per se will have generated strikes, riots and civil disorders to such an extent that a lapse into sound judgement may be a reprieve from more serious chaos.

1988 AD Five years later the conjunction of Saturn with Uranus in Capricorn shows the breaking up of structures, mental and physical. Saturn rules Capricorn, lending extra force to the fact that they both rule the skin – the Earth's crust being the skin aspect of the

Earth. Earthquakes are more likely at this time because the friction of Saturn's immovable mien objects to Uranus' irresistable force and indicates that something's got to give! And that something may be of Earth-shaking proportions. This could well be the time of geographical upheavals and continental break-ups which Edgar Cayce spoke of so vividly. As already noted regarding his predictions, Uranus is a factual element in the timing and mechanism of earthquakes. Skin diseases may abound, and this is already potentially accounted for by man-made depletion of the Earth's delicate ozone layer. Trees which would normally compensate for the increase of ultra-violet radiation reaching the Earth, continue to be clearcut, especially in the Amazon and tropical zones where they are not being replaced. Drought-caused forest fires have been on the rampage the last few years and man-made ecological imbalances have produced immense infestations such as the gypsy moth, tussock moth, spruce budworm and southern pine beetle which have destroyed millions of acres of trees each year. In their official report on the subject the National Academy of Sciences states that as the ozone shield dissolves skin cancer increases. A more recent bulletin from the University of California says a 10% decrease in the ozonasphere is equal to a 40% increase in skin cancer. This implication also ties in with the *Revelation* prophecies of a skin plague. Such conditions will be associated with scarcity and possible world famine as Uranus passes through Capricorn during March 1988 until 1995 when a lack of stability will create problems on all levels. New patterns, solutions to problems and prototypes in the political arena appear unable to fulfill the promise of their inception. Many and various *internal combustions* will break loose with physical extremes, tremendous unrest and chaotic conditions. We are reminded of the possibility of a new moon being wrenched from the Ring of Fire. Influences appear to abound which could bring about the political and social unrest predicted in *Revelation*. Fortunately, by this time, public leaders will be wiser and more enlightened to lead us through these crises.

The dismal implications of the future will, however, be accompanied by miraculous progress within individuals who understand what is happening. These events will surely bring out the very best and the absolute worst in us as we rise to meet, or resist, the challenge of the future. The frightening events will be offset by a marvellous flowering of the human spirit amongst people who can relate to what is happening in a positive way. In times of calamity and stress people have always been more closely involved with each other in mutual support, and when Uranus conjuncts with Neptune in **1992-93 AD** Capricorn for almost two years during 1992-93, it could be the turning point in the recorded history of this civilization. Since Capricorn represents what one consciously tries to control, it would tend to indicate societal structure and a humanity intensely, maybe desperately, trying to comprehend the spiritual laws represented by Neptune. We may finally realize there is a greater power than ourselves and that it functions through us and for us. The chaotic conditions in the physical world will force us to realize that God's will be done, not ours. The unity produced by scientific discoveries and the tremendous increase in human understanding will prepare the way for harmonious world unity. Globalism – the exploitation of the Earth – will be replaced by the biocentric integration of 'planetism', a concept reflecting our unity and interdependence. Uranus' destruction of the obsolete in order to make way for the new and more vigorous will upset the Capricorn power-trip. Experientially, this means that many geniuses will appear amongst those who can give up their ego and let the will of God and the visionary force transform them. Insanity caused by pollution and mental purification is equally likely amongst those unwilling or unable to understand or cope with this heavy energy combination. This is consistent with the Bible prophecy of mass insanity in the 'last days' and also the Hindu 'guna' principle whereby satvic or pure natures will benefit from the increased cosmic vibration and tamas or impure characters will gradually become panic-stricken, disoriented, violent and finally insane.

1995-2000 AD 1995 to 2000 sees Uranus in its own sign, Aquarius. All the afore-mentioned transitions should be almost established by then. After all the Saturn resistance to the Uranus changes, we may now say that, symbolically, the lion and the lamb can lie down together. Since Aquarius rules astrology, its reinstatement as an occult science can be expected, together with that of the other metaphys-ical disciplines. Aquarius rules the light, and intensification of the light during this decade will burn off remaining negative dross from the Earth plane. Purification by fire will almost be accomplished as

Jupiter conjunccs Uranus in Aquarius during early 1997, bringing sudden changes again and some more upheavals, serving to bring new concepts into focus and bring about re-evaluations.

Neptune   Neptune's attributes are mystical. It rules ideology, inspiration, dreams, etc. Its form is elusive, at once encompassing the everything and the nothing of Nirvana. As a dissolver of illusion, and delusion, it works to transform our fixed beliefs, the lead of our personalities, into the gold of understanding and wisdom. Neptune rules water – illusion/maya – because water is symbolic of the living spirit and can carry one on beyond the limitations of the finite world and illusory existence. As a universal solvent, Neptune melts away the remainder of what Uranus shattered (the Saturnian influences of ego and conceptual rigidity) including humanity's sense of security and addiction to obsolete institutions and ideologies. It replaces them with more inclusive and universal systems and values. With Neptune's discovery in 1846, the international influences of the industrial revolution and colonialism were introduced, but at the same time we saw the counter-vision of Thoreau and Marsh and rediscoveries of natural law.

Neptune first moved into Scorpio during 1955 to prepare the way for higher consciousness to start filtering into those fertile recesses of the brain. Being the sign of transition and enlightenment, Scorpio brought rejuvenation, but because a vibratory increase can polarize consciousness (i.e. the light that illumines can also blind), it also resulted in degeneration, to the same power amongst conditions unready and people unwilling to be influenced in a positive direction. During those years many of the potential New Age leaders were born and by the time cataclysms begin to occur, these persons will have begun to occupy leadership and government levels where they can establish themselves as sources of strength and wisdom when we most need enlightened leadership.

1970-85 AD   In 1970 Neptune moved into Sagittarius, the sign of philosophies, foreign affairs, religions and higher education. It also facilitates the working out within oneself of one's relationship to the cosmos. It will remain here until 1985, so during the coming decade our attitude to religious orthodoxy will be undergoing its greatest evolution. We see the forces set in motion for a merging of

179

traditional established religions with the more living and experiential faiths of the coming Age of Light. Laws of nature and the 'mysteries' spoken of earlier may well be introduced into the general educational field. As psychic and subtle energy sciences are developed they will unite us more closely into a truer 'family of humanity'.

Neptune, as the planet of secrecy and exposure, has been active in recent years to expose multi-faceted corruption in high places, government and business. We can expect to see nations losing their authority figures to mere figureheads as Neptune goes into Capricorn (stability, security, ambition) in 1985, and people will become ever more disillusioned. In a recent British poll only 10% of those interviewed felt government to be the real power in England. 66% thought it was the unions, and many Americans already feel the same way about the multi-national corporations. The words 'disillusion' and 'dissolution' sound almost identical and it is strangely ironical how closely they are associated, one giving birth to the other. Disillusion of the public over the corruption of the establishment and its inability to fulfil its obligations to them, will give way to dissolution of establishment power and the general impulse of people to rely upon their own community groups and taking responsibility for themselves. Paramahansa Yogananda, the great Yogi who brought Hinduism to the West, said that the way of the future would be for world brotherhood colonies to spread throughout the world 'like wildfire'. The ocean will be tapped for resources *1988* AD and development of natural energies. By 1988, world famine (influenced by Saturn in Capricorn) will be a very real possibility, intensifying research into the ocean as a food source.

Pluto Pluto was discovered in 1930. Under this planet's influence superfluousness is neutralized. Unresolved matters are reduced to an undifferentiated state, and finally regenerated in a negative or positive form. Naturally, such random states, lacking initial cohesion and order, are susceptible to the influences of those most aware of the opportunity to take control. The discovery of Pluto coincided with the depression, when Hitler and Mussolini were on the rise and communism under Stalin was spreading. Solidarity gained by such means always ends in disaster and so did the Third Reich. Pluto (named after the Roman god of the underworld – the unconscious) motivates the masses, working on the deeper levels of the subconscious mind, so it is not surprising that Hitler rose to power in answer to just such a collectively subconscious need. He was apparently well-schooled in astrology and metaphysics.[2] There is an interesting case to be made that Hitler was an adept of the dark forces. He knew that around this time in history a 'new man' and a 'master race' would inherit the Earth and sought to corner the market by selectively breeding genetically superior children. World domination on behalf of the dark powers was his goal and the master race was needed to accomplish these ends. What he did not realize was that the 'master race' would be the children of light and not of the darkness, and that the spiritually evolved master race of the New Age can only be seeded by the new and evolved souls incarnating right now.

The glyph of the phoenix is used to represent Pluto and to indicate the new birth which this planet finally brings. The refocalization of new forms, which results from such disasters as major wars, can serve to further negative and antiquated interests or to bring forth evolutionary change and the kind of radiant regenesis found throughout nature. Perhaps this is why Pluto also stands for humanity's ultimate triumph of universal brotherhood. As the outermost planet, its changes are slow and its complete cyclical action affects generations rather than individuals.

1971-83 AD   Uranus' energy is going to open us up to tremendous spiritual Truths and Pluto will arrive to put them all to practical use. It has been in Libra (harmony/balance) since 1971 and will progress into Scorpio by 1983. Because of the positive aspect of Pluto's destructive and purifying nature, combined with the fairness and judicial penchant of Libra, it is no accident that things which had probably been happening for a long time have been suddenly magnetized into the light. Since the beginning of this phase we've had the 'Pentagon papers' incident and Viet Nam; un-presidential behaviour and Watergate; CIA assassinations abroad and domestic spying; IRS harrassment and corporate bribery on a massive scale. Everyone's willing to confess and the left hand is finally discovering what the right hand has been doing all this time – hiding yesterday's dirty laundry or eating a lot of junk food which turns out to have been carcinogenically improved with various additives.

This, too, is consistent with the teachings of Meishu Sama who pointed out that as the divine light continues to increase it will illuminate the darkness, separating more clearly the negative from the positive until they polarize far enough to culminate in the ultimate 'conflict of forces' or battle of Armageddon. As individuals we have felt the process too and realize that immediate and concentrated effort to clean up our collective act is necessary if there is to be any bright hope left for the future.

Extensive political reform is likely between now and 1983. We see new relationships forming amongst people as we learn to become less judgemental – especially of things like sexual deviations from the norm which tend to isolate society into coteries and factions. Pluto in this sign makes the male and female roles 'fair' in their relationship to each other, attaining the ultimate yin and yang harmony which nature intended. As Pluto transits into Scorpio we'll no doubt see some pretty radical changes involving sexual mores, the emphasis being displaced from gender-oriented roles to individuals freely relating within open and loving relationships. Self-healing will increase as we learn to take responsibility for our own welfare. Medicine will become less preoccupied with drugs and symptom-treating and allopathy will fail to help the new and more intense diseases and purifications which will arise. Purification of the physical body will no longer respond to suppression by normal medical means and psychic and extra-sensory energies will be researched for healing. Natural and holistic approaches to sickness will be embraced, treating the whole person, spiritually, mentally and physically.

1983-95 AD At the end of 1983 Pluto enters into Sagittarius until 1995, representing the philosophical application of the new physical awareness gained while in Scorpio. This will bring about use of the new biochemical research and the discovery of many Earth resources to replace current dwindling energy supplies. Pluto will be regenerating its energies through the higher cosmic ray of Jupiter's

1994 AD influence as they come into conjunction at the end of 1994 and bring about a profound enlightenment on all social and religious levels. This time will be a preparatory opportunity for being our brother and sister's keeper, as Jupiter, sign of the higher mind and philosophies, expands the general acceptance of new knowledge and

Truth. This is the beginning of awareness that the chaos will pass and of hope for a new world order.

1999 AD By September 1999, Mars will indeed 'reign for the good cause' as predicted by Nostradamus. It will conjunct with Pluto, stimulating and attuning everyone to moral evaluations and the understanding of higher spiritual relationships. New and world-wide codes of ethics will result. The nations, allied more truly than ever before, will share new healing techniques and natural resources made possible by research into the various energy fields from non-depletable sources.

By December Mars moves forward to join forces with Neptune and Uranus, firming up the unifying growth initiated by their earlier conjunction in 1992-93. Being the planet of pure energy, Mars infuses these three planets of transition with a rush of expanded awareness, building faith in our future. Religious and spiritual unity will be made likely by humanity's inner knowing by that date that separations are illusion and that we are, indeed, One.

Bearing all this in mind we can see why some of the prophetic and astrological implications for the remainder of the century appear spectral. In the short term, and under our present collective condition of consciousness, world government and world religion seem like the worst disaster. A totalitarian nightmare. But if one projects to the future, we are strangely relieved at the vision of world unity and universal brotherhood with national boundaries and personal distinctions dissolved by harmonious cooperation; even love?

Two Stelliums Two major stelliums (more than three planets in one sign) before the end of the century clearly imply definite and strong influences at work to unite the Earth. By seven planets in Sagittarius we see the way prepared in 1983 for organized religion, as we now know it, to be superseded by a synthesis of spiritual principles; and growing socialization. Six planets in Aquarius during 1998 (the follow-up to an earlier preparatory cycle of 1962 which set the forces in motion with a similar stellium) will help people confidently begin to gain mastery over their emotions. The potential is vividly apparent for humanity to experience a truly loving attitude toward all others, all races; all superficial differences fading. Animals and plants will be recognized and revered in a special way. The 'New Order of the Ages' will be on the way, from that dark place in the pocket book, to the heart.

If the consciousness of the planet is ready, everything will be wonderful when it comes to political and religious world unity. If not, it'll be hell. Timing is obviously important for we approach a time of eccentric activity and extremes. We cannot doubt that sooner or later this will come to pass by one means or another. Let's hope it's later rather than sooner, so we may be quite ready. It does seem logical, however, that a single seat of church and state may well be prematurely generated by the economic need for nations to survive. Or it could be accomplished by despotic ('Beast-ly') force. If this should happen, as the *Revelation* prophesies so clearly, we can at least remember that the creative intelligence of the universe knows what it's doing even if we don't:

Pluto, working to clear up the pieces from Uranus' radical surgery, may see a negative world power sneak in and run with the ball for a while. (This is, after all, a battle between good and evil being played out on the physical plane.) With the new form of government established – even if it is too soon for comfort and under horrendously terrible conditions – it is divinely ordained that as the battle progresses and global purification takes its toll upon the domain of the Beast, there will be a postive refocalization of the freed energies.

As the Plutonian cycle culminates, the fledgling Phoenix will preen the ashes of death and destruction from its beautiful feathers and fly off into the settling dust of a murky sunrise. A new culture *will* emerge. After all, who can hold back the dawn?

References
1. Dane Rudhyar, *Astrological Timing – The Transition to the New Age* (Harper Colophon, 1969).
2. Trevor Ravenscroft, *The Spear of Destiny* (Putnam, 1973).
    Pauwels and Bergier, *The Dawn of Magic* (U.K.) or *The Morning of the Magicians* (U.S.) (Avon, 1960).

Part Four

Emergency Stops

14. How the Forces Work

When the wind whispers gently
it persuades faded leaves
To float quiescently
From the bough, muttering softly
As they rustle comfortably
Into the carpet of

Nature's richest colours.
When turbulent
It fells in a single storm
Great trees
That have weathered
The flow of centuries.
Blown by playful winds
Small messages of seeds
Whirl, dizzy,
Into dark repositories
Moist pockets
Of the Earth-Mother
And pollen love letters
Into fields of giggly flowers.

In the affairs of the world, the winds that blow are the tides of consciousness, stirring deep within the human psyche. The winds of fortune or disaster prevail in response to undercurrents of collective mood, bringing weather for all seasons and all reasons. It's a strange business, and yet an integrity prevails which allows no change without consent, no structure too oppressive without a just and submerged agreement from our deeper levels of being.

For instance, tremendous amounts of psychic energy are generated and released when thousands come together to share in a single emotional reality – major sporting events, Woodstock, *Jaws, The Exorcist,* or inflation. This is especially true when the action is carried by the media into the homes of millions more, who vicariously share in and contribute to the energy generated by involvement with the event. Games, of course, provide an emotional outlet for spectators, and the energy of one side's supporters is offset and neutralized by the other side. It is a healthy and innocuous phenomenon. However, what happens when entire populations from Third World nations struggle continually for their very survival, for freedom from hunger and oppression, from exploitation? What happens psychically when the power-structures of the world, built upon such inequality, attain the technology and manpower to maintain their position? All the hates, angers, resentments and hostilities amass in the spiritual and mental realms before they take form and action in the physical world. Frictional pressure builds and spills over into other levels and two main things occur. Susceptible physical conditions succumb to the boil-over of extra-sensory energies. Turbulent weather and geographical catastrophes are the pressure-vents whereby the negativity is released, or it may take the form of natural disasters or outbreaks of disease. The second natural result is that the psychically generated neagtive energy is harnessed and utilized by the dark forces for destructive and counter-evolutionary enterprises, to confuse and decimate life-forces seeking perfection. The power that sustains the physical atom is etheric energy. It is formed by and susceptible to creative consciousness. It is responsive to impulses from the spiritual level which impress it as a magnetic energy matrix for matter, thus attracting things into existence. Although the majority of German people were not fully aware of, nor condoned, the activities of the Third Reich, they would never have been possible if national emotionalism had not been forcefully stimulated and profoundly stirred by the ego mania of leaders, long before the infamy began. On the spiritual level, national psychic energy was utilized and made manifest on the physical plane by the 'principalities and powers' referred to earlier, working through the ignorant and those of ill will.

As another example, Meishu Sama, who taught ordinary people

how to be channels for the divine light of the New Age, said science was the strongest weapon of the negative force. While humanity had received many wonderful benefits from it, the evil forces have attempted to make everyone totally dependent upon technology with the aim of using it to acquire absolute world power.

Throughout nature, higher and more developed life forms live and feed upon the less evolved and more vulnerable species. Big fish eat smaller fish and so forth, and although humans are not exactly food for the gods, it is our energies, attitudes, desires and aspirations that nourish divine involvement, providing the psychic energy necessary for help or intervention in personal and world affairs. We have free-will and there is no celestial commitment to humanity without invitation. Prayer, invocation and affirmation evoke the grace of divine response above and beyond one's normal karmic dues.

In the world today we observe an apparent ideological struggle between two great and powerful systems: free-enterprise and communism – actually, capitalism and dictatorship by the state. Nowadays, both systems are sufficiently close to the turning point of their cycle that each has begun to take on the characteristics of the other. The fault lies not within the relative merits or weaknesses of either system, but within the average consciousness of the people of the world themselves.

Pir Al-Wahshi, the Sufi master, has expressed the situation very clearly. He says, 'As we grow in consciousness and knowledge, so it is reflected in the world around us. The world one sees is a mirror of the self – only when one changes will the world change. One cannot change oneself by changing the world; but one can change the world by changing oneself.' In the same way, Don Juan told Castenada that when we change our vision of the world, the world will change.

15. The Economy

'For we wrestle not against flesh and
blood, but against principalities, against
powers, against rulers of the darkness
of this world, against spiritual wicked-
ness in high places.'
St. Paul (Ephesians 6:12)

The dollar affects world economies and when the U.S. sneezes the
rest of the world catches cold. At the time of writing, the American
economy and the world economy approach a state of unprecedented
chaos. It is not likely that the present economic system will sustain
its holding pattern much longer. More likely is the eventual
emergence of an entirely new mode, a blueprint for which already
exists within the prophetic record. So, rather than elaborating
upon existing information about preserving assets until they can
be reliquidated, our intention here is to alert the reader instead
to crucial *trends* which might otherwise go unnoticed for what they
are. Although the implications of these stirrings, at this stage, may
only be apparent if one knows something about prophecy to begin
with, they relate directly to the phasing-in of a new political/
economic world order according to various predictions – particularly those of the Bible – concerning the future.

These trends, already strongly in motion, will ultimately affect
every individual, as well as the fate of nations.

The United Nations and the International Monetary Fund are
committed to formation of a new international economic order

beginning with global economic development strategy for the 1980's as well as a single European parliament. Economic relief and a politically united Europe before the end of the decade is also the goal of the European Common Market.[1]

A sound economy in Western culture is the health and mainstay of a nation's equilibrium, and until now we have believed that an individually competitive and collectively capitalist system was the right diet for a 'chicken in every pot'. Money is the life blood of technological civilization. As long as it circulates to all parts of the body, nourishing every cell, civilization is healthy. When greed and monopoly block or congest the flow, sickness sets in and symptoms of hunger, poverty and deprivation affect its people. Stagnation, inflation, recession and bankruptcy affect its business and industry. Thus one can reconcile the fact that there is not, in fact, a chicken in every pot and that in the so-called free world entire governments are permeated by the influence of the multi-national corporations and dominated by enterprises such as General Motors (a private business, yet only 18 nations in the whole world have a GNP as large).

Corporate greed and government treachery are no longer purely moral issues but survival problems, and we are seeing the beginnings of a strengthening and reinforcement of monopolies. Antitrust laws have become an ineffective farce. Like the forest that cannot be seen for the trees, the roots of 'Big' (capital B as in Brother) business—the cartels, conglomerates, consortiums and multi-national corporations—have by now ubiquitously penetrated into the very infrastructure of world society. Consequently, it is not surprising that precious little is generally known about those trends which form the *context* within which future world economy and/or government may be electronically solidified: items like TLC, EFTS, SWIFT, etc.

TLC: 'Tender loving care?' you say? Try: Trilateral Commision — a consortium of 'distinguished private citizens', international bankers, industrialists and multi-national corporate magnates of North America, Western Europe and Japan. According to the

Encyclopaedia of Associations the organization was established (by David Rockefeller) in 1973 'to foster closer economic and political cooperation among these three areas of the world'. The strongest statement we shall make here is that existence of an organization such as the TLC automatically consolidates the power base of a wealthy elite.

In its controversial annual report of 1975, 'The Crisis of Democracy', the Commission pronounced the nation as suffering from 'an excess of democracy' and that it was America's inherently *un*democratic aspects which enabled it to function. It pointed out 'potentially desirable limits of political democracy' and said that 'the vulnerability [of democratic government as a viable system in the future] comes primarily from the dynamics of democracy itself'; also that 'the areas where democratic procedures are appropriate are, in short, limited', etc. Certain startling recommendations were made for limiting the existing 'excess of democracy' by restricting freedom of the press — an alternative to which would be government regulation of the press; instigating policies of governmental secrecy, and centralization of power within Congress; a program to reduce the job expectations of the college educated; and centralization of economic and social planning — the modus operandi of State Socialism. (State Socialism, however, appears not to be the totally preferred alternative.) The most prophetically relevant part of the whole report was its prediction that *the post industrial era, dominated by electronics, would 'evolve into new social structures' which would progress 'beyond traditional democratic forms'* (emphasis added).

According to the basic programs of the TLC we may expect to see a gradual reduction and limitation of democracy at home and accommodation of undemocratic regimes abroad. In 'Multi National Corporations: Why Be Scared of Them?' John Diebold wrote in *Foreign Policy* (Fall 1973) 'the logical and eventual development [of the increased role of multi-national corporations] . . . would be the end of nationality and national governments as we know them'. In the short term, then, multi-national interests seek to avoid constraints of government regulation and taxation and are gradually shaking themselves free of Federal Trade Commission regulation too; in the long term the TLC entente is to influence national governments to enforce TLC policies—externally through economic domination of economies and internally through political connections.

Ex-President Nixon appears to have paved the way for this particular path of influence by creating a 'Trojan horse' for large corporations to permeate government when he set into motion the President's Commission on Personnel Interchange in 1969. Since then countless business executives have been placed in key positions within government policy councils where they can help their company affiliations.

In 1974 only two of the Commission's U.S. members were a governor or a senator and they happened to be Carter and Mondale. A member of the task force which produced the 1975 'Crisis of Democracy' report was its chairman Zbigniew Brzezinski who, but a year later, became National Security Advisor under the TLC's successfully sponsored presidential candidate, Jimmy Carter. Such an election could, itself, be construed as a 'limitation of democracy' since the prestigious media publicity of that candidacy was planned and carried out under TLC auspices. A number of top media executives are themselves members of the TLC. By 1977 25% of the North American TLC members had key positions within the Federal government administering U.S. policy—and especially foreign and monetary policy.[2]

When one realises that the Rockefeller family alone has banking and business assets in 125 nations it is obvious that the combined assets of all TLC affiliates may well be impossible to inventory. It does, however, explain why the need to control U.S. foreign policy is a paramount consideration of the Commission, no matter which party or political system operates out of the White House. Economies can plunge and wars can ravage but those who are really at the helm of money and power prosper no matter what, because the industries they control can produce medicine, munitions or agricultural petrochemicals with the raw materials, resources and chemicals they also control – it is all a matter of focus in the win-win game of worldly power wielding.[3] In the case of multi-national banks and corporations, patriotic allegiance to the U.S. is diluted by virtue of their international context. Common financial interests unite these entities across national boundaries.

In line with the electronics dominated society we observe growing daily, we can point to existing computer usage as well as planned systems which will provide, we are told, economy and convenience – in exchange (we ask) for a mandatory and symbiotic indenture to and dependence upon 'the system'? The power of the computer to transform us into a 'cashless, digital' society is enormous. Consolidation of information about people is already being stored in massive computer 'data banks'.

Truncation is the banking word used to describe the non-return of cancelled checks to individuals and their microfiling for central storage by the receiving bank. A cassette tape four inches in diameter can store some 40,000 chronologically microfilmed checks which can be individually and electronically retrieved in seconds – usually for a fee. A national truncation system is the goal of the American Bankers Association in conjunction with the National Standards Institute. We're advised this will save time, money and person-hours and that the savings will be reflected in bank service charges to customers. That doesn't sound so bad, but a disquieting pulse communicates itself when a top banking executive states, 'We're preconditioning the market for a paperless world. . . .'[4] So, we look at the larger system of which truncation is a small component – EFTS. Electronic Funds Transfer System.

EFTS embodies a more sophisticated and far-reaching structure of efficiency and economy measures. It involves the use of computer technology and high speed electronic communications to facilitate bank transactions and the eventual withdrawal of cash money from the public's hands to further the goal of a cashless society.

Some of the changes proposed by EFTS which will specifically affect individuals include direct deposit of paychecks to employee bank accounts (conceivably, you had better *have* a bank account if you want to get paid in the future); pre-authorized debits to checking accounts for bill paying; transfer of funds at supermarkets and retail store checkout counters from the individual's checking account. No actual money will be involved. Cash, checks and personal credit cards are expected ultimately to be replaced by the advent of a single, plastic, all-purpose debit/credit card which will be acceptable as cash or credit anywhere in the nation, and parallel systems are planned for other countries. This will be each person's key to the network system of computerized ledger entries. When this system is fully operable the only way to transact business will be through participation in and connection to the EFT system.

10 01 0145131 8

Conversion to the new electronic mode is moving more slowly than anticipated, however, because as far back as 1976 the Knight News Service circulated a feature article entitled 'All Purpose Credit Card Predicted (by bankers) Within Four Years'. *A Readers' Digest* article entitled, 'Coming Soon: Electronic Money' (Nov. 1976) stated, 'In this new totally electronic age, the enforcement of financial obligations will present few difficulties, since failure to pay up could be disastrous. The culprit might even be forced to undergo what EFT men call "plastic surgery"—cutting off his bank cards. Economically speaking, this would make him a non-person.' The EFT system, in concert with the Universal Product Code (those computerized lines printed on merchandise), comprise the basis of the newly emerging and revolutionary cashless money method. The individually numbered debit/credit card will be each person's only key to the system. (As St. John predicted, 'And no man might buy or sell save he had the mark, or the name of the beast or the number of his name.' *Revelation* 13:17.) In *The Mark is Ready—Are You?,* Ron Steel explores the existing possibilities of invisible laser tatooing for identification purposes and implantation of transponder devices for tracking.

EFTS is a cell in the body of a much larger, international electronic banking network based in Brussels. Brussels is a center of immense importance in the scheme of things to come. As a politically neutral country it is the seat of both NATO and the European Common Market—and the SWIFT network—Society for Worldwide Interbank Financial Telecommunications.

SWIFT was also conceived by the progenitors of the Trilateral Commission and was birthed in the same year as the TLC. It represents the formal linking of the international banking community in order to realise more effective computer usage. Interbank transactions now synaptically spark at speeds up to 30 times faster than any previous system. SWIFT currently has 20 member countries (including most of TLC territory—Western Europe, North America and Japan) who key in their own terminals to 'concentrator' centres in every member country. Each operating facility has a duplicate centre as a security backup. Approximately 600 banks are plugged into the SWIFT network and IBRO (Inter Bank Research Organization) looks to the eighties for establishment of a multi-bank network.[5]

In the final overview the international banking community (the prime clients of which are the multi-national corporations) itself is largely controlled by TLC affiliations.

Edgar Cayce, who had also accurately foretold the economic crash of October, 1929, attributed the division of this country (which he predicted for around this time) to 'fear on the part of those who control capital investment' and a lack of universal oneness of purpose. Krondratieff, the Russian economist who developed data on financial cycles, predicted a short recession in 1975 and the greatest crash of all time in the early 1980's. In this vein, Reginald McKenna, Britain's Chancellor of the Exchequer in 1916, declared that 'They who control the credit of a nation direct the policy of governments and hold in their hands the destiny of the people.' So, who controls the credit of this nation? We can trace back the establishment of a Central Banking system to the Federal Reserve Act of 1913 when the intent was to mobilize reserves and increase confidence in the American banking system. It was set up to be under *public control*. This is still the *declared* intent, yet the American Bankers' Association textbook, *Money and Banking* (p. 234) says, 'The member banks own the 12 Federal Reserve Banks.' From these 12 banks is formed the 12-member Open Market Committee which acts on behalf of the Federal Reserve System. The U.S. government publication *Money Facts*[6] reads, 'Congress has never given authority for determining money policy to the Federal Reserve System—and certainly not to a committee within the system containing members who owe their selection to private bank interests.' In defining what the Federal Open Market Committee does, this publication says, 'It determines the amount of government securities the Federal Reserve will buy and sell, in order to influence the level of bank reserves. In essence, the Committee determines U.S. monetary policy.' The Federal Reserve, therefore, fulfils a function it is neither constitutionally nor legally authorized to perform and its hierarchical structure can be traced directly back to TLC sources. As this update goes to press (1980) we note that the Federal Reserve Chairman and the U.S. Treasury Secretary are both members of the TLC.

While the nation's media is understandably focused upon events and policies crucial to the eighties, certainly the 'energy crisis', one can observe that banking, communications and agriculture appear to be major targets of TLC control.

With respect to media control, literally thousands of publishing houses, newspaper chains, magazines, film companies, radio and TV stations across the nation and across the world have been systematically absorbed by multi-national corporate interests. The danger this poses to freedom of speech is that political or business opinions contrary to the interests of the parent corporation obviously will not be aired by the subsidiary media company.

On an individual level, an important innovation to be aware of is the two-way cable TV system of Warner Communications which will eventually be available nationwide. Its name is QUBE. QUBE has been referred to as 'undoubtedly the most awesome political tool ever developed by modern technology'. Viewers' opinions can be polled on virtually any subject by pressing one of five buttons which feed answers to multiple-choice questions back to the mainframe computer. National elections and crucial political issues can be put to public referendum. QUBE is only one example of the technical merging of TV with the computer and telephone. While the creative and positive aspect of QUBE is that it communicates *with* viewers instead of *at* them, there is also some concern about its potential to psychologically manipulate public opinion by its programming content. TLC (Rockefeller) banking entities are alleged to have bought corporate control of all three major television networks in addition to the Warner QUBE system.[7] We cannot help but wonder whether QUBE is intended to be instrumental in shaping and evolving those 'new social structures beyond traditional democratic forms' which the TLC apparently seeks to instigate via its top government and business positions.

As far as agriculture and big business are concerned, the same corporations who already own the agribusiness farms, supermarkets and petrochemical industries (to name just a few) have been buying up seed companies to gain global control of seed supplies.[8] Control of seeds, of course, can lead to control of the entire food system and, as if that weren't bad enough, official reports estimate that by the end of the decade the food industry could be monopolized by a core of 50 major companies.

'Technotronic' structuring to shore up the society of a decaying economy awaits us as inevitably as the skeleton awaits the decay of the body. It already exists. And it currently evolves toward its most productive capacities. Nothing, however, is likely to constrict the closing circle of the computer state and accelerate public acceptance of it faster than great national crises and the breakdown of world economies. With the exception of invasion by a foreign power (and foreign powers have been buying heavily into U.S. industry and business for a long time now so that domestic control of the economy is being lost), inflation is the most destructive factor as it completely dissipates essential order. In such cases and at such times authoritarian government measures are a natural outcome. Joel Stein's informative booklet, *The Human Potential Movement*,[9] points out that 'What is developing today is a *potential* system of total social control. In such a society, every resource and every human being would be programmed into a complete system of computerized control in which everyone *could* be manipulated according to the requirements of the state' (emphasis added).

There are, as yet, no easy answers to our growing dilemma. The obvious response to the sheer pervasiveness of the problems, barely touched upon here, might be 'to suffer the slings and arrows of outrageous fortune or to take arms against a sea of troubles and by opposing end them' — options that didn't help Hamlet either. The most difficult, yet only realistic type of constructive action available is one to which only a few may actually be advanced enough to truly respond. Such action is radically different from anything previously postulated or even recognised for its potential as a solution until recent times. Two courses of action become necessary — one to be sought within by working on one's inner development in order to become ever more loving, open, clear and attuned. The other course is to work on an external level, ideally as part of a group expression (one such group currently working to 'spiritualize' government is NOVUS, P. O. Box 32422, Washington, D.C. 20007), whereby one purifies karmically through constructive service in life-affirming ways. This creates the new and brings about in the material (matter-real) world necessary transformations to negative conditions. To the extent that transformation can

199

be accomplished by each of us we lessen the possibility of ultimate negativity manifesting in the world.

In a not-so-distant future which we cannot deny *may* be dominated by electronic control of 'the system' there will be a number of people who have seen clearly the signs of the times, prepared themselves accordingly in all the important ways and who *will* survive outside the system. When such people are drawn together as aligned groups, and similarly motivated associations form networks, a powerful and transformational magnetic grid emerges which has organic life and growth potential of its own, equal to any force of nature which draws upon the life principle of the universe.

The Piscean age, characterized by a strong spirit of competition between people, is now shifting to the Aquarian paradigm of co-operation for mutual benefit. Instead of isolated families digging themselves in for the duration of hard times with stockpiled supplies and ammunition to ward off marauders, the *ideal* situation is one where communities of like-minded people everywhere work *together* in preparing to meet future needs and demands. The best way to see that our *own* needs are met is to see that *everyone's* needs are met, and to work at that level.

Community Skills Bank One's own skills are an important survival resource. Any job, trade or service that enables a person to find work in any location or situation, no matter how bad the economy, is absolutely invaluable. Learning new crafts and areas of expertise now will insulate many from much potential hardship in the future because viable survival abilities will be acceptable as a means of barter when money may not be available or acceptable, but perhaps food, medication or other materials will be. All kinds of maintenance and repair work will be at a premium in the future, and the ability to provide an inexpensive substitute for something that is now costly is worth its weight in gold. Homegrown produce and food preserving, clothing, footwear (à la rubber tyres and canvas), animal husbandry, alternative and natural methods of healing, learning the uses and applications of herbs and how to forage for wild edible plants, are just a few pursuits which are rewarding in and of themselves, and not just as a precaution against future needs.

Those who can see the gestalt forming as our culture arrives at an impasse know that we live within the stomach of the Beast. Now is the time to solidify bonds with friends and sympathetic groups, and through mutual goals and understanding, establish the new order. These will be needed to buffer the shock when the old system collapses beyond help, releasing its rigid frame and iron grip, spewing us all from its dark confines into an alien and unstructured freedom. Valuable time is being spent trying to shore up the crumbling empire. People are much like sleepwalkers trapped in their own nightmares and unaware that it is *their* dream. Fortunately, as the light increases people everywhere are helping to wake each other up to the significance and potential of the times in which we live, and are using this period of grace to explore new frontiers of knowledge, make inner journeys and generally build the foundations of the new order. In city and country, new lifestyles are being created, experienced and sought. Communities in the cities are learning to become independent of the commercial centralization of supply and demand patterns and are transforming the technology to new life-affirming purposes.[10] As Chogyam Trungpa advises, 'cutting through materialism' is an essential part of it.

The subtle thing about money is that ultimately you only get to keep what you give away. This is the metaphysical aspect. When one keeps the flow of green energy circulating (like electricity) a vacuum is created which can then be refilled with new input according to one's needs or desires. Hoarding and monopolies are what stop the flow and cause problems. After all, prosperity already exists on all levels and in all combinations as an objective state and it is but a matter of allowing and freeing oneself to tap into it. Because prosperity is only possible to the extent that we believe ourselves worthy to receive, careful introspection is necessary to examine and deal with all hidden attitudes and beliefs which have programmed us to underachieve in terms of general prosperity. Consciousness must then create the belief in one's ability to have—whatever. Creative consciousness is a matrix which has

201

magnetic attraction for the circumstances that come to us, and the experiences we undergo. 'As a man thinketh, so is he.'

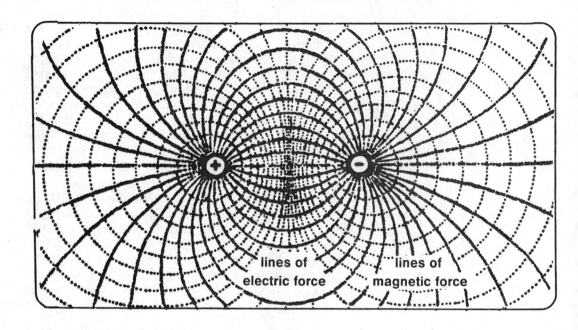

lines of electric force   lines of magnetic force

Manifesting Prosperity

Each person is a point through which the infinite energy of the universe flows, becomes transformed by the individual's consciousness and radiates out according to his or her creative will. It's that simple. Temporarily detained in atoms, bone and sinew, we human spirits have all created our own subjective worlds as a result of the kind of energy we have transmitted and created. People are not lucky or unlucky, fortunate or unfortunate by random chance. Everything unfolds in perfect harmony according to Law. We receive the fruits of our own returning karma and creative abilities. As co-Creator apprentices, human way-stations where the creative force of the universe can take on form and see Itself/Himself/Herself in 3D and living colour, we have forgotten that we *are* that source. If you need something, do not try to draw it *to* you by an act of will. Your creative will is the *source* of it. One's thought impulses are a kind of wave-form which ripples out into the ethers, the subtle energy resource pool, where they attract the kinds of energy necessary to give impetus and eventual form to that original thought impulse. To want something and know that it is yours *already* will manifest it in your life far more surely than hoping for it to come *to* you. Werner Erhard says, 'You don't get to vote on the way it is. You already did.' Christ said that we '. . . see as through a glass, darkly' because unconscious impressions, negative programming and conditioned responses cloud our vision and distort our energies.

Michael Phillips' book, loosely based on some Taoist wisdom and called *The Seven Laws of Money* (Random House) explains how money will come if you are doing the right thing. Don't predicate your actions upon first having enough money, but set the ball rolling and see what the energy draws in the way of needed finances (irresponsibly creating debt or rationalizing rip-off is not part of this method). Venturing out on a precarious limb on more than one occasion to test its validity, I have found this principle works and have used it successfully. For this reason, it is a particularly pernicious fallacy that work (i.e. what you do for a living) and money are inseparably related. From the perspective of cosmic principle, real work is service; it is love in action. By doing what you enjoy most and do best, it is possible to break through the puritan work ethic to a place where responsibly doing your own thing becomes an extension of universal harmony. Admittedly, in today's stressful job market people with family responsibilities and financial commitments cannot so abruptly turn the faucet of the cosmic resource pool. The transition from one definition of livelihood to another requires a great deal of fortitude, optimism, energy and resourcefulness. But it can be done with patience and careful planning and by developing sensitivity in decision making and attunement to opportunity.

The acquisition of money is still viewed by our society as an end in itself, and people who feel this way are usually not aware of how identified they become with the means they have selected to generate it. So, naturally, it's important to do only the kind of work

203

you believe in and feel good about. It's karmically untogether to support an exploitive industry with one's daily efforts just for security or a fat paycheque.

It is not clear what emotional scars the depression left upon the mass psyche, but there's probably a good case for a relationship between the rigours of that period and the preoccupation amongst those old enough to have experienced it with 'security', 'nest-eggs' and 'money in the bank'. The irony is that we are quickly approaching a time when these things will provide no security whatsoever. They are already shrinking in value and becoming increasingly dwarfed by inflation. Frustration runs high, for instance, at supermarket checkout stands when people must part with their paper value symbols, 'Aw heck, Myrtle, there goes another $20.00!' The attention is not upon the bag of groceries which *is* the $20.00 in terms of three-dimensional, living-colour, real life havingness, but upon attachment to the *idea* of the money itself which, (a) represents no intrinsic value, and (b) the value of which can only be realised at the time of exchange. This is the ephemeral aspect of money. Having a lot of it for the security, power or the material wealth it *represents* is the essence of the Great American Dream and shows us how important symbols are in our society and how the economy, the very foundation of our culture, is as insubstantial as a dream, an elaborate fantasy of our own creation.

The real esoteric scoop (if there is such a thing) is that the universe is the source of our prosperity, not the financial structure of society as we have come to understand it.

Seed Money and Tithing Christ said, 'Cast your bread upon the waters and it shall return to you after many days,' and books have been written on the law of tenfold return. Here is how you get to keep what you give away; reap what you sow. Donating to worthy groups or helping financially when the situation calls for it, on whatever level, activates the economic echoes back to the source. This is 'seed money' in action.[11] Many religious orthodoxies have traditionally encouraged their members to pay for the prayers said for them, and to tithe 10% of their incomes. But human nature being what it is, this has resulted in too many men of the cloth wanting better cloth and storing up treasures on Earth as well as in heaven. Consequently, the business of money and the church got a lot of bad press. This is unfortunate because in the process, the real and dynamic principle of ten-fold return has been lost. Now, when it is explained to us by the more enlightened amongst our present spiritual leaders we somehow can't hear what is being communicated. The moment the kindly and respected lips form the sounds 'money' or more especially 'your money', we run the message through our filter of preconceptions and our mental reflexes snap into conditioned response with 'Oh no! It's that old ploy to get my money again!'

When giving of one's substance, either randomly or as tithe (which is contributing to the source of your spiritual nourishment or whatever makes you feel good about yourself, inspired and high, but not necessarily 'the church'), it is very essential to 'give and not to count the cost, to labour and not to seek for any reward save that of knowing we do Thy will'. These higher principles of universal subtlety are very sensitive to negative vibration when they are set into motion, and if one gives with selfish or ulterior motives the energy simply dissipates off into the ethers instead of bringing back the boomerang. Giving freely in an attitude of gratitude is where it's at and to know that just being alive and having a physical body is the most incredible gift, and that all blessings are *already* yours. You have but to put in your claim. When articulating your needs, come from a place of fulfillment and abundance so that the pattern is already complete and existing outside of time and space, and has only to manifest physically.

The idea of a world government and a world economy is, in a sense, like the Rorschach psychological ink-blot test. There is no fixed reality to it; it is simply a vehicle for each person's own projection. Interpretations range from that of national leaders who see it as the best way for nations to survive; business corporations who see it facilitating expansion and international trade; and others who may see it as an unfolding sequence of Orwellian dimensions. But any way you view it, the time *is* upon us for world unity and we move inexorably in that direction. Cosmic sources inform us through Spangler's *Revelation: Birth of a New Age* that the world consciousness has already changed from one of separation to one of attunement, communion and wholeness. It remains for personal consciousness to make that complementary change. The founding of the Baha'i faith in Persia in 1844 (recorded in the prophetic chronology of the Great Pyramid) was specifically to lay the groundwork for bringing world unity and world government to the highest purpose. A planet functioning as one harmonious unit is what the New Age, in its fullness, *is* destined to be. Therefore, computerization of a crowded global village may be as inherently OK as it is not OK, and its potential to serve or bind humanity may ultimately be as positive or as negative as those who control the system care to dictate.

The disadvantage in discussing who might *have* that control is that it is easier not to confront it at all, to dismiss the subject as paranoia or the ravings of 'conspiracy theory'. We do not write of these things but of people with the same values who tend to behave in the same manner, pursue the same goals and eventually organize and work with others toward the same ends. The results of collectivism, vested business interests, political alliances on up through to the consortiums and cartels is not so much 'conspiracy' as simply *the way it gets to be* at that level of unified power. The Bible's *Revelation*, however, describes as 'once the great men of the world who deceived all the nations with their sorceries' those kings of the Earth and merchants who deal within the system of the last great world power (defined as the modern Babylon, the 'whore' city devoted to materialism and sensuality) and who were made rich by her. The architects of the United States Constitution never envisioned democratic free enterprise as leading to the phenomenon of the multi-national corporations; and neither did Karl Marx. Perhaps St. John, the *Revelation's* author, did, though. Chapter 18 describes the merchants of the latter day Babylon as dealing in resources, precious metals, gems, grains, animals, chariots, ships, slaves, oil . . . 'and the souls of men'. God's people are told to 'come out of her [Babylon]' to avoid the pestilence, death, famine and burning which will destroy in a single day that city 'which had corrupted the Earth' for so long. As the mighty city is consumed with flames and thick smoke, the world's merchants view the conflagration from a distance in fear and torment, lamenting their ruin, 'for no man buyeth their merchandise any more'.

Our salvation, so to speak, lies not in opposing a pervasive (and predominantly unenlightened) power structure by force, revolution, violence or radical means, but by seizing and liberating key images, myths, archetypes, ideologies, established and protected mystifications and monopolies so that the light of truth may finally reveal and anchor on the planet the order of the universe—unclouded. As the *Astrological Predictions* chapter concludes, there are intensely powerful and positive celestial influences waiting to refocalize the chaos if we don't manage it by ourselves. The prophecies indicate that things will get worse before they get better, but after Babylon's demise the *Revelation* describes a mighty angel who symbolically sums up the action by hurling down into the sea a great boulder, like a millstone, crying, 'Thus with violence shall that great city Babylon be thrown down, and shall be found no more at all . . . .'

All cycles have their completion, even the negative ones. In the *I Ching* Hexagram #36, Ming I (Darkening of the Light), speaks of this process with a quiet clarity:

> The climax of the darkening is reached. The dark power had first held so high a place that it could wound all who were on the side of good and of the light. But in the end it perishes of its own darkness, for evil must itself fall at the very moment when it has wholly overcome the good and thus consumed the energy to which it owed its duration.

References
1. *European Community Magazine*, Dec. 1972.
2. Richard Raznikov, 'Bad News About Jimmy', *Marin Life*, Sept. 1977.
3. G. Edward Griffin, *World Without Cancer* (2 Vols., American Media, 1974).
4. *Press Democrat Parade Magazine*, July 15, 1979, 'Here Comes Truncation'.
5. *Datamation Magazine*, Oct. 1978, p. 53.
6. *Money Facts—169 Questions and Answers on Money—A Supplement to A Primer on Money*: Chairman Wright Patman—Subcommittee on Domestic Finance, Committee on Banking and Currency, House of Representatives, Sept. 21, 1964.
7. Washington *Spotlight*, Dec. 15, 1978, p. 10.
8. *CoEvolution Quarterly*, Winter 1979/80, 'Plant Patenting'.
9. Available from Truth Forum, PO Box 2946, Grand Junction, CO 81502.
10. *Beyond Isolation*: The West Coast Collective Food System as We See It by People's Cooperative Communities Trucking Collective (Free Spirit Printing Collective, PO Box 24112, Main Post Office, Oakland, CA 94623).
11. Jon P. Speller, *Seed Money In Action*, 1965.

16. Food

The food crisis – that is, the quality, price and availability, affects us all. The very rich may simply suffer the inconvenience of having to open cans of food for their pets instead of tossing the customary fillet succulents. But meanwhile, many of the poor in this country are eating canned pet food themselves – when they can afford it, and in other parts of the world they're eating the pets. Many have nothing. Many die.

The Malthusian dictum that the law of rapidly diminishing returns takes over when population exceeds food production is becoming a reality in our time. This law of diminishing returns is seen rampant everywhere. The process is gathering momentum and is compounded by changing weather. Most of our farms have become energy drains, requiring more energy input than they can quantitatively produce. Twenty calories of fossil fuel are now needed to produce one calorie of food. This is biologically unsound but representative of modern agriculture. Even so, the West has not yet felt the full impact of the scarcity which is freaking much of the world's population. Only small ripples, called 'fear-of-scarcity' lap gently at our toes. We ignore the incoming tide, attempting to deal with it by rhetoric.

Even under present conditions there is still enough food to go round. With some radical changes there could be enough to avoid a crisis entirely. Unfortunately, the United States is the major proponent of a system which has contributed to (and apparently intends to continue) the colossal inequities of food in the world today. For this reason, and others which we shall explore, the years of prophesied famine seem inevitable and should be taken seriously:

America has always been aware of the delicate politics inherent in its position as the world's largest food producer, and dominance as a major world power is not separate from the U.S.'s role as the good fairy with the big bread-basket. In actuality, the fairy is a myth and her goodness tempered by interests not wholly altruistic.

According to ex-Secretary of Agriculture, Earl Butz, 'Food is a weapon. It is now one of the principal tools in our negotiating kit.' This is no voice crying mean things in the wilderness. A Political Research Department report of the CIA, which was released in 1974, concluded that world grain shortages which are likely to increase in the near future 'could give the U.S. a measure of power it had never had before – possibly an economic and political dominance greater than that of the immediate post World War II years.'[1] That food is a weapon has already been amply demonstrated by regular news items concerning America's continuing role in toppling foreign governments and influencing the policy of other nations by withdrawal of aid. During Allende's efforts to nationalize industry in Chile, agricultural loans and food assistance from the U.S. were halted. He was assassinated by a CIA-backed coup which put a fascist government in power and restored U.S. copper control. Several American food corporations have been recently exposed bribing foreign governments in order to gain economic and political advantage. And in 1974, Bangladesh was told by the U.S. government that unless it discontinued exporting locally-made gunny-sacks to Cuba it would be ineligible for further loans on easy terms to buy American food. In Orwellian irony, nearly half the American 'Food for Peace' shipments during 1974 went to South Viet Nam and Cambodia. The dictatorships then sold the food on the open market and bought arms to continue the war efforts of both countries. The 'Food for Peace' programme sells food to many poor nations to help the 'world hunger situation' – a situation which it is, itself, perpetuating by its political preference for capitalist inroads for American business, which keeps people in bondage at low wages, producing things useless to their own needs.

An important aspect of the world food imbalance is caused by the land of many under-developed countries being monopolized to grow cash crops for multi-national corporations and the wealthy few, for crops like sugar, coffee, tea, cocoa, tobacco, etc. Consequently, these countries must import their own grain when they could be growing it. Local farmers cannot compete with the low cost of U.S. food and are forced off the land, which is then bought up by the corporate interests. The 'green revolution' has made the underdeveloped nations dependent upon the West by using fossil fuels, fertilizers and energy, rather than labour-intensive, methods. 80% of the U.S. exports for aid go to political allies and friends and we actually import more protein from under-developed countries than we send out – mostly to feed livestock for meat production. We actually discourage nations from becoming independent, from the benefits of land reform, from a better quality of life for their people, because the American way of life and its luxuries are largely dependent upon their dependence upon us! It's a vicious cycle, begun and perpetuated by the corporate interests of 'overdeveloped' countries such as our own. Many under-developed nations remain so also because they are subjected by an oppressive feudal system. Meanwhile, at home, it is the giant corporations who control commercial farming – Bank of America, ITT, Prudential Insurance, Tenneco, etc. They create monopoly-inflated prices in exchange for poor quality, expensive food.

A U.S. Department of Agriculture report leaked to the Washington Post in October of 1974 (that Pluto in Libra influence at work again) and states that the 'food gap' between rich and poor countries is growing wider every day and is primarily the result of economic and political decisions, not natural causes like drought and population. So, there you have it from the source. While growing populations and changing weather are undeniably related to famine, they are consistently used by the powers that be to camouflage (yes, you guessed it!) the corruption, mismanagement and outmoded practices which have made the planet so extremely vulnerable to these disastrous catalysts in the first place.

Fluke Weather Because of imbalances, natural and manmade, one can observe multiple problems which will surely develop historical precedents in starvation if they are not handled, by developing new approaches and making radical changes in the existing system. Unfortunately, it may be too late already. It remains to be seen.

Weather Change   To start with, our entire agricultural technology is based upon a fluke of good weather. The past thirty years has been a period of rare good weather – the best in a thousand years. Practically all of our present genetic strains of high-yield crops were selected to give maximum productivity under a limited range of environmental conditions, generated by a few sunny decades. Now that the weather patterns are changing, we find that most of the basic grains from which these present hybrids were taken, have not been saved by the United States Seed Bank (which, incidentally, has not received a budgetary increase in fifteen years).[2] Consequently, agri-business farms, growing hundreds of thousands of acres of a single hybridized crop, are vulnerable and entire crops can be wiped out by blight or inclement weather. The Great Plains provide 60% of

Seed Bank Depletion   world trade wheat and almost all animal feed. Throughout the Bible we see that ancient peoples saved excess grain in times of plenty for years of famine. They understood the law of rhythm and knew that fluctuations in yield were part of nature's cycles, and they prepared. Modern governments have not been so wise, and when the new 'miracle' strains, heavily dependent upon pesticides, were developed the old ones which were hardy and resistant to stress were mostly discarded. If the scientists knew anything about the laws of nature, they would have allowed for the cyclical nature of things and not counted on good weather and programmed seeds for ever. A food shortage is inevitable for the following reasons:

Pollination   It was so long ago that most of us learned about the birds and the bees that we have forgotten how dependent we are upon those little creatures, the honey bees, to pollinate our food crops. 20% of them have been killed off during the past decadee by pesticides and many farmers have had to purchase or rent bee colonies to get key food crops pollinated. Virtually all fruits and berries and many vegetables are being affected, and some livestock forage. No bees, no crops. Because this is a serious and increasing problem, work is now under way to have the honey bee declared as yet another endangered species.

Fertilizer Shortage   Petrochemicals are needed for the manufacture of fertilizers and natural gas is required to run plants. Many plants are presently closed until new sources of natural gas are discovered. Initially,

212

Soil Depletion one pound of fertilizer yielded up to 25 lbs. increase; now the same amount produces a maximum of only 5 lbs. because the natural fertility of the land has been leached by synthetic fertilization. The way things have been set up, a 3.5% increase in fertilizer per acre only adds a 1% per acre yield increase, and takes the equivalent of 88 gallons of gasoline to produce one full acre of corn. By the same token, because of chemicalization of the soil, American wheat which used to contain 15-17% protein now contains only 6-10%.[3] Americans will not eagerly reduce their consumption of 1.3 million tons of fertilizer which is spread each year on lawns, golf courses and cemeteries; an amount which would produce a year's supply of grain to feed about 65 million people in the underdeveloped countries!

Grain Misuse Also, it's very sobering to realize that animals in North America are better fed than most of the world's population. They consume 78% of our grain, as it takes approximately 21 lbs. of protein to produce 1 lb. of meat.[4] And how much grain is used the world over for liquor production? One can only guess. Grain itself is monopolized by six large dealers who buy up 90% of all the grain produced. Two of them, Cargill and Continental, control 50% of the world's grain shipments. When the export payments were around 50c a bushel recently they sold to a 'foreign' Panamanian company and collected $1 million in government subsidies (taxpayers money).

Monopolies The Panamanian firm was a Cargill subsidiary and the wheat never went to Panama. It was resold instead, and shipped to Switzerland at 10c above the U.S. domestic price. The 'big six' set the prices that will be paid for a farmer's grain as they control shipping and storing facilities and the farmers are dependent upon them.[5] The infamous grain deal with Russia was another in a series of travesties.

Shrinking Acreage Another important trend to be aware of is that small farms are going out of business at the rate of 1,000 a week in the United States. They are being forced out of business by the big agribusiness farms and tax-loss syndicates. Their valuable land, which could be used for growing a variety of crops to feed local populations, is being used up by highway expansion interests, shopping centres and housing developments at the rate of 600,000 acres annually. Other valuable land is used for non-essential and non-nutritive cash crops.

213

Production Snags   There are other problems too, conspiring to cause domestic food shortages which may be severe and prolonged, or last for only a few days or weeks. Either way, they are bound to cause extreme hardship if people are unprepared – strikes involving workers at petrochemical plants, farm workers, food processors, warehouse stockers and especially truckers. Any disruption of service could halt the production line from the grower to the consumer, and in the cities this would be an acute problem. The energy crisis – always hovering around the corner – could critically disrupt farm work, processing and distribution of foodstuffs. Cities depend upon uninterrupted service to keep retail shelves stocked. Once shelves thin out, buying rampages and hoarding panics begin. The American railroads have already become crippled and largely bankrupt in recent years and conveyancing of goods by land from the gigantic, central growing areas, to processors, packers, warehouses and retailers has become increasingly expensive and dependent upon gasoline availability. An alternate system exists in California. [6]

Deliberate Waste   To dispose of the incredible over-abundance of food which the early 'green revolution' produced in this country, farmers were paid huge subsidies to hold one in four acres of land fallow while ploughing under excess crops. The rest of it went to beef-up livestock and thus was promoted a larger per-capita consumption of meat by the industry. It's easy to see how this system was responsible for the poor of the nation still not being able to afford adequate food, because the prices were maintained artificially high to ensure profits and large segments continued to go hungry in America and to die of starvation in distant lands. The same is even more true today, although the fallow land has now been put back into operation.

There is still sufficient food and food-growing potential for every person on Earth to be adequately fed for a long time to come. The only thing that prevents this is the rigidity of the systems we have established, predicated upon maximizing profits as a way of life and at all costs. The system of institutionalized waste is 'so ingrained into our agricultural practices and in our attitudes and nutritional doctrine that we are all but blind to it' says Frances Moore Lappe,[7] author of *Diet For a Small Planet*.

Protein   Because of the high probability of drastic food shortages if basic systems remain unchanged, it is wise for people to address themselves to that possibility before it happens. It's soft-pedalling the issue, actually, to talk of food 'shortages' only. They will be but the first signs of massive and enduring periods of world famine affecting the entire planet, not just the poverty pockets.

At one time the recommended daily allowance of protein intake, published by the National Academy of Sciences, was 70 grams. In 1968 it was reduced to 65 grams and in 1973 it was again cut back to 56 grams for the average adult male. Right now most vegetarians daily ingest far less than that and maintain apparently good health. So, as food becomes scarcer we can expect to be told that we really don't need that much protein after all. We probably don't. American livestock, on the other hand, consume as much protein in a year as the entire populations of India and China combined,[8] and, tragically, there is no sign of that abating. Less meat consumption is a step in the direction of freeing land for food production and grain for needy humans instead of animals. Live simply so that others may simply live!

Food Storage   Storing food in times of plenty is not only prudent, it is essential when they are times like these. However, it's called 'hoarding' and 'immoral' when done in times of scarcity. The Mormon Church has always advised its members to store at least a year's supply of food for their families, and there is certainly historical precedent in this respect. However, in America, the land of plenty, people are not accustomed to thinking in these terms and, in spite of mounting signs to the contrary, resist the idea by denying that it could ever happen here. However, there is ample evidence that the stage has already been set for a big drama. The catastrophic expectation of many that if they had some food stored for emergency use it would be forcefully taken by desperate neighbours or plundering hordes, is not necessarily true at all. Starving people are not energetic because apathy and weakness, not to mention ill-health, set in very quickly. If a real famine were to hit, there would be a 100% chance that those who were unprepared would eventually perish. The chances of survival, healthy survival even, with stored food are certainly more

Complete Protein Vegetable Combinations

Beans	+ Corn		Soybeans & Wheat
	Milk		
	Rice	*Sesame	+ Beans
	Sesame		Milk
	Wheat		Rice
			Soybeans & Peanuts
Milk	+ Beans		Soybeans & Wheat
	Corn & Soybeans		
	Peanuts	**Soybeans	+ Corn & Milk
	Potatoes		Peanuts & Sesame
	Rice		Rice & Wheat
	Sesame		Sesame & Wheat
	Wheat & Peanuts		
		***Wheat	+ Beans
Peanuts	+ Milk		Cheese
	Soybeans		Milk
	Soybeans/Wheat/Rice		Peanuts & Milk
	Sunflower seeds		Soybeans & Rice
	Wheat & Milk		Soybeans/Peanuts/Rice
			Soybeans & Sesame
Rice	+ Brewers Yeast		
	Legumes (Beans)	*Sesame — spread, seeds or meal	
	Milk	**Soybeans — grits, meal, flour, tofu	
	Sesame	***Wheat — bulghur, flour, sprouted	

than that. After all, we buy insurance not because of total certainty of loss or accident, but 'just in case'. Food will never be cheaper than it is now, so if the worst does not happen, one can always eat one's investment – profitably. There are several reputable companies that produce emergency storage food plans,[9] and many excellent books on the subject which give instructions for successfully compiling one's own storage programme.[10]

A year's supply of food on hand is certainly not too much, but even a few weeks' worth of supplies might make the difference between calm survival and the stark panic which could result from a relatively minor cause such as a national trucker's strike, or some other short-term cessation of food availability affecting cities. For those who believe, implicitly, that 'the Lord will provide' regardless of their own efforts when food is suddenly no longer there, His provision will no doubt be to soften the heart of a friend who *has* stored food. They will take from their own families in order to give to the passive 'believer'. The triumph of true faith, or the ultimate rip-off? Do these people sit at their tables each evening and say, 'If God wants me to have food He'll provide' and then wait for Colonel Sanders to appear at the door with complimentary chicken? No, they do what everyone else does; they go to the store. If God has foretold the difficulty of the last days through his various prophets it was because he intended that those who would listen should be prepared – or why else mention it? Bear in mind that some major cities have been quietly training their police specifically for food riots, according to the Los Angeles Times. As Howard Ruff, Mormon and author of *Famine and Survival in America* put it, 'I'm going to act as if it's all up to me, and when I've done as much as I possibly can, I'm going to act like it's all up to God.'

Seed companies throughout the world are being bought up in a concerted effort by multi-national corporations in the petrochemical, drug, pesticide and fertilizer industries. Their new subsidiaries breed plant varieties increasingly dependent upon artificial pesticides and fertilizers. The U.N. Food and Agricultural Organization estimates that by 1991 three fourths of all *natural* vegetable varieties now grown in Europe will be extinct because (like the fast food chains) 'agriseed' cartels can invade with massive advertising and PR, making swift take-over inroads where the original, traditional varieties now predominate. Just as certain popular herbs and healing plants have been discredited, outlawed and supplanted by the patentable drugs of orthodox medicine, the agribusiness seed industry is moving, at this writing, to patent major hybrid vegetable and fruit species. Legislative efforts have begun for the U.S. government to join an international agency that coordinates plant patenting laws worldwide. In Europe growing or selling the seeds of any plants not contained in the Common Catalog of the European Economic Community is illegal. In a deliberate attempt to clear the market as quickly as possible for the new patented varieties, sometimes hundreds of varieties a month are deleted from the Catalog and violators are being prosecuted.

Modern agricultural technology seeks to make all crops as uniform as possible, eliminating the natural profusion of varieties found within each plant species. With the Green Revolution farmers and growers all over the world began to plant the same narrow range of hybrid seeds produced by the major seed companies. People simply stopped growing their traditional seeds, an infinite number of which promptly became extinct. Intentional elimination of genetic diversity is the real threat to future world food supply because infestation and climate change can wipe out in a single growing season not only an entire crop (the Great Plains grow 60% of the world's wheat, for instance) but also the possibility of replacing it with a more resistant traditional strain or breeding into it survival qualities from a related variety. As an example, the U.S. has only two types of peas and they comprise 95% of the total acreage devoted to that crop; there are only three kinds of millet to account for 100% of that crop, although there may have been thousands at one time, according to the Graham Center Seed Directory. If the traditional varieties are not *saved* by individuals and concerned organizations it may not be possible to breed resistance back into the limited and uniform quality hybrids now dominating.

Whoever controls the seed — the beginning of the food system — can control the entire system. The seeds of hybrid species cannot be saved and are not resproutable!

You don't need a computer to project that the outcome of such an unchecked trend could mean a virtual end of nature's infinite bounty as a free and self-perpetuating food source. It could be usurped, in a comparatively short time, by compulsory dependence upon the multi-nationals' expensive supply of sterile hybrids — a situation ripe for exploitation and fulfillment of the Biblical prophecy wherein a suppressive government removes seed sales from the market and only those bearing the system's official identification number ('mark of the Beast') would be able to buy food — especially during the global famines which could result from the lack of genetic diversity described.

Original open-pollinated varieties *are* still available from a handful of family-owned seed companies, collectives and old time growers. A catalog of such sources is available, together with information on political resistance to plant-patenting legislation.[11a] ('Original' refers to indigenous traditional plant strains which have evolved to successfully survive stress, climate variation and pests. 'Open-pollinated' means the seeds can be saved, usually up to two years, and replanted to continuously perpetuate their strain.) As a very real survival resource in terms of future food needs and also as a valuable instrument of barter in rough times, these original open-pollinated seeds have their place in every family's survival and storage plan.

Learning how to grow one's own food is not only economical and convenient, it is better food and an investment for the future. The present solution to the food crisis, posed by authorities and government agencies, is to step up production, mechanization and chemical use. This is, at best, buying time only and helping to postpone future crisis by sweating harder and faster on the treadmill. There are viable alternatives available for the taking, but they are not considered a realistic solution by the majority who hope the existing system can accommodate necessary changes according to the present rules. This way, the fringe benefits which accrue to the nation who monopolizes 60% of the entire world's resources can be sustained.

It is not the intent of this chapter to itemize intricate solutions to problems which are, after all, infinitely complex, but it is apparent to even the most humble layperson that something is terribly wrong and that some very obvious and viable solutions are being ignored and resisted because of vested interests.

We can understand, of course, how the necessary changes would completely disrupt and undermine the entire fabric of life as we have come to know it in the West. And that is surely why far-reaching changes of similar magnitude have only come about, historically, by revolution. Since revolution is so bloody-wasteful

> *If the world*
> *were a global village of 100*
> *people, 70 of them would be unable*
> *to read, and only 1 would have a college*
> *education. Over 50 would be suffering from mal-*
> *nutrition, & over 80 would live in what we call sub-*
> *standard housing. If the world were a global village*
> *of 100 residents, 6 of them would be Americans. These 6*
> *would have half the village's entire income; and the*
> *other 94 would exist on the other half. How would the*
> *wealthy 6 live "in peace" with their neighbors? Surely*
> *they would be driven to arm themselves against*
> *the other 94 . . . perhaps even to spend, as we*
> *do, more per person on military defense*
> *than the total per person income*
> *of the others.*

and wasteful of blood, and the majority of people pacifists by nature, if not by conviction, it would seem inappropriate to pursue such a solution. Instead, there should be a way for folks to accomplish the desired ends by unorthodox and joyful means. Means which would get everyone high instead of rich or fiscally secure.

'However' seems like a casual enough word to introduce the statement that there *is* a revolution under way at this very moment. It is a (r)evolution of consciousness, the most integrated and important aspect of which began some time around the mid-sixties and became manifest as the 'internal revolution'. This was a term generated by the natural foods movement which was largely responsible for the sap rising within a great number of attuned people, who thus began the movement from the cities back to the land to create simpler, healthier and more bio-conscious and self-sufficient life-styles.

'Group Think' It is not necessary, of course, to live in the country or even desirable for everyone. It's quite possible to be 'in the world but not of it' and the ancient Hindu writings tell us that in this, the Kali Yuga, enlightened men will be householders, not ascetics. By seeing and understanding the error around, one can break through the myths that dictate that things are just so and must remain so. Society is rather like the fish in Lake Tanganyika in West Africa. At noon the sun is directly overhead, and it is then that the fishermen row to the centre of the Lake carrying a lattice between two boats. Because of the time of day, the sun casts a vertical shadow down through the lattice into the water so that shoals of fish beneath the surface believe themselves to be caught in a net. Slowly the boatmen ease in to shore, and as they go the fish swim along, within the confines of the lattice shadow. The fish are then trapped in the shallows by waiting nets and harvested. People are also trapped and helpless within their own cultural myths until understanding the truth of situations eventually sets them free and they begin to extricate themselves from what are, in reality, the confines of their own group thoughtforms. We're only as free as we think we are, and for most of us that isn't very much at all. One particularly insidious group thoughtform is that modern diet and foods are desirable and that people who eat whole, natural, unadulterated food are faddists!

In speaking of changing the state of the world today, philosopher Michio Kushi says, 'Modern man has lost his intuitive self-direction and tends to become a robot within industrial society because his internal compass, his innate judging ability has declined under the influx of artificial and chemicalized food . . . To meet such a critical situation, metaphysical encouragement is unable to appeal to everyone. Since the cause of the present crisis is more or less of a biological nature, we must begin by restoring our dietary patterns. The reconstruction of humanity must begin with the correction of what man is eating.' He's right, of course.

Survival Diet In *Natural Sources,*[11] a volume on cancer prevention, the author has already extensively covered a wealth of material relating to diet transformation, healthful eating and long life. Most meat contains additives and hormones, fish contains levels of mercury contamination and commercial chickens are pumped full of hormones. Produce is chemicalized and sprayed. Suffice it to say that eating, whole, natural, organically-grown and unadulterated food will serve you well and that one is then spared the risk of selecting food from the confusing roster of cholesterol-building, cancer-causing, fat-making, brain-dulling, allergy-causing, health-impairing foods which form the commercial grocery inventory.

However, the only 'proper' diet is the one that works well for you, according to where your head is at and the feedback your own body gives you. Nourishment is the art of paying attention to these signals and the quality of input.

Community Resources Now, while food is abundantly available, it is important to take advantage of good eating habits and build a sound foundation for health and increased awareness. Many communities are forming food conspiracies (neighbourhood bulk buying clubs) [12] and food co-ops which control the quality and price of their food. [13] In San Francisco, non-profit community stores have sprung up in key neighbourhoods. They are cheaper than co-ops, more convenient than conspiracies and run by volunteers. Most major cities have begun to sponsor community gardening projects, [14] utilizing vacant lots where people can renew their sense of community and become involved again with the cycles of the soil. Judging by the number of publications on how to grow in your own garden or rooftop, indoors and in containers or in window boxes, it should no longer be necessary for anyone not to have cheap, fresh and good quality produce in season.

Don't Blame the Bugs Petrochemical use and synthetic fertilizers negatively polarize the soil and attract bugs and insects which are scavengers and have been programmed by nature with an affinity for confused plants of negative frequency. It is their dharma (life pattern) to feed off imperfection and keep the natural world in balance. Because the human race have failed so miserably as stewards of the Earth and created so much pollution and imbalance throughout the land, the insect population has proliferated to keep up with the demand. Not understanding that they are simply keeping up with the havoc we ourselves have wrought, we call them pests and infestations and blame *them*. A healthy plant would, by definition, have been produced by completely natural means and will absolutely not be attacked by blight. Mulching, composting and complementary planting will minimize bug problems and organic gardening is something that everyone can do individually to produce the best food possible for themselves. Remember, soil takes up to seven years to regain organic integrity after petrochemical husbandry.

The Hunger Project In the meantime, readers should know about the immense power of individuals to make a difference in the world when they have an idea whose time has come. Considering the implications of this chapter, there could be no better time for individuals 'to create, within themselves, the context of food sufficiency and an end to starvation on the planet as a manifest reality by the end of the century.'

In little more than a year since its inception almost 300,000 persons from many countries have become The Hunger Project.

Within three years of its inception a million persons from many countries became The Hunger Project. This project is unique in that it is not an organizational matrix *within* which its members function, but individuals who are simply *being* The Hunger Project in their own way by doing what they can. At all levels, from just telling others about it (to strengthen and expand the thoughtform and generate its reality) through to working at the highest legislative levels, each person's commitment and intention to end world hunger and scarcity in the next 20 years is forming a collective resonance, a manifesting force for change.

The principles involved in this process are those necessary to make the world work. There *is* a shift in the wind . . . and an idea whose time has come. You are invited to make it happen.[15].

References
1. *San Francisco Chronicle*, March 12, 1975.
2. *Community Nutrition Institute Weekly Report,* May 1974 (1910 K Street NW, Washington DC 20006).
3. *East West Journal*, Dec. 1974, p. 24.

4. Frances Moore Lappé, *Diet for a Small Planet* (Ballantine/FOE 1971).
5. Lobenstein & Schommer, *Food Price Blackmail* (United Front Press, San Francisco, CA, 1973).
6. People's Cooperative Communities Trucking Collective c/o PO Box 24112, Main Post Office, Oakland, CA 94623.
7. *Harpers Magazine Fantasies of Famine,* Feb. 1975.
8. Ibid.
9. *Co-Evolution Quarterly,* Summer 1974, p. 15.
10. *NASHA Survival Catalogue.*
11. Timms and Zar, *Natural Sources* (Celestial Arts, Millbrae, CA, 1978).
11a. Graham Seed Center Directory ($1.00), Frank Porter Graham Center, Route 3, Box 95, Wadesboro, NC 28170. For information on political resistance to plant patenting: National Share-croppers Fund, 2128 Commonwealth Ave., Charlotte, NC 28205.
12. *Food Conspiracy Cookbook & Members Manual,*
    Preparation & Organization of a Community Buying Club.
13. *Food Co-operatives, How to Start One & Make it Prosper,*
    Organizing a Food Co-op,
    Food Co-ops for Small Groups.
14. *Gardens for All.*
15. The Hunger Project, 81 Piccadilly, London W1V 9HF, England. The Hunger Project (International Headquarters), 1735 Franklin Street, San Francisco, CA 94108.

17. The Environment

'The Earth does not belong to man: man belongs to the Earth. All things are connected like the blood which unites one family. All things are connected. Whatever befalls the Earth befalls the sons of the Earth. Man did not weave the web of life: he is merely a strand in it. Whatever he does to the web, he does to himself.'

(Chief Seattle)

The original inheritors of this land were the Red people. They were the Earth Mother becoming conscious of herself in the corner of the great Earth and sky which this mighty continent represents. First asking pardon, they sought to liberate the spirit of all creatures and sentient life forms which they took for their use. Nothing was wasted. As part of a living network, each of the many tribes were sustained by the life-support systems found within the pockets and richly diverse folds of the Earth Mother's lap. In nature, then, the memory lingered of beauty experienced and regenesis to come, but in the world of today the beauty has all but vanished and undying artefacts are omnipresent. For many people, even the memory of how nature was is fading.

Scars of early error and the beginning of this continent's contribution to ecocide lie buried somewhere around Wounded Knee, Sand Creek, Powder River and the many places where the things that have ripped the web of life to the shreds it's now in! In the ecological scheme of things, humanity can currently and accurately be defined as a plague upon the Earth.

People are taking more from the environment than they are collectively replacing and at the same time creating more waste than can be disposed of: from over 100 billion beverage cans discarded annually to a premature proliferation of nuclear power (plants, bombs, breeder reactors) which threaten genetic biocide from 'no deposit, no return' radioactive wastes for the next 250,000 years! Environmentalist Gil Bailie addresses the issue this way, 'Maturity is the wisdom not to use all the power you have. Taboo is what to do while you're waiting on the wisdom. It's not like law exactly. Laws are political; taboos, religious. If a taboo is to work, something has to be sacred.' The human race is scheduled in the course of events to lose its dominant position in the organic complex. It is a transitional species which may be succeeded by weeds and termites. As H.G. Wells once said, 'It's a race between education and catastrophe.' The price system and the industrial state can only mine out the resources and move on. What backup systems do we have for when they're gone? Will we be left like trapped rats in a sewer? You decide.

All the pollution and exploitation inherent in a culture so out of harmony with the universe as ours is points out that homo-sapiens as a species is not yet housebroken. Still in its evolutionary infancy, it has barely progressed from that childish stance of hysterically insisting that this particular planet is the centre of the entire universe. Now that this curious species has become only a little more aware, it still officially insists that its own habitat and kind are the only planetary culture in the universe and that it is the master of that sphere, (but not, apparently, the most responsible).

Beings from more advanced planets than our own have been visiting Earth since we were mere protoplasmal, primordial, atomic globules, sloshing around in a swamp. But the main purpose behind the flurries of sightings and contacts with UFOs in recent decades is – observation. It is of universal, cosmo-geological interest when a leading species, a planet and a solar system are in a crisis and at the same time due to experience some accelerated and drastic evolution-

227

Marsh was ahead of his time (a 'head' of his time?) and because he was from Woodstock, Vermont (then a village of some 50 frame houses) he might even have enjoyed being called 'far out'. He was concerned about anything and everything that related to environments. He was particularly intrigued by the massive outflows of silt which he observed from the Italian Alps and Apennines, and which he calculated to amount to 220,000,000 cubic yards annually – enough to cover 360 square miles with seven inches of silt! In his travels to various parts of the world he noted that most of it was swept toward the equator, which led him to deduce that the equitorial diameter of the planet would be increased and its centre of gravity eventually displaced, thus affecting its rotation. As noted in the Pole Shift chapter, an accumulation of scientific data supports this kind of possibility.

It is significant to realize that today's pollution problems are derived mostly from the use of energy stores that were produced during previous historical cycles – the Noachian deluge, which may have been the time of the last pole shift. Since then, coal, the fossil product of plant and animal life, and oil, mostly of marine life, have gestated within the Earth. This means for at least as long as the approximate 7,000 years of recorded human history. During that time human activity was sufficiently slow not to disturb the overall ecological balance. Yet within the last 150 years we've managed to use up practically all of those resources. The Great Spirit is recorded in the Hopi tradition as cautioning against using the Earth's stores from their territory before the 'great purification' as they would only be used 'for selfish purposes and evil gain'. The Red people obeyed, but the pale 'hairy men from the East', as the Indians called them, arrived to divide and conquer them and sub-divide and conquer their land. Forests and grasslands, the hair of the planet, were successfully shaved and converted to profits, dust bowls and semi-desert. Mineral and energy resources were gouged out to the point of depletion and whole species have now been exterminated with more continuously endangered. The solution proposed by world leaders to supporting an increasing world population of 20 million a year, and coping with 'sudden' world dilemma is to find newer, more creative and ingenious ways to *continue* doing the very things that have ripped the web of life to the shreds it's now in! In the ecological scheme of things, humanity can currently and accurately be defined as a plague upon the Earth.

People are taking more from the environment than they are collectively replacing and at the same time creating more waste than can be disposed of: from over 100 billion beverage cans discarded annually to a premature proliferation of nuclear power (plants, bombs, breeder reactors) which threaten genetic biocide from 'no deposit, no return' radioactive wastes for the next 250,000 years! Environmentalist Gil Bailie addresses the issue this way, 'Maturity is the wisdom not to use all the power you have. Taboo is what to do while you're waiting on the wisdom. It's not like law exactly. Laws are political; taboos, religious. If a taboo is to work, something has to be sacred.' The human race is scheduled in the course of events to lose its dominant position in the organic complex. It is a transitional species which may be succeeded by weeds and termites. As H.G. Wells once said, 'It's a race between education and catastrophe.' The price system and the industrial state can only mine out the resources and move on. What backup systems do we have for when they're gone? Will we be left like trapped rats in a sewer? You decide.

All the pollution and exploitation inherent in a culture so out of harmony with the universe as ours is points out that homo-sapiens as a species is not yet housebroken. Still in its evolutionary infancy, it has barely progressed from that childish stance of hysterically insisting that this particular planet is the centre of the entire universe. Now that this curious species has become only a little more aware, it still officially insists that its own habitat and kind are the only planetary culture in the universe and that it is the master of that sphere, (but not, apparently, the most responsible).

Beings from more advanced planets than our own have been visiting Earth since we were mere protoplasmal, primordial, atomic globules, sloshing around in a swamp. But the main purpose behind the flurries of sightings and contacts with UFOs in recent decades is – observation. It is of universal, cosmo-geological interest when a leading species, a planet and a solar system are in a crisis and at the same time due to experience some accelerated and drastic evolution-

230

ary changes. Do you not suppose that in one of those far-off planets a humanoid culture flourishes in harmony and at peace? Is it really so naive to envision a planet with a history free of nationalism and ideological bias; with geographic boundaries instead of political perimeters to divide the lands between the waters? Instead of centralized national governments, isn't it remotely possible to conceive of regional, indigenous, governments in touch with the needs and ways of the specific locations of each society populating that planet? Could regional self-sufficiency ever replace the industrial state, and could the provision for needs instead of desires ever really satisfy populations better than growth economics? And, could a technology even a little more advanced than our own, not harness the universal flow of life-giving energy as it radiates from a sun, a wind, a tide (of water or consciousness), from the ethers – on whatever planet, somewhere in space?

The fledgling human race is about to learn one of the greatest lessons a child can learn; that of responsibility for its own actions. When an infant abuses its toys it has nothing to play with and laments the pieces, and when it puts everything in its mouth to experience pleasure it can get sick. The awareness is dawning that by consuming all we are becoming sick. The planet suffers. We are the planet and there's no separate existence.

Culture as a Trip The drug culture has opened up awareness to that very educational and basic element of perception, the 'trip'. At first, the subjective psycho-active experience seems like the sole reality, and then comes the realization that there are as many 'trips' or perspectives on so-called reality as the human mind can conceive – and more besides, all equally valid. Our entire economic culture is really a spin-off of a great many possibilities for regulating a society. Our present one is simply the full-blown expression of a single perspective. Yet people are behaving as if it were the only one possible and as if their lives depended upon it. This is true, of course, for those locked into the experience of the present cultural viewpoint or trip as the only possible model, as the sole reality. It's still an inconvenience for the others, who acknowledge it as a powerful trip (a power-trip) but their vision is creating another.

231

A successful culture is a semi-permeable membrane between the human and natural worlds. They are not different. *Planet/Drum*,[2] (a bio-conscious information network of ecotone overtone) explores the shift from the political and ultimately suicidal view of 'world-nation' to the essentially organic perspective of 'planet-region' emphasis. Organic growth should be the goal of a truly civilized society instead of economic growth fed by power demands and productivity.

Eco-Systems   The randomness of nature is contained within 'the law'. The law is simply the form through which life manifests itself for its own benefit and a perfect example of this is the ecosystem. This term was proposed back in 1935 by A.G. Tansley as a name for the basic unit of ecology – ecological communities and their physical environment – being considered a unit for all levels of biological organization. The biosphere itself is a giant ecosystem, as are Boise, Idaho, The Rolling Stones, a community garden or two people in love. All ecosystems are basically open systems, continually drawing in and releasing energy and matter. Like the semi-permeable membrane, the pathways of loss and replacement frequently connect one ecosystem with another. Ecosystem ecology is contrary to standard scientific modus operandi which considers parts first and what makes them operable, and wholes last. 'The creation ... of this new science of ecosystem ecology is, without doubt, the most important single event in the twentieth century' says Dr. S. Dillon Ripley, Secretary of the Smithsonian Institute. 'It may be the most important event in all history. It is our attempt to avoid the fate of the other great civilizations.' The Indians lived within ecosystems, the Chinese today are doing it. The West is not.

The present definition of logic does not include the concept of nature as a model for culture because the modern mind has been nourished on concrete. Concrete (the adjective) is a metaphor for concrete (the noun) which is as concrete as you can get. Logic is concrete; concrete is concrete. It seems that the failing of concrete-style logic is that it is unable to embrace the simultaneous sensory awareness of complex inter-relationships. The complex of ecological relationship does provide the ultimate logic of integration: individuals join to form species/populations; populations form

232

community/ecosystems; ecosystems join to form the biosphere, and if we wish to integrate our cultures within nature we do so at the level of the ecosystem which everywhere has a common structure and progression, but varies in composition and function, according to time and place.

McLuhan was the first to isolate the printing press as the invention responsible for launching civilization in its linear-oriented direction. This orientation has seduced society into giving it exclusive rights as the primary means of digesting knowledge and understanding of the external world. We like to have something substantial on which to rest the mind – preferably geometrical or mathematical in nature but, above all, linear. The compulsive penchant of science for detail analysing at the expense of overview has prevented our civilization from ever really seeing the whole gestalt of any issue. Consequently, the majority of our technological inventions are really marvellous, in the short run, but absolute disasters in the long term – precisely because the science that sired them was so deliberately myopic and because the universal laws we already know were not taken into account. Yesterday's solutions have simply become today's problems; an ever-expanding bubble about to burst.

Whole Systems Understanding whole systems is of prime survival priority for civilization right now. The attitude which fosters material progress and waste in the name of free enterprise is the same fragmented approach which idolizes the pursuit of eternal youth. It has relegated old people to isolation as useless rejects within society. No wonder the West is a culture afraid of death. Because it was profitable and because it stimulated basic human insecurity, commercial advertising and the media have sublimated the insidious myth of youth-fixation into the mass psyche. This is one small aspect of mind pollution more lethal by far than that of the environment. The former keeps the human soul in bondage to illusion and the latter environmentally imprints and conditions the mind into acceptance. This is how the negative power works.

Future Primitive The modern mind has also been conditioned to disdain the unsophisticated ways of successful adaptive cultures as 'primitive'.

233

While it seems likely that creative achievements of intellect, technology and science are desirable exercises along the evolutionary path to Godhood, many so-called primitive peoples are still close to the natural world from which they have emerged. They have not yet experienced the loss of primal innocence which such progress inevitably brings. We can look down from the top of the Empire State Building with our diet cola in one hand and a telescope in the other and observe what appalling ignorance and superstition is the lot of aboriginal culture. Perhaps it is not apparent from such lofty heights of judgement that these peoples have much to teach us.

The successful birth-control method of Polynesian women has mystified anthropologists for centuries. It is simple enough, in that their cultural paradigm dictates that pregnancy occur only when the spirit of the unborn is invited by the woman into her body, so that's how it happens.[3] The Tassaday tribe, recently discovered in the mountainous jungles of Southern Mindanao, are believed to be 'the most primitive human beings so far discovered' according to *Time*. Yet their tribal commandment is 'Let us call all men one man.' They have no weapons, and no words for 'bad', 'enemy', 'war' or 'kill'. The Bambara of the West African Sudan believe that the correct balance of the entire cosmos depends on their speaking good words. For them, speech carries part of the vital energy present in all matter. How's that for primitive?

The 'primitive' is something to be recaptured as the evolutionary spiral swings us back to our genesis, the primal state, but at a higher level of understanding than when we took our leave of it many eons ago. That state is called 'future primitive'. As Lao Tsu phrased it, 'The purpose of contracting (returning to Nature) is served by expanding (emerging out of Nature in the first place)'.[4]

From the more limited perspective of our linear twentieth century scientific heritage, we are finally learning that ecological stability = diversity, and that if that diversity is lost so is the ability to sustain populations and their life support systems under varying cultural and natural pressures. This diversity has already been dissipated throughout most of the civilized world, but nowhere more crucially than on the North American continent, with its massive centralization of crops, production and distribution centres and services. Those who can 'hear the drum' and understand the pulse of the times should prepare to rely on their own inner and local resources and upon cooperating networks.

Up to now, science has neatly inventoried the known world of what is possible into such a tight little box that most of us cannot cognize or experience phenomena outside its rigid and factual dimensions. The senses will not compute what the mind cannot comprehend, so now is the time for all visionaries to come to the aid of the planet. As the late Dr. Jacob Bronowski put it, 'Beyond facts, we describe not more facts, but images. We can only understand the information by analogy from the factual world.'

Intuitive Faculties It is now time to wean the mind from facts, logic and reason as the sole criteria of reality, and finally divest language of its prime rating. This simultaneously liberates other levels of mind and other ways of knowing. Perception is sharpening, intuition is becoming keener. Just feeling things on a gut level with that inner knowingness is hovering all around – an untapped resource waiting for us to recognize and use. As this ability, common to animals and 'primitives' develops, the human organism can become more sensitive and aware, integrating and transcending mundane limitations of consciousness. We can become less dependent upon the pedantic tyranny of words fed into the eye or ear, single file, to be received, interpreted and computed in orderly fashion by the brain. *Revelation is now possible.*

This approach to life has worked throughout the ages for autochthonous societies, humble extensions of the natural world, who have been schooled by crawling things and fish, the taste of the wind, the moods of the seasons and the light on the water. They survive intact until absorbed by the twentieth century. It is then they dissipate, become sick and degenerate. Technological power and ecological ignorance does this to people.

Perhaps this is the message behind the Beatles' song 'Let it Be'.

235

We certainly must begin to do that with nature. How else can there be attunement to her subtle and complex laws or understanding of the energies we observe at work. A culture of communities is necessary where these two vectors cross – the mystique of nature and the creative/practical possibilities of science/technology in the service of humanity and the planet. This can only be accomplished by an aware culture, by aware people.

This way lies transition.

.... And the end of all our exploring
Will be to arrive where we started
And know the place for the first time.

T.S. ELIOT

References
1. George Perkins Marsh, *Man & Nature: Physical Geography as Modified by Human Action,* 1864.
2. *Planet/Drum,* Box 31251, San Francisco, CA 94131.
3. French anthropologist Charles A. Muses at 1975 annual Conference of American Anthropology Assn. 'Parapsychology, Psychotronics and Anthropology'. Dec. 2-8, 1975.
4. Lao Tzu, *Tao Teh King,* Ch. 36.

18. Heal Ourselves, Heal the Earth
(or, 'Look Ma, no Planet!')

A long time ago, a distant planet in some far off solar system destroyed itself. It wasn't an accident, exactly, and it wasn't sabotage either. What happened, quite simply, was that over a period of historic time it had become confused. Instead of preparing itself for a splendid and glorious evolution, as any decent corner of the universe should, it ate itself up, imploded with an enormous burp, and became a Black Hole. The particles that escaped became an asteroid belt around the sun and remained there until some errant cosmic wind reduced it to dust .... but all that was a long time ago; 'once upon a time' you might say.

Technologist Buckminster Fuller and humanist Lewis Mumford represent two diametrically opposed philosophies about the best route to that glorious evolution. Both agree, however, that before a valid global order can be established humankind's spiritual and intellectual relationships with the natural, machine-made and physical environment must be profoundly refined and revised. They are talking about an eco-logical, harmony-oriented, scientific-spiritual transformation which is quite impossible while operating under the old priorities – priorities which include ripping off the environment and its creatures to maximize profits, preserving the illusion that making money and owning things are essential to happiness and welfare; political priorities which render a clean environment a threat to so-called free enterprise.

Writer/researcher Tom Tarbet views the present crisis as the culmination of ever more bizarre attempts to interfere with, or even replace nature by analytical technology. The 'tech/no-logic' approach is employed to repair the mounting damage of which *it* is the cause. It stubbornly insists that this is the cure for, rather than the cause of, planetary dilemma.

We have reached a point in history, you see, when we ought to have attained a higher level of consciousness to deal with the karma (Newton's law of motion) that is now catching up with us. Human level consciousness by itself, apparently, can no longer resolve the complexities it has created. Environment shapes consciousness just as surely as consciousness creates environment. Where the external world is out of harmony, our inner beings are proportionately stressed. As a self-perpetuating cycle each is the extension of the other. Consequently a great majority of modern disease and dis-ease is directly related to the imbalance between nature and the man-made environment, between ideologies and nature, and especially between our degree of spiritual awareness and nature. Where the two meet is called 'the Tao' or the 'Way'.

Since mass transformation is needed far more urgently than mass transportation, the metamorphosis can start immediately – from the inside outwards. If changes in nature occur first within the seed, then transformation can begin now, and within you: you must view the mess 'out there' from a perspective of inner ecology (egology?).

Elements and the Body The cardinal elements of earth, air, fire and water underlie all cosmology and the metaphysical sciences (where physics is now leading, by the way) and we are concerned with how these elements involve our environment, and ourselves as individuals within the greater whole. From the esoteric traditions we learn that the elements have their counterparts within the human body. Air and the mind are related; water and the emotions; the Earth and the body are of the same substances; fire and the spirit.

The following sections are presented to help get those basic human instincts out of mothballs and to stimulate the not-so-common-sense which we were supposedly all born with. By keeping plugged in to nature, or at least recharged by it, you may be spared the scientific and un-natural solutions to scientific and un-natural living. 'Not blind opposition to progress, but opposition to blind progress.'

19. Earth

It was an old Wintu Indian woman who said that the spirit of the Earth hates the white man because everywhere he had touched it was sore. She did not live to witness the recent seeding of a pervasive and deep impulse to return to nature, to be suffused by it. An ever-growing number of organic farmers, homesteaders, growth communes and spiritually oriented communities have the motivation and ecological sensitivity to nurture the land back to health, to again regard it as the Mother. Although the planet is now labouring in extremis, the increasing light of the New Age is again revealing the ancient knowledge which was dissipated before the dawn of this particular civilization and, like a small flame, secretly preserved only by those affiliations of higher consciousness. Timeless and profound truths are now being publicly released for people of good will everywhere to use with wisdom and speed. As humanity expands its collective awareness truth in an unprecedented measure is now discernable to the open mind and is readily attainable by individual effort, which in turn contributes to raising the level of the mass mind and, therefore, the planetary body.

Planetary Grid In healing the Earth it is necessary to know that it has its own energy points and 'ley lines' very similar to the meridians and acupuncture points of the human body. Continuing discoveries behind the Iron Curtain have shed some light on the nature of a grid system which overlays the Earth. Although new to the reality registry of science, this planetary grid was part of the occult body of knowledge which persisted in metaphysical lore for centuries. Plato

239

(an adherent of the Pythagorean School) who often dropped pearls of wisdom, knew of the sinking of Atlantis, the reversal of the Earth's poles, and was apparently also familiar with the grid system. 'The Earth,' he wrote, 'viewed from above, resembles a ball sewn from twelve pieces of skin.'

According to the journal of the USSR Academy of Science, *Chemistry and Life,* Plato was right. Examination of the Earth's surface from space photographs reveals that the planet projects from within itself to the surface, ridges and geophysical features which form a dual geometrically regulated grid of twelve pentagonal sections superimposed over a system of 20 equilateral triangles.

Planetary Grid

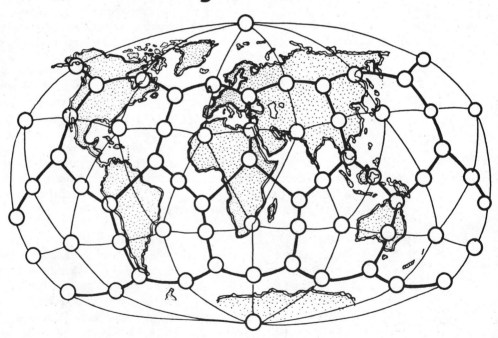

It took public knowledge of extensive psychic discoveries by the military in the Soviet Union to bring Western science's occult experiments out of the closet into the public arena. However, it is the new age publications who usually present such information publicly, well in advance of cautious official sources. According to *New Age Journal* No. 5, colour photographs from the Gemini spacecraft also indicate the presence of geological structures encircling the Earth. The ribs of this network coincide with mid-oceanic ridges, core faults and zones of slowly heaving topography within the ocean depths. Nodes of the grid frequently coincide with areas of minimal and maximal atmospheric pressure. Hurricanes appear to originate at these nodes, their paths tracing the ribs of the lattice, as do many of the prevailing winds and ocean currents. Geothermal activity coincides with large deposits of mineral ores and natural Earth resources lying along the faults and folds of the Earth's crust, often following the grid spokes. Where they intersect, several oil fields are evident. The 1973 International Volcanological Symposium in Bucharest[1] featured a presentation on 'The Planetary Network of Faults and its Significance in the Prognosis of Ore Deposits'. If energy resources are involved in the grid we can be sure it will not be long before the subject of this network is fully acknowledged and exploited by all countries. The slowly edging tectonic plates associated with the proliferation of volcanic and seismic activity are also found to be largely located along the grid's triangular edges. So much for the physical aspects.

Most people are accustomed to thinking in purely physical terms. Things are either alive or they're inanimate. In actuality everything is the manifestation of some form of living intelligence. Our own sun is the divine focus of a highly evolved, creative Being of great power and majesty. This Being, known as the Solar Logos, is hierarchically sub-ordinate to the Central Sun Logos and the Powers beyond. Our own Earth and sister planets are each the physical form of their respective planetary Logos. Currents of specific energies and power flow from the sun and between its planets to nurture environments and physical/spiritual energies suitable to the evolution of each. In his book, *The Magic of Findhorn,* Paul Hawken explains the role of the cosmically-attuned intelligences of the nature world known as

241

Devas and Elementals. These nature spirits assist the Earth Logos by working on the etheric energy levels to preserve harmony in the environment upon which the evolution of physical life forms depend. (Where there is a physical body or form there is also a spiritual one. There cannot be a materialization without the energy frequencies which allow for materialization of matter.) Contact with these nature beings has been established for over a decade now at the Findhorn Gardens in Scotland (where 40 lb. cabbages once grew in sand and roses bloomed in the snow) where truth seekers from all over the world have formed a New Age community dedicated to expressing the divine consciousness released at this centre via the Earth's power points and fostering the link between the natural and spiritual worlds.

Earth is the physical form of the Logos who is the source of ordered energy and patterning known to us as 'nature'. This planet is endowed with the same energy systems, physical and subtle, as the human body that evolved out of it. There is only one life.

Since ancient times it has been esoterically known that there are natural force lines, related to the Earth's magnetic field, connecting places of high vibration all over the planet in an etheric web. These are the spiritual or energy-level counterparts to the physical form of the grid. Such places are the sites of many sacred centres and shrines.[2] It is apparent that the ancient peoples of the Earth who located these sites (whether by geomancy or inspiration) knew what they were doing. Their cosmology was accurate and intact. Stonehenge was erected, not just as an observatory, but in a formation related to the etheric energy chain of the English countryside. The massive stones were placed to harmonize the natural energies of the Earth at that key point, just as acupuncture needles would be inserted in the body. Many such historical settings were chosen for geodetic and geographical purposes, in direct alignment with fixed stars. (We are beginning to learn that a relationship probably exists between the nodes of the grid and force-line projections terminating as Black or White Holes.) Specific energy force-fields released at these places made attunement to the higher forces there possible. The Indian nations of the ancient America came from all over the

242

continent to meet at the Medicine Wheel, unifying and radiating energy from the Wheel over the great land.

Now that this information can be fleshed out with some scientific evidence it is apparent that the focal points of the network do coincide with many places of occult and religious significance:

Nodes   The Bermuda Triangle, one of 12 major energy-vortexes on the planet, is at the centre of one circle with a forceline running Northwest intersecting Black Mesa (the spiritual centre of the continent designated by the Hopi Indians) on its way to San Francisco, a hub of New Age activity. The node in the North American Great Lakes area is the site of as many plane and ship disappearances and catastrophes as the Bermuda Triangle, according to Jay Gourley's book *The Great Lakes Triangle.* The line of zero magnetic deviation, where a compass points true North, veers Southeastward along the connecting ley line to the Bermuda Triangle. The Western Himalayas, seat of Buddhism for centuries and retreat of evolved mountain yogis, is seen as the hub of another wheel. One of its spokes intersects close to Lhasa, Tibet, historical residence of the Dalai Lama until the Chinese invasion of the fifties. At the spoke's Western peripheral node is the Great Pyramid of Giza, that massive energy transmitter/receiver located at the centre of the Earth's landmass at a point where the magnetic fields under the Earth, those on the surface of the Earth, and those of the celestial fields all cross so that the fields of alignment are direct, says J.J. Hurtak in his *Introduction to the Keys of Enoch.*

The etheric city of Shamballa, the heart chakra of the planet, lies over the Gobi Desert on the node of the Eastern spoke. The West Coast of Scotland is the site of yet another power point, coincident to the Isle of Iona, alleged resting place of King Arthur, and the early Christian site of St. Columba's Abbey. Another etheric retreat of the spiritual hierarchy is located over Lake Titicaca in the Andes. The Incan Empire originated in this region between Peru and Bolivia and the grid schematic shows another point here. Kyoto, the 'city of Shrines' in Japan is indicated at yet another point.

Forgotten for so many centuries, this dynamic network is today being re-energized and revitalized by centres of consciousness throughout the entire world. At the various loci of the web, magnetic radiance resonates ultimately to unite and elevate all forms once more to harmony and realization of their divine potential.

Cities, those concrete labyrinths of congested energy, interfere with the flowing of natural force lines which are the vital power of the Earth and its sentient beings. Geographical areas where the life-chain progression has been regressed or arrested by eutrophic swamps, sink-holes, pollution, waste-disposal, building development and freeways, are also violations of the land's numerous delicate forcefields and channels. They become, instead, acute sources of negative energy. All life suffers in proportion to the Earth's distorted energy flow, creating sickness in the planetary and human bodies.

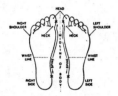

Consequently, the vast majority of people who live in the cities are unknowingly dreadfully out of balance in many respects. Visually and vibrationally, they are cut off from nature's nurture in the most profound of ways,

Living in cities, our feet seldom touch the Earth; our eyes are shielded from the light and we eat polluted and artificial foods unless we know better. Existing within an environment of concrete and glass, the negatively polarized vibrations of aluminum and plastic, fluorescent lighting and synthetic fabrics is to be insulated from the Earth; improperly grounded, electromagnetically imbalanced.

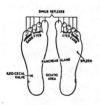

Energy is absorbed by the body from above and from below. The electromagnetic energy from the ground is channelled up through the soles of the feet for optimum functioning of the body. However, concrete is an insulator from this natural and necessary grounding process. Astronauts develop problems after long periods of weightlessness for this reason. When the electrical charge of the body becomes distorted and weakened through insufficient grounding it gets run down and fatigued. There are reflex points on the soles of the feet which correspond to the major glands and organs. These reflexes are analagous to acupuncture points, and stimulation of them for toning and correction of health problems is known as

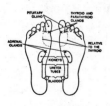

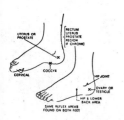

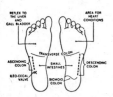

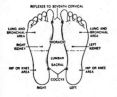

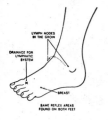

Reflexology. The ungrounded conditions of urban living make the soles of the feet vulnerable to tiny crystalline deposits of toxins which are formed because circulation is slowest at the lower extremities. Through their plentiful perspiration, the soles are discharge points for toxins. The electromagnetic flow to the body is weakened when deposits accumulate. Then energy flow to corresponding parts of the body is blocked and symptoms develop. Pressure-point massage of these foot reflexes is one way to compensate for this propensity.

When the Indians became sick, one of the first things they did was to enter the forest, rich in negative ions, where they would breathe deeply and sit with their back against the trunk of a tree. This way they grounded themselves, 'sitting in the lap of the Mother' as they put it, to receive healing. Walking barefoot on the Earth and running at the beach are effective ways to restore grounding to the body, and provide stimulation of the feet to break up any forming deposits.[3] By all means 'bare your sole!'

Clay has been used for centuries for curative purposes. French naturopath Dr. Raymond Dextriet, author of *Our Earth, Our Cure* says, 'Everything unhealthy and emitting negative vibrations is irresistibly attracted to clay (a brilliant positive pole) and becomes subject to immediate elimination.' In the *Essene Gospel of Peace* (translated from a third century Aramaic text discovered during the 1930's in the Vatican Library) we read that Jesus counselled the sick in the use of earth, air, fire and water for healing and restoration: 'Sink your feet in the mire, that the embrace of the angel of Earth may draw out from your bones all uncleanness and all disease.'

The Earth *can* most powerfully heal us if we let it, just as it is within our own power to heal the Earth.

References

1. *New Age Journal,* No. 5, p. 36.
2. John Michell, *View over Atlantis* (Ballantine 1972).
3. Fred Rohe, *The Zen of Running* (Random House, 1975).
   Mildred Carter, *Helping Yourself with Foot Reflexology* (Parker, 1973.
   Eunice Ingham Stopfel, *Stories the Feet Can Tell/Stories the Feet Have Told,* PO Box 12642, St. Petersburg, Florida 33733.

20. Air

Ions   At the end of the last cycle we are told that Noah, et al, took refuge in an ark. With the twentieth century penchant for innovation it will have to be something different this time around. Therefore, the latter day ark may well come as the new model 'P' – the Park . . . . where trees and living green things exchange pollution for pure air and produce negative ions in abundance. Negative ions are molecules with extra electrons. They are found wherever the air is fresh and clean. Negative ions have been found to accelerate the healing process, increase resistance to disease and infection, fatigue and hypertension as well as enhancing learning ability and the sexual drive.[1] Positive ion environments have bad effects on living organisms. They stifle the life-force and contribute to sickness and asocial behaviour. The density of smog-bound freeways and industrial areas, polluted city air, air-conditioned atmospheres and stale, uncirculated air deplete the brain function and energy levels. NASA has found that plastics and air-conditioning in spacecraft absorb and block the passage of negative ions so important to the crew's health and mental state. We also know that such conditions deplete the body's vitamin reserves and create a condition of stress. Electrical sources such as heaters and appliances, domestic and industrial, generate their own electrical fields and produce positive ions in the immediate atmosphere. All this indicates a case for increased intake of B vitamins to help handle stress; vitamin C to aid the body detoxify inhaled pollutants and prevent oxidation of extra vitamins E and A which are needed to increase tissue oxygenation and the permeability of capillaries to provide a better delivery of oxygen to the cells. Foods rich in these vitamins (or natural organic supplements) should be concentrated in diets of all city dwellers and trolls who hang out under freeways.

Electrically-charged, high velocity winds accompanied by sudden temperature increases and drops in humidity bring an excess of electrically-charged positive ions. [2] Air ions (not unlike LSD) affect seratonin metabolism in the body, producing radical changes in adrenal, pituitary, endocrine and thyroid function. They drastically affect the central nervous system and influence adaptation to stress and development of mood. According to Dr. Albert Krueger, professor of Bacteriology at the University of California, Berkeley, negative ions act to reduce blood-levels of seratonin in the mid-brain, thus tranquilizing a person from the emotional behaviour, anxiety and aggression produced by ambient positive ions. Negative ions influence survival in respiratory diseases, burns, and can affect thirst, appetite, sensitivity to pain, psychomotor performance and sexual behaviour. Through this process of ionization they cause erratic and extreme behavioural impulses and biochemical anomalies such as preventing the proper coagulation of blood. Doctors in Switzerland do not operate during a windstorm and the authorities are more lenient about crimes of passion at these times.

Israeli scientists have identified a common 'irritation syndrome' which accompanies the ion change in the air just before these electrical winds begin. [3] Clinically known as the 'seratonin hyper-function syndrome' it manifests as insomnia, migraine, nausea, oedema, palpitation, diarrhoea, tremors and vertigo. With it comes irritability, tension, depression, apathy and extreme fatigue.

Lunar Influence The possibility of future celestial disturbances preparatory to shifting of Earth's axis would be associated with wind-borne positive ionization. As mentioned earlier, massive electrical winds would also result from shock waves of a celestial body transiting close to the Earth. Like the moon, its positive electrical field would repel the positive field of Earth's outer ionosphere (the inner side is negative), thereby 'squeezing' our enveloping ionosphere closer to the Earth's surface. (When the moon is in its full phase this occurs and causes changes in air electricity so that it becomes more positively ionized, hence the origin of the word *lunacy* and the full moon's apparently mysterious influence on mental states.) This phenomenon would be intensified if the hypothetical body were closer or larger than the moon and, coupled with the hysteria such an event could generate, could well account for the mass insanity prophesied by the Bible.

There *is* a concentration of positively ionized air over much of the world right now. High velocity winds blowing over the current drought areas of the world and wind currents produced by the increase in frequency and intensity of earthquakes and volcanic eruptions are a major source. Wide-spread, irrational, confused and violent behaviour, triggered by this ion saturation is a growing and unrecognized social problem. Understanding the phenomenon and knowing how to contact antedotal negative ions is important survival information.

Negative Ion Sources
There are great concentrations of negative ions in the wilderness areas and along the sea coasts, swept by uninterrupted winds from the ocean. Mountainous regions are also rich in these beneficial ions and it may not be coincidence that geographically high cultures have been culturally high as well: the Incas of the Peruvian Andes, the Buddhists of the Tibetan Himalayas and the Hunza kingdom of the West Pakistan Himalayas where cancer is the exception and longevity the rule. In cities the places to seek are parks and gardens. The forests and woodlands of the suburbs are ion-rich in a beneficial way. Even a few little plants in a room raise the vibration and release their negative ions to create beauty and healthier indoor atmospheres. Asparagus ferns produce more negative ions than other plants. Large bodies of water, lakes and waterfalls are also associated with negative ions and so are cold showers taken in the home (the cold pipe is grounded whereas the hotwater pipe usually is not). Ion generating machines and electrostatic units are now available on the retail market.[7]

As one of nature's healers and sustainers, fresh air is a human birthright which the wilderness, forest and ocean still freely dispense. 'Seek the fresh air of the forest and the fields and there in the midst of them shall you find the angel of air . . . then breathe long and deeply that the angel of air may be brought within you. I tell you truly, the angel of air shall cast out of your body all uncleannesses which defiled it . . . ' says the *Essene Gospel's* account of Jesus' counsel.

Practical Applications In terms of increased food-growing possiblities for the future, there are definite implications for the role of ionization. Fifty years ago large-scale tests were being conducted with ionization therapy on food crops. Results showed that 80% of the experiments increased the yields up to 30% [4] Now that recent experiments at the Air Ion Laboratory at the University of California in Berkeley have shown that both negative and positive applications of ionization enhance plant production up to 50% (growth is stimulated by negative ions while positive ions cause leaves to retain more moisture and become more fleshy) we see here a practical means of developing increased food production modes. It is also possible that economically successful use of air ions will be made in the future of aviculture (bird raising) and related fields, areas already pioneered by the USSR. [5]

Prana In addition to the benefits of negative ions, there is another important component of air. It's called prana. Prana is the Sanskrit word for the subtle life principle permeating the universe. It is the underlying (etheric) energizing factor in air and water, and 'prana-yama' is the control of this cosmic life-force through breath. No scientist can yet give you the full lowdown on prana because its properties are too subtle to be analysed by instruments, but Soviet researchers refer to it as bioplasmic energy. Prana remains the domain of the yogi and the man of knowledge, but, we suspect, not for much longer. Science is hot on its track.

Prana can be stored by the body: deep breathing of fresh air suffuses the blood stream with the vitality globules of prana which are carried throughout the entire system. Not only does this increase circulation, but, by exchanging oxygen and carbon dioxide through the lung walls, it cleanses the blood of toxins, purifies and energizes the nerve channels. Yoga masters say that the cleansing and rejuvenating benefits to the body will outweigh unavoidable inhalation of polluted air.

The ancient practitioners of medicine understood the pranic process very well – the entwined serpents of the Caduceus (Hermes' staff – the symbol of the medical profession) represent 'serpent power', otherwise known as Kundalini/shakti force which originates

250

up from the energy centre at the base of the spine. The coiled serpent of mundane consciousness is gradually awakened by yogic discipline, personal evolution or through the help of an evolved teacher. With inner progress it is eventually raised by the interaction of the pituitary and pineal glands. This enables awareness to become stabilized in the higher centres of consciousness. When it reaches the top of the head (Crown chakra) illumination occurs.

The marriage of the physical and divine forces within us combines the inner and outer realities in divine synthesis, creating new consciousness, the new Being. This is the meaning of the Biblical exhortation to be 'reborn' and explains the mystical union of the Hindu Shiva and Shakti, formerly believed to be the pornography of a degenerate culture. This is the evolutional maturity required for New Age citizenship.

Kundalini The All-India Institute of Medical Sciences and the Max Planck Institute are currently undertaking a special international project for the study of the kundalini in which yogis and scientists of all nations have been invited to participate [6]

Shiva and Shakti The ida and pingala are the names of the pranic nerve channels symbolized by the snakes and they relate to the sympathetic and parasympathetic nervous systems. They flow around and synthesize within the central nerve channel of the spine (Shushumna) shown as the central rod of the Caduceus. The knob atop the rod represents the pineal gland or third eye (seat of consciousness called Ajna chakra) nestling between the wings or frontal lobes of the brain. Although this symbol has, appropriately, been adopted by the modern medical profession, their official leaflet on the Caduceus' significance states that they do not know what it means or why it eventually became affiliated with the medical profession. They regard it as 'controversial'. The significance is simply that the established healing arts are, as yet, still in their infancy. When the profession as a whole comes into a true understanding of the whole person and his/her relationship to the cosmos, they will simultaneously arrive at a comprehension of the esoteric symbolism which has, (like true success in healing) thus far, eluded them.

References
1. H. Lueder, *Biologische Workamkist Atmospharischer Ionen In Medizinischer Und Pravenhomedizimscher Licht.* phys. Med. und Rehabil., 11, 5:96-101. (1970)
2. Some of these winds are The Khamsin, Sirocco, Sharav, Zonda, Foehn, Chinook, Mistral, Santa Ana, etc.
3. Shulman, Levy, Pfeifer, Suparstein, Tal, Air Ionometry of Hot, Dry Desert Winds and Treatment with Air Ions of Weather-Sensitive Subjects. *International Journal of Biometeorology* 18:313-318. 1974.
4. V. H. Blackman, 'Field Experiments in Electro Culture'. *Journal of Agricultural Science*, 14, 240-267. 1924.
5. *Scientia. Revue Internationale de Synthese Scientifique.* Sept-Oct. 1969. 'A Preliminary Consideration of the Biological Significance of Air Ions.'
6. Write to Kundalini Research Foundation, 10 East 39th Street, New York, NY 10016 for free introductory book on the general concept of Kundalini by Gopi Krishna and Prof. C.F. von Weizacker, Director of the Max Planck Institute.
7. Information from Cosmic Creations, PO Box 99433, San Francisco, CA 94109.

21. Fire

There is more to light than meets the eye!

Jesus said, 'The light of the body is the eye' (*Matthew* 6:22). Today, and two thousand years later, scientists are able to confirm it. The eye absorbs the full-spectrum light rays from the sun into the body for its vital functioning while the feet draw in electromagnetic energy from the ground. The light 'eye-food' is as necessary to health as mouth or belly food.

The poultry industry knows this and has proved that light received through chicken eyes stimulates the pituitary gland and increases egg production. Therefore commercial layers are exploited and allowed only two hours' sleep in every twenty-four. Light entering the pupil causes nerve impulses that influence the lower brain and pituitary which stimulates hormones. The pineal gland, seat of consciousness, is also indirectly affected by light through the retinal receptors, according to 1970 Nobel Prize winner Dr. Julius Axelrod and others.[1] If the basic chemistry of the body is responsive to glandular actions triggered by the pituitary and pineal glands responding to light, then the characteristics of the light are also important.

Light Effects In his book, *Health and Light,* John Ott (pioneer of time-lapse photography with plants and founder of the Environmental Health and Light Research Institute) elucidates finely for the layperson. He reports, with photographic evidence, that after six months of controlled experiments with mice under pink-toned fluorescents, their tails developed lesions, became gangrenous and finally fell off.

253

Calcium deposits formed in the heart tissues, they bore smaller litters and developed behavioural problems. Under purple-hued lighting the mice lost their fur, developing bald spots; dark blue light caused their cholesterol levels to increase. Research results obtained by the Boston Veterans Administration and the School of Dentistry in 1970 had disquieting implications for humans: hamsters were fed a high sucrose diet. Half of them were exposed to lighting which approximated daylight (ultra-violet added) and the other half were under cool white fluorescent. The group under the full spectrum light averaged 2.2 cavities and the other, under normal artificial lighting, had 10.9 cavities, three times more severe. Additionally, this second group showed retardation of sexual maturity. Another study at the Chelsea, Mass. Soldiers' Home showed that the body absorbs calcium more efficiently under full spectrum light.

It is a fact that artificial lighting illuminates with an imbalanced spectrum. It is particularly deficient in ultra violet. We may well ask what effects, in addition to depleting the body of vitamin A, fluorescent lighting has upon office workers and people forced to spend long periods in such light. We know that such lighting also produces the positive ions which are not beneficial.

Glass does, through the eyes, what concrete does through the feet It deprives us of essential natural energies to the body's organs and glands. There are so many new diseases plaguing society today that the following study may provide some insight into the type and nature of contemporary pathology: New Jersey farmers were experiencing difficulty with squash growing a few years ago because of increasing virus problems which could not be traced to insect pests. Scientists at the U.S. Dept. of Agriculture and Rutgers University finally traced the problem to the recent reduction of sunlight reaching the Earth. Aluminum foil was then used on the ground to reflect more light and particularly the ultra-violet. This cured the problem and follow-up studies revealed a five-fold increase in yield. Other virus studies have been done related to lack of light. And since the introduction of sunglasses to native cultures in tropical climates, health problems have proliferated significantly.[2]

The point is, a great many people are caught up in the kind of life-style which habitually cheats them of the full-spectrum and ultra-violet rays. Living and working in offices and homes with commercial glass is unavoidable for most, but spending time indoors for entertainment, wearing glasses and sunshades of various tints, travelling in cars and buses for long periods, can almost totally deprive one of any real exposure to natural, full-spectrum light. For this reason plastic eyeglasses and contact lenses have now been designed by industry which admit almost the full spectrum (including the ultra-violet) and neutral grey sunglasses which reduce the brilliance of all rays evenly. Plain glass screens out ultra-violet.

A full-spectrum artificial light is now produced in incandescent and fluorescent types. Commercial tinted grey glass which admits full-spectrum rays is also available and should show the 'Full Spectrum Seal of Approval.'

Inner and Outer Illumination To quote again from Jesus words in the *Essene Gospel,* 'Put off your shoes and your clothing and suffer the angel of Sunlight to embrace all your body. Then breathe long and deeply, that the angel of Sunlight may be brought within you .... (and) shall cast out of your body all evil-smelling and unclean things which defiled it without and within .... None may come before the face of God whom the angel of Sunlight lets not pass. Truly, all must be born again of Sun and of truth, for *your body basks in the sunlight of the Earthly Mother, and your spirit basks in the sunlight of truth of the Heavenly Father.'* (emphasis supplied). The physical body receives light through the eyes from the sun of our solar system. The spiritual body receives its light via the third or spiritual eye from the spiritual sun, ('If thine eye be single thine whole body shall be full of light' *Matthew* 6:22) located at the consciousness centre known as the Ajna chakra, site of the pineal gland. The more this eye becomes receptive to the divine light, the greater one's spiritual unfoldment.

'Haven't you noticed the days
Somehow keep getting longer
And the spirit-voices whisper
In us all
Haven't you noticed the rays
The "Spirit Sun" is stronger
And a "New Day" is dawning
For us all.'

– *Hummingbird* by Seals and Crofts
based on the Bahai scriptures

References
1. *Experientia* 26, 'Electrophysical Evidence for the Action of Light on the Pineal Gland,' 1970. p. 26.
2. John Ott, *Light and Health* (Devin-Adair, 1974).

22. Water

Although the Earth's surface is more than two-thirds water, its entire immensity is almost all polluted. Draining to remove surplus water from the Earth's surface has resulted in a lowering of the water table. And because such large areas of plant cover have been destroyed a more rapid runoff is permitted, which means that less water seeps into the ground to replace the underground sources which have been depleted by wells and pumping operations. We are using up more water than can naturally be replaced. The spectre of drought, aggravated by wayward and eccentric weather, is an increasing and real global threat.

The Oceans In his eloquent plea on behalf of the seas and the creatures who inhabit them, Jaques Cousteau writes that our destinies are linked with theirs in the most profound and fundamental manner. To help save the oceans, from which all life originated and upon which all life depends, he has formed the Cousteau Society.[1] The ocean acts as the Earth's buffer by maintaining a delicate balance between the many salts and gases which make life possible. Every river that flows near an urban or industrialized area carries pollutants to the open sea and as a result the oceans are dying. Only radical measures will prevent the Mediterranean becoming a dead sea within 20 years, say scientists. As the seas gradually die the buffer effect declines and the carbon dioxide of the atmosphere increases the 'greenhouse' effect. This means that heat radiating out from Earth into space is blocked by the CO_2, and sea temperatures increase. One catastrophic effect of this is the melting of the Antarctic icecap by warm underground currents. Another deadly effect of the sea's heating is the extinction of its vegetation, decreasing available oxygen on the

257

planet, numbing the food-chain. *Revelation's* future warning about a third of the creatures dying in the sea (8:9 and 16:3) may now be read with a little more credence than before. The Smith's book, *Minemata* reports that mercury poisoning in the village of that name in Japan, caused fish and octopuses to move in the seas as if they were drunk. Huge amounts of dead fish floated on the water's surface and crows fell from the sky. Cats went mad and died in agony. What it did to the people who ate the fish of those waters will leave a dark stain in the annals of human history. Similar cases of this horrendous 'Minemata' malady of the central nervous system have been recently reported amongst poor Ojibway Indians eating fish from the English-Wabigoon River in Ontario. Perhaps the infamous 'soylent green' may be a *safer* food resource of the future than those offered by the sea.

Like the Earth, our own bodies are largely composed of water which is needed to flush and cleanse, nourish and provide energy and prana. Pure water is essential to health, and it is disappointing to learn that it is so hard to come by!

Drinking Water On April 18, 1975, U.S. National radio and press covered a report released by the Environmental Protection Agency that all 79 of the nation's drinking water systems which it had tested, including San Francisco, contained measurable amounts of potential cancer-causing chemical substances, several of which are formed by the chlorine which is the standard water purifier. Nevertheless, the U.S. Government Printing Office continues to circulate reprints of an FDA *Consumer* article on bottled water, which says, ' . . . All agree (Public Health Service, Environmental Health Service, FDA) that most public drinking water is perfectly safe, in spite of harmless aesthetic shortcomings in some areas.'

By the same token, an article appearing in the L.A. Times on February 21, 1974 entitled 'Fluoride in Fresh Water on the List of Pollution Hazards' quoted experts from 55 countries who opposed the hazards of fluoridation. On the same day the same paper ran another story attacking the anti-fluoridationists for protesting against the addition of more fluoride to fresh water.

258

Fluoride   A glimpse of the fluor-ride upon which most of the U.S. is coasting has its place in any consideration of health and environmental data. It's an important issue and one vitally connected with the nation's welfare. Ingested chemicals have subtle and far-reaching effects on the consciousness as well as the body. Here is the story on water:

The International Society for Research on Nutrition and Vital Substances and the Diseases of Civilization was co-founded by the late Dr. Albert Schweitzer in 1954. Its present honorary President is Dr. Linus Pauling. Its members come from major academic institutions in more than 75 countries and 98% of them voted against fluoridation in 1966 after considering the great body of evidence about it. The National Health Federation has also been studying fluoridation and after a recent study of 25 major cities with fluoridated water, has *unequivocally* concluded that 'Fluoride in the amounts added to public waters causes cancer and/or increases the growth rates of cancer cells.' [2] And independent studies by the University of St. Louis agree. [3]

These findings render fluoridation a violation of the Delany Amendment to the Food, Drug & Cosmetic Act, which prohibits the use of any carcinogenic substances in food or drink. It also violates the U.S. 1974 Safe Drinking Water Act. 'No national primary drinking water regulation may require the addition of any substance for preventive health care purposes unrelated to contamination of drinking water'. Since fluoride is added for so-called health purposes only and is not used for water purification it is clearly a contradiction of this Act.

Cancer Link   During the period which San Francisco has had fluoridated drinking water, the *New England Journal of Medicine* reports a 400 per cent increase in thyroid cancer in that city. There have been *many* studies proving that fluoride is related to thyroid malfunction. [4] Compared to the non-fluoridated West Coast cities, San Francisco has a 23% higher cancer death rate. [5] Nationwide, fluoridated cities have a 20% higher cancer rate than the non-fluoridated ones. People with kidney disorders, [6] urinary tract problems, diabetes, hypothyroidism or hypoglycemia, [7] are especially susceptible

259

to the destructive action of fluoridated water because their ability to excrete salts is impaired. There is also evidence that fluoridated water can cause kidney disease.[8] The Mayo Clinic has discontinued the use of fluoridated water for all kidney patients, and especially for dialysis machines, because of the development of symptomatic bone disease amongst those patients on fluoridated water.

According to the late Dr. K.K. Paulev, statistical analyst for the General Electric Company, official charts give the statistical illusion that fluoridation prevents cavities. What really happens is that in their early years, fewer children *have* teeth, because fluoridated water delays their growing-in by one to three years. Statisticians from several other countries have agreed with these findings, which is probably why most of their countries want no fluoridation.

Hardening of tooth enamel is actually a symptom which develops on the way from the standard one part per million, to mottled teeth and other signs of fluorosis (fluoride poisoning) in dosages from two to eight parts per million, at which time osteoporosis and bone degeneration set in. Dr. Hugo Theorell, Nobel Prize winner for his enzyme chemistry work, says the toxic effect of fluoride is first detectable in lipase (pancreatic juice) inhibition at one part in five million, but several earlier studies on enzyme inhibition put it at one part in 15 million.[9] Our standard drinking water dosage is one part in *one* million! The U.S. Water Quality Standards of 1975 designate the upper limit of permitted fluoride as 2 ppm. More than 2ppm has been legally condemned by these Water Quality Standards as unsafe.

The government reference book for pharmacists, as early as 1952, warned that fluoride depletes calcium from the body. As an environmental pollutant, fluoride does the same thing. It leaches copper from pipes and has other corrosive effects. The Ohio Sierra Club has filed a $9 million suit against the Harshaw Chemical Company, charging that fluoride emissions from its plant have destroyed the Harvard-Dennison Bridge over the Cuyahoga Valley. The bridge was closed in 1973 after engineers found much of it had been eaten away.

A Poison The fact is, fluoride is classified along with arsenic and cyanide in the Pharmacy Law as a dangerous poison. (The sodium fluoride used for drinking water is also used as a rat poison. Hydrogen fluoride, the industrial pollutant, has been classified as one of the major threats to wildlife, and what it does to animals it does to humans). According to our drug laws, it is a legal offence to sell or even give away one fluoride pill (1 mg.F), yet that is approximately the amount of fluoride found in each quart of fluoridated water. One can only draw the conclusion that adding fluoride to the water is, by legal definition, a poisoning of the water supplies, and that anyone who drinks more than two quarts of fluoridated water daily exceeds the toxic level. Boiling fluoridated water for cooking also increases its concentration because some water evaporates and fluoride is a salt.

Fluoride is a cumulative poison. It is absorbed from a variety of sources, including toothpaste and pharmaceuticals, from foods and beverages processed with fluoridated water and grown in areas near steel, aluminum, ceramic and phosphate industries (140 ppm has been found in Oregon crops). It is breathed in air pollution from those industries and from pesticides, herbicides, gasoline and aerosols.

How It Started The fluoride issue appears to have started back in the early 1940's when the aluminium industry's imagination. was sparked by a widely circulated magazine article in *Colliers* and *Readers Digest*. Dr. George Heard, a dentist of Hereford, Texas, published 'The Town Without a Toothache' questioning the relationship between his lack of business and the presence of naturally occuring fluoride in the local water. The Texas Health Dept. conducted a survey which tentatively confirmed that a relationship existed. However, several years later Heard wrote a disclaimer (but by then fluoridation had begun to proliferate): 'The dental investigators made a serious mistake when they gave fluoridation the credit for our good teeth. They overlooked the food grown in our rich, well-mineralized soil. It is these minerals, of which processed foods rob the body, that build health and good teeth. As the town grew and people began to live on processed foods, tooth decay increased by leaps and bounds in spite of the fact that people were drinking the same water.' [10]

261

The story is pieced together from the Congressional Record [11] that in 1944 the Aluminum Company of America hired an attorney at the astronomical salary of $750,000 a year, although there was no litigation pending to speak of. After a few months that gentleman became Administrator of the Federal Security Agency (now HEW). He immediately began plans to negotiate an arrangement with the aluminium industry (apparently triggered by the above publicity) who were then in a fluoride dilemma because it was not allowed to be disposed of in rivers and fields due to its high toxicity. The attorney in question began the promotion of fluoridation and the Aluminum Company of America began selling sodium fluoride tablets to put in drinking water. (In recent years the aluminium industry fluoride has been largely replaced by the cheaper sources from the fertilizer business.) Propaganda expert Edward L. Bernays (nephew of Sigmund Freud and inventor of the term 'public relations') was then retained for his services. In his book, *Public Relations and the American Scene* (Rumford Press, Concord, NJ) Bernays states, 'The conscious and intelligent manipulation of the organized habits and opinions of the masses must be done by experts, the public relations counsels. They are the invisible rulers who control the destinies of millions... the most direct way to reach the herd is through the leaders. For, if the group leaders accept our ideas, the group they dominate will respond... all this must be planned... indoctrination must be subtle. It should be worked into the everyday life of the people – hours a day in hundreds of ways... A redefinition of ethics is necessary... the subject matter of the propaganda need not necessarily be true.' Is this why the government, the medical and dental professions, and most of the public have come to believe that fluoridation is really desirable?

A P.R. Job

Dr. Frederick B. Exner of Seattle who testified at the 1966 Los Angeles fluoridation hearings said, 'If American industry had to stop polluting our air, water, and our countryside with the fluoride fumes and fall-out, and to dispose of its fluoride wastes without creating a public hazard, it would cost, not mere millions but countless billions of dollars. And therein lies the explanation for the utterly relentless drive to fluoridate our water supplies by any means, fair or foul, and many otherwise puzzling aspects of the drive to fluoridate.'

To sum up on this controversial issue, 91 nations, including the U.S., signed the Clean Seas Pact in 1972. This pact prohibited oceanic dumping of certain poisonous wastes, including fluoride, without special permits. Like the lethal radioactive waste, fluoride is a contaminative byproduct of industry which cannot easily be disposed of. The U.S. violates this prohibition by subversion, however. It is channelled first through the nation's drinking water and thence on to the open sea. In this diluted form an estimated 50,000 tons at least are eventually disposed of annually, and 100,000 into the air.

It is no secret that so-called primitive or indigenous peoples, living close to nature with a natural diet, do not have the enormous dental and health problems of so-called civilized cultures. There is evidence that in Haiti, for instance, the teeth and health of the people rapidly deteriorated once they began to eat the foods which the white man and modern culture provided. The same is true for the American Indians.

Side Effects Even if fluoridation did, absolutely, eradicate caries from the human race, it would still be unacceptable to many of us for the same reasons that pesticides are unacceptable. The toxic side-effects (a side-effect being something that we ignore the presence of for as long as possible) of both take too heavy a toll on the natural and human worlds. Is the possibility of stronger teeth worth the possibility of cancer and other symptoms? Refined foods and heavy sugar consumption are what cause most cavities and much of modern society's ill health. If the public believes that fluoride controls cavities in the young, the pressure is off the processed food and sugar industries, and fluoride waste is successfully disposed of by industry. This is a major triumph for the dark forces.

All that can reasonably be said now is that if there is any doubt in your mind about the quality of the water you drink and its relationship to your wellbeing, there are a number of viable alternatives available. Bottled spring water, the label of which indicates its actual spring source, is one of them. Distilled water from the large bottling companies is another. But for long-term investment and eventual savings, a home distilling unit, purchased for your family or together with neighbours is also sensible. Oxygenation and prana can be restored by pouring the water back and forth from one container to another before drinking.

As to the relative merits of distilled vs. fresh spring water – some say that distilled water eventually leeches the minerals from the body. Proponents of distilled water say that only the excess minerals are removed, such as those from arthritic deposits, gallstones, kidney gravel, etc. Those who favour spring water regard it as a source of valuable minerals, while those who oppose it hold that these minerals have accumulated in the water from its contact within the Earth and they they're not soluble in the body and contribute to mineral deposits such as the above complaints. The argument then goes that springwater was originally distilled by nature in the form of rain and the rejoiner to that is that if nature provides completely for one's needs one can hardly imagine the 'noble savage' boiling his/her water to stay well. Aboriginal cultures are strong and healthy for the most part and the abnormal stones accumulated in modern bodies are due to a combination of factors, including the consumption of city water. The top experts on health and nutrition do not agree on this subject.

What they do agree upon, however, is that either type of water is far superior to any city water. Take your choice.

The standard prescription in society today for the prevalent conditions of anxiety, frustration, hopelessness and inability to cope (which doubtless act as the seeds of later illness) is a 'visit to the doctor'. The doctor, in turn, prescribes the necessary tranquillizers, phsychic energizers, stimulants, drugs or placebos to cope with the situation (mostly by removing it from one's awareness). Illness is primarily caused by germs, viruses, pollutants and other physical manifestations attacking the body, they say. Andrew Weil, MD, author of *The Natural Mind,* speaks for the New Age consciousness when he views germs as *agents* of disease rather than its cause.

Organic farmers view insect pests in the same way. The established medical profession does not yet consider the whole person as the focus of his or her whole environment, physically, mentally *and* spiritually. The state of the art is still very primitive in that respect and the mystification, money and power which accrues to the profession and its practitioners is not easily relinquished to methods which whould necessarily involve people in learning to take responsibility for their own health. Most folks prefer not to take that responsibility upon themselves, anyway, and thus has come into existence a very 'scientific' but not very enlightened medical powerstructure.

The scientific preoccupation of today's medicine has resulted in doctors of naturopathy (nature doctors) being outlawed in many States. Apparently, science won't move until all the facts are in on 'nature' before it will concede that sun, fresh air, pure water, diet, etc. are related to health in anything but the most peripheral of ways. Nothing could be further from the truth.

> . . . . Only with the heart can one see rightly;
> What is essential is invisible to the eye.
> *The Little Prince*

> The truth is what is; not what should be.
> What should be is a dirty lie!
> Lenny Bruce

References
1. The Cousteau Society Inc., Box 1716, Danbury, Conn. 06816.
2. *National Health Federation Bulletin*, July/Aug. 1975, p. 2.
3. Ibid.
4. *Journal of the American Dental Assn.* (Editorial), Oct. 1944.
    Clinical Nutrition, Vol. 6, 1958, p. 459, Dr. H. Follis.
    Medical World News, July 2, 1972: Drs. T.K. Day and P.R. Powell-Jackson, Guys Hospital, London, England.

Hearings, 82nd Congress, 2nd Session, Pursuant to House Res. 74 & 447 Pt. 3 (p. 1517), 1952: Robert S. Harris PhD, Director of Nutritional Biochemical Laboratories, Massachusetts Institute of Technology.

5. *National Health Federation Newsletter,* July 1975.

6. *Journal of the American Medical Association,* Nov. 13, 1972, reported kidney damage by fluoride.
    'Fluoride and the Kidneys – a Review', Dr. Yudkin, reported at 5th Annual Conf. of International Society for Fluoride Research, Magdalen College, Oxford, England, April 1973. (Reported in the society's official journal *Fluoride.*)

7. John Yiamouyiannis, PhD, *Fluoridation* (NHF, PO Box 688, Monrovia, CA 91016).

8. *Journal of the American Medical Association,* Nov. 13, 1972, 'Renal Failure & Fluorosis' by Drs. Juncos and Donadio.

9. *University of New Mexico Bulletin,* Aug. 1, 1938, 'Menace of Fluoride to Health'.
    Physiology Review, Vol. 13, July 1933, 'A Review of Fluoride and its Physiological Effects'.
    Nature: New Biology, Vol. 231, June 2, 1971, p. 159, Dr. D.B. Ferguson, University of Manchester Medical School.

10. Ibid.

11. From the testimony of Florence Birmingham on May 25, 26, 27, 1954, on behalf of 50,000 women, as President of the Massachusetts Women's Political Club. It was published in a special Congressional Record book printed for members of the Committee on Interstate and Foreign Commerce, who held fluoridation hearings. Quoted in *Fluoridation and Truth Decay* (Ibid.).

Part Five
Coming Home

23. The Six O'Clock Bus

It was during one special Saturday evening in the August of 1969 that this book was conceived in the Berkeley Hills of California. The idea came as such a profound inspiration that my sense of amazement continued for some weeks. (I was surprised and intrigued when I learned, some time later, that the impulse had come at a time when the Zoroastrians hold their fire ceremony; a short period when the spiritual realms are said to be closest to the Earth plane.) However, as the demands of my job and everyday living caught up with me, my energy for the project soon waned. I wasn't really sure if I was copping out or whether it was just not the right time, but I put aside the research with the proviso, 'Well, if it's meant to be written, I hope I'll be alert enough to know when the right time comes.'

Several years and many changes later a close friend told me of a very disturbing dream he'd received the night before. Its meaning was immediately clear to me. I was amazed. Whether my interpretation of the dream was true I didn't know, but I did know that it exactly symbolized the subject that I had intended to write about. If the translation had any validity at all, it confirmed the dream of one man as a conduit for the collective unconscious. Being aware of cosmic reality at all times, it sends information through to the subconscious mind in the form of symbolic and metaphorical dream references. In the same sense, recent films like *Earthquake, Tidal Wave* and *Meteor* are all bubbles surfacing from the group unconscious, expressing latent themes of the future.

I felt very strongly that my friend's dream was a message of the urgency of the times and resumed work immediately. It wasn't until the volume was completed and the chapter sequence changed around a few times that I realized the similarity of this dream to the content of the chapter on Involution/Evolution concerning the significance of six, the number of return; the number of the bus.

Here's an account of that dream:

The dreamer found himself, reluctantly, in a dark basement. Someone lit a fire in the fireplace and he was surprised how brightly it burned, filling the whole room with light. It was a beautiful room, and although the furniture was very old it was all of good quality. A mutual friend from a monastic order was there.

The scene changed and now showed a young girl who was drugged and undergoing spasms. She was being held down by friends who acted as if nothing were wrong. The dreamer was shocked. The girl said she had been with someone in a dark alley, waiting to jump out on a passer-by to force them to open a bottle of drugs.

In the next scene the dreamer was sitting in the middle of the road. He knew that if he sat there with his back to the oncoming six o'clock bus it would take him back to town where he was to play Jesus in a pageant. He was worried that even if he got to the pageant no one would know he was meant to be the Christ because he had forgotten to bring his costume – a white cloak and scarf. He then realized that the clothes really didn't matter, because regardless, he would just 'be Him' in the part, and people would know. However, he eventually tired of waiting in the road for the bus and became afraid he would be run over if the driver didn't see him. So he wandered off to an area where he found an old abandoned bus in a state of disrepair: ripped seats and old newspapers lying all around. To his surprise, he suddenly discovered some cigarettes in his pocket and couldn't wait to light one.

As he was puffing away he noticed, as if by a revelation, that he had a watch. It was 7:30pm and he realised to his dismay that he'd missed the six o'clock bus.

In confusion and frustration he rushed from the old bus. Running along, however, he found himself in an area enclosed by a very high wire fence. He could have climbed out, but felt too lazy and indecisive about whether to make the effort. At that moment, a large dog, like a Doberman Pinscher, appeared. He had huge jaws and was jumping up and down. From a distance he looked friendly. Then, just as the dreamer took one last look at the top of the fence, the dog saw him and leaped toward him, snarling and growling. The high fence prevented his escape and the dreamer put his hands out in front to defend himself – noticing as he did so that they were clasped in the attitude of prayer. The dog immediately attacked him and began to gnaw ferociously at his hands.

The dreamer woke up in a sweat, whimpering and with his hands clasped.

. . . And a translation:

The dreamer is in a dark basement, unwillingly.

The unconscious – people tend to resist it, even fear it.

Someone lights the fire, and he is surprised how brightly it burns, filling the whole room with light.

Illuminating the unconscious and revealing

It is a beautiful room, and although the furniture is old, it is all of good quality. A friend affiliated with a monastic order in 'real' life is there.

a beautiful place. Ancient in origin are its contents but all valuable. The friend represents the spiritual link between the conscious and unconscious mind.

A young girl, drugged and having spasms. She's being held down by friends who act as though nothing were amiss. She said she had been with someone in a dark alley, waiting to jump out and force a passerby to open a bottle of drugs.

Humanity (the friends) accept suffering as natural, unaware that it is caused by illusion and the karma of our own ignorance and mistakes. Humanity is also drugged (under the influence of maya/illusion of matter) and in a dark alley (the world today), waiting for someone (technology, politics) to open their bottle of drugs (apparent solutions).

The scene changes. He's sitting in the middle of the road.

The 'middle way' between extremes taught by the Buddha; the road to higher consciousness.

He knows that if he sits there with his back to the on-coming six o'-clock bus it will take him back into town

where he is to play Christ in a pageant

He's worried that even if he got on the bus no one would know he was meant to be Christ as he had forgotten to bring his Jesus costume.

But he realizes then that the clothes really don't matter, because regardless, he would just 'be Him' and the people would know.

Nevertheless, he tires of waiting and becomes afraid he will be run over if the driver does not see him.

He wanders off and finds an old abandoned bus in a state of disrepair with ripped seats and old newspapers.

To his surprise he suddenly discovers cigarettes in his pocket and can't wait to light one.

As if by revelation, he notices he had a watch all the time. It's 7:30 pm and he realizes he has missed the bus.

Waiting for the future (it is unseen). Returning to the town – returning to the 'garden'/Godhood/evolving back to perfection. (See chapter on Involution/Evolution for six, the number of return represented by the bus.)

wherein he would manifest the Christ-consciousness.

His ordinary outer consciousness began to doubt the validity of what he was doing,

but insight tells him he need not convince anyone by external means, as the inner essence would communicate itself and be all sufficient.

He loses faith in 'the way' and the promise of the future, feeling unworthy.

He discards the 'real thing' for an unreasonable facsimile as people tend to do in life,

settling for the mundane sense-pleasures which cloud the spirit

and forgetting the lateness of the hour (*Luke* 21:34) although guidelines (the watch) to our divine heritage have always been there. (The *I Ching* says in 'Fu' the hexagram of 'the turning point', 'If a man misses the right time for return he meets with misfortune. This misfortune has its inner cause in a wrong attitude toward the world. The misfortune coming

In confusion and frustration he rushes from the old bus. Running along he finds himself in an area enclosed by a very high wire fence.

He could have climbed out, but felt too lazy and indecisive about whether to make the effort.

A large Doberman-like dog appears, jumping up and down. From a distance he looks friendly.

As the dog leaps toward him snarling and growling, the dreamer takes one last look at the top of the fence, realising escape is too late.

He tries to defend himself, putting his hands out in front and notices that they are clasped in an attitude of prayer. The dog attacks, viciously biting and gnawing at his outstretched hands.

The dreamer awakes, whimpering.

upon him from without results from this wrong attitude.')

He (representing humanity in general) begins to feel trapped.

The fence is life's illusions of limitation (maya again!) and the inertia of people toward overcoming them or finding solutions.

An obvious symbol of danger, which viewed from a distance does not immediately seem threatening (the world situation).

The danger approaches and escape is no longer possible, although it was earlier.

He (the world) is defenceless and engulfed by the danger (the great purification) and by that time it's too late for prayer or religious postures.

Your next question is precisely the right question . . . .

273

24. On Survival

'Let us not look back in anger, nor
forward in fear, but around in awareness.'

(James Thurber)

In view of the preceding chapters and the uncertain quality of the
future, anxiety about survival is natural. Personal survival, preservation of civilisation, the human species and the planet are
questions which surely plague all of us. Is there death after life? Did
Mu and Atlantis really exist? Was terrestrial life seeded here by
interstellar parents from the galactic network? Is the asteroid belt
between Mars and Jupiter the remains of an advanced planet called
Maldek which blew itself up? And will history repeat itself?
Enquiries of this nature are valid, but fear really isn't, because when
you're living within 'the Law' survival *occurs* in the same way that
money becomes available when you're doing the right thing. You
can never objectively pursue the kind of survival necessary for the
future because it is ultimately inherent in the course of living
right-use-ly, sensibly and in attunement with divine will. It's also a
matter of karma.

To people who are not, to some extent, spiritually awakened any
advice on this subject may sound unrealistic or foolish. Therefore, it
is of little constructive value to suggest any measures to them.
People who are conscious in that sense already know by inner
signals that preparation is necessary for the transitional phase
ahead, or are instinctively making the kind of changes in their lives
which will automatically put them on course. The inevitable wave
of cataclysm can only be surfed to safety upon the raft of the Law.
There is no other way, realistically speaking, that will carry a
person through.

Attunement To think of current and future world crisis exclusively in the physical terms of food and energy panics, economic and political chaos, international conflicts, environmental devastation and looming catastrophes is to miss the point entirely and fall short of a recognition of the even deeper issues involved. Not until we can see these events as part of an epochal change in human consciousness arising from the interaction of our innermost beings and cosmic timing can we fully comprehend the crisis in its true and holistic perspective and remain relatively calm in their midst. To concentrate on the stormy physical details of the coming rite of passage is to become open to fear. This can only block the flow of spiritual intelligence which will show from within what to do, where to go and how to act. Divine impulse is received through meditation, prayer, dreams and in the form of inspiration and receptiveness to direction. Worrying about the physical body's survival and mental fretting leads to confusion and a distorted scattering of judgement. But being concerned first with the spirit will allow the physical and mental needs to manifest for one's highest good, creating resilience to fear and repelling it from the aura.

One can avoid becoming overly anxious about the future, its possibilities, probabilities, dangers and threats—which may or may not ever happen—by learning to concentrate fully and immediately upon being here now and in present time, completely. Training the mind to 'heel' is a facility which will insulate one from the future tense and the preoccupation with fearful details which can only give them energy. Prepare to take care of future food needs in whatever way seems appropriate to you but let it not become an obsession. The same applies to other basic needs. Centering one's attention upon the *flow* of events within a far wider context, that of the whole 'master plan', will provide energy to cope with trials and fortitude to sustain one's centre in the face of difficulty.

Emotional Body When the involuntary emotional body becomes overstrained there is a burden on the mental and physical bodies, and a mental or physical breakdown is likely. Therefore, the emotional body must be strengthened and disciplined to rule the other bodies. The physical body, as the 'temple of the spirit' must be purified and kept in shape for the light to flow through, otherwise it will be impeded by the impurities and become sick. This means developing the tools and abilities for health and spiritual strength now, in order to become strong and knowledgeable before these abilities become necessary to survival. In 'Wei Chi/Before Completion', the *I Ching* says, 'Now is the time to lay the foundations of power and mastery for the future.'

The divine radiations brought by the increasing light come from the flow of universal life energy. This flow is expressed as the 'Chi' of ancient oriental origin and can be harnessed within the body by such disciplines as Tai-Chi, Akido and other martial arts. Various yogas can also sensitize one to this process by activating kundalini energy. Meditation, attunement to nature and the many spiritual disciplines put one in touch with it.[1] Purification and attunement are always the goals.

Preparation The great cosmic law is that the spiritual precedes the physical. Spiritual preparedness is what is needed for ultimate survival. However, because most people think in the reverse sequence confusion is created. If this were true and the physical could manifest before the spiritual or mental realities, only the wealthy and cunning would survive the times ahead, and that's certainly not the way it will be. Adequate material necessities, food and tools are essential when you know that for a while scarcity is in the nature of things, but beyond that is the next level involving actual survival skills. Living from nature, on the move, perhaps; foraging and growing; shelter construction; understanding weather and using wilderness knowledge far above the boy scout level, is something many of us know nothing about (although we'd be wise to learn). If survival totally depended upon these skills, the rednecks who shot 'Easy Rider' would be the most likely to make it. We know of a Californian who has stashed a ten-year food supply on his private property. He has it cordoned off by barbed wire, plans to plant a minefield and has enough ammunition to keep the Weathermen happy for a long time. He may survive for a while. He may also be the kind of person whose property will be swallowed up by an earthquake! So let us state it very clearly: those who embody the consciousness of the New Age and are performing greater services to humanity will receive divine protection. 'Hurt not the Earth, neither the sea, nor the trees, till we have sealed the servants of our God in their foreheads.' (*Revelation* 7:3). The good shepherds know their sheep and the light from the spiritual eye in the forehead identifies those on the journey home. The stormy channel from this age of sorrows to the New Age cannot be navigated by life-forms of unrefined vibration. This is the Law.

Inner Connection In a storm, a reed is flexible and can bend with the wind; the oak, being rigid can only be uprooted. And in the times ahead those who are flexible and have prepared themselves will find that the accelerated changes to come will not manifest so much as a strain upon them but more as a profound opening of consciousness.[2] Spiritual survival qualities are in the range of the inner spectrum: love, faith, understanding and affinity for others; being compassionate and mastering emotions, self discipline, responsibility, strength and courage. Being able to hold one's centre, to go within for what is needed and make the cosmic connection, to utilise subtle energies of body, mind and spirit, is to be able to survive. And to be of One mind, to attune to the master within, the Christ consciousness, to the Father. The ascended Masters in their communications to the Earth plane, do not prophesy dire calamity because the planet's ultimate fate depends upon humanity itself from moment to moment. What they do affirm is our divine destiny which is inherent and expanding at all times. In an interview with the United Press during the 1950's, Paramahansa Yogananda said that no break-up of the Earth was in sight and that another two billion years of equinoctial cycles remain to the planet in its present form. *(The Road Ahead* discusses other future world prophecies by Yogananda.[3])

In translation from V.17 of the glossary of Crowley's *The Book of the Law* we read, 'The infinite unity is our refuge, since if our consciousness be in that unity, we shall care nothing for the friction of its component parts. And our light is the inmost point of illuminated consciousness.'

Eileen Caddy, a founder of the Findhorn Community in Scotland, received the following words of divine guidance for the future, 'Now is the time when all shall be revealed, when those who truly know

277

the meaning of one-ness with all of life and live and demonstrate it will find they are indeed in the eye of the hurricane and that nothing will be able to touch them, no matter what is going on all around. "A thousand fall at thy side, and ten thousand at thy right, but it shall not come nigh thee." Why? Because your faith and trust is in Me and Me alone.'

Communication with the divine force personified as Limitless Love and Truth is revealed by David Spangler in his inspirational book, *Revelation: The Birth of a New Age*. The transmissions repeatedly emphasise that they are not prophesying destruction, nor trying to focus peoples' attentions on the negative aspects of change or on the old; rather, they are trying to encourage an attunement to a building, creative Presence. The message is not to judge, not to separate into the saved and the lost, not to be concerned with one's own salvation, but to turn one's energies towards service and holistic, inclusive creativity:

'I am with all. None are saved. None are lost. There is always only what I Am, but I have revealed Myself in new Life and new Light and new Truth. Those who attune to that will not be saved. They will only be attuned to what I Am in My new revelation. And those who heed Me not, but follow the downward course as human level consciousness unwinds itself and enters a new cycle, they are not lost. They only attune themselves to what I will become in a future revelation to them, but apart and separate from what I Am now.

'This new man (of New Age consciousness) filled with My presence, cannot be touched by whatever falls upon the old. Should nuclear devices be used, the energies will be the revelation of Me. All that will remain is of what I Am and all that is not of Me shall disappear, to follow another law and another destiny.

'No man knows the time of My coming. I Am already revealed all about you, if you will look within and about yourselves and see Me. See naught but Me, and know My presence with you. There is no waiting, but for those who choose to wait for the hour of My universal revelation, they will know when it will occur. Behold! In the next second, I AM.'

References
1. Spiritual Community Guide for North America: Box 1080, San Rafael, CA 94902
2. *Season of Changes, Ways of Response,* (Associations of Light Morning, Box 32, Virginia Beach, VA 23458. Heritage Press. 1974)
3. Swami Kriyananda, *The Road Ahead,* (Ananda Publishing, Nevada City, CA. 95959).

25. The New Age

'Be not conformed to this world; but be
ye transformed by the renewing of your
mind.'   *Romans 12:2*

Earlier chapters referred to the merging of our solar system within
the higher vibration of the Central Sun's aura. The cosmic
summertime converges again upon this corner of the cosmos and
upon all levels of terrestrial life as our world becomes more closely
aligned with the regions of the centre of the Milky Way. The mighty
radiance of the Central Sun is invisible to scientific sensors because
this confluence of celestial and physical energies takes place beyond
the ultra-violet reach of the spectrum. (Light comes into the
spectrum at the ultra-violet end and passes out via the infra-red
end. This 'Doppler Shift' is used by science to detect the advance or
recession of celestial bodies.) Nevertheless, the blossoms of human
consciousness have been embraced by its warmth and are even now
unfolding instinctively to the light, harmonizing and raising awareness to a new evolutionary level.

A New Colour The Oriental cosmology gives a fuller understanding of this phenomenon, and has traditionally divided the polar opposites of nature,
matter and spirit into the opposing complements of Yin and Yang.
As far as the physical spectrum is concerned, Yang, at its most
earthy and masculine is denseness, infra-red, while Yin at its most
feminine and spiritual (refined matter-energy) is expansively ultra-
violet. The forces in movement at this moment, gestating beyond
the ultra-violet of deep space, are evoking the energies of a new

cosmic ray into the spectrum of consciousness. Accordingly, the Yin, feminine aspect of nature is stirring with a new vitality. On the human level it is manifesting in an explosion of creativity and in the form of the Feminist movement. Its purpose is to balance out and harmonise perfectly by its Yin-feminine forces the traditional aggressive Yang-masculine emphasis of a culture based on logic, production, the physical sciences and political technology (refer to chapter on Spirals).

In *The Book of Revelation*, Chapter 12, a divine woman is described. She's clothed with the sun and wears a crown of twelve stars in her hair. The moon is under her feet. As she gives birth to a male child a great red dragon waits to devour it, but the child is caught up and spirited to the throne of God. This surreal reference is a metaphor for the ascendency of the Feminine Ray which will bring forth the birth of the Christ Consciousness upon the planet. Although the negative force in the form of the dragon is 'loitering with intent' as they say in England, trying to prevent this birth, he does not prevail.

The new Feminine Ray enters manifestation as an extension of the ultra-violet and will profoundly influence consciousness as it continues to take form. Many natural events now beginning to occur will augment this process. For instance, the coming alignment of the solar system's nine planets in 1982, according to NASA, will bring an increase of up to 20% in solar activity which will coincide with an unusually long solar cycle. The result will be phenomenal storms on the sun which will emit intensified ultra-violet radiation. The effects of radiation upon terrestrial life will depend upon the strength of the protective ozone belt which is already leaking in excess ultra-violet due to manmade causes. Solar activity influences the Earth's magnetic field which directly affects the body's bioelectric field and thence the nervous system which responds to impulses from this energy field. Ultra-violet rays affect the oxidation processes and increase the exchange of gases in living nerve tissues. Electrical charges within the brain both activate and respond to various levels of consciousness. Disturbances in the heavens, as predicted, will be related to the incredible leaps of consciousness and the radical changes which will envelop humanity toward the culmination of the century.

The place humanity is heading towards is at once a kind of hazy Shangri-la of the mind, beyond the usual separative distinctions, and yet also a new state of reality which can be tapped into at will. Up to now, human identity has been experienced in a fragmented way like the pieces of a jigsaw puzzle jumbled upon the table of life. Always deep within its psyche was the knowledge of an interdependence, a oneness, and the possibility of unity. This was accomplished on a limited scale when some of the pieces came together, creating a perfect expression of a small part of the overall picture. But the theory was never fully realised, never clearly understood in a functional way – until now.

Manifesting the 'Real' World

Now the human mind is becoming free of the illusion that the skin separates us from the 'outside' world. As philosopher Alan Watts would say with a chuckle, 'Is my head in the world, or is the world in my head?' Indeed, it is both. There *is* a real world around us which many dimly perceive and of which some even have subliminal glimpses. Only the 'superior man' (as defined by the *I Ching*) is sufficiently free of the world's illusions to see clearly the 'real world' and to function within it. Cutting through that illusion is what Castenada's mentor, Don Juan, meant by instructing him to 'stop the world'. The mundane world is what we have unconsciously created and what we perceive it to be through the filters of our own projections and the distortions of the mass mind. The *real* world is, quite simply, the state of affairs that exists within complete universal harmony. It's run by the creative intelligence of Beings of Light (enlightened ones) who function beyond the duality of that group consciousness, and the range of the five senses.

When we breathe in it could be said that the world is in our head: that which exists *is* because we subjectively perceive it to be. We contain the universe within the limits of our consciousness of it. In a sensory deprivation chamber, during sleep and after death it continues in another fashion, but ceases to be in the form which the five senses apprehend and habitually compute to the brain's receptors, the bio-computer.

Conversely, when one breathes out, a seemingly objective world comes into being all around. We are specks, overwhelmed, within an infinite universe. 'The Dance of Life' is aptly named, because the whole of conscious existence is one of shifting focus, like a mirage, between the inner/subjective reality different to each of us, and the outer/objective verity which no one subject to involuntary subjective states can even identify as such. Somewhere between lies Truth, the absolute attunement of what is so at any given time. The knowledge available to humanity at this time and the tools it is discovering will provide the wisdom to use both in the service of the one life. This will lead to fuller knowledge of Reality in the future.

Above all, the New Age is an era when inner and outer realities may be held as historical concepts only. We are destined to progress from the present cold plateau of division and separateness of traditional 'I/Thou' relationship and outer awareness. We shall reach heights very soon where only a synthesis exists which is not associated with inner or outer anything, but only oneness with and flow between.

In a similar sense (sigh?) choanalytical approaches to integration are aimed at the deeper levels of mind to aid the separative personality or ego to sustain its own imagined security or self-esteem. But, as Gina Cerminara points out in *Many Mansions*, although they are justifiable goals, they fall short of real integration at that most crucial level beyond the strata of the mind: the spiritual. Spiritual objectives beg the acquisition of soul qualities and the learning of spiritual lessons. Ego really blocks the view because in order to see Truth a person must be able to penetrate the limitations of individual ego, no matter how well adjusted that ego may be. When both these integrative approaches are combined and directed to the highest good of the individual and all of life, inner evolution unfolds much more swiftly because the outer personality (which is only the costume which each soul wears) undergoes less inner resistance to the educational but often unpleasant experiences of life.

In his amazing biographical work, *Memories, Dreams, Reflections*, Carl G. Jung states, 'Only here on Earth, where the opposites clash together, can the general level of consciousness be raised. That seems to be man's metaphysical task – which he cannot accomplish without "mythologising". Myth is the natural and indispensable intermediate stage between unconscious and conscious cognition.' This civilization is now preparing to bridge that intermediate stage, literally bringing to light and into the conscious mainstream of life those things which have hitherto been submerged within the darkness of the unconscious and of unconsciousness itself.

Redirecting Consciousness

Human laws and technological creations are an (albeit deluded) way of exercising creative Godhood: mastery over mass, energy, space and nature. You could call it a kind of evolutionary adolescence accompanied by the same self-assertiveness and obstinate need to prove independence from the parents – in this case, the Heavenly Father and the Earth Mother. Modern WoMan *has* the consciousness required to manifest desires, it's just that they have apparently been the kind of desires which create problems. Thus far the universe has been dealt with through reflection. Consciousness has been externalized and used to develop scientific and technological prowess in the physical world, as well as attempting through science to understand its parts. The direction of this consciousness can be creatively and positively rechannelled by any collective act of will.

Outer Limits

Civilization's energy resources are being used up, economies struggle under the tremendous weight of voracious production needs, and it is becoming apparent that the incredible energies which were harnessed built but a one-way street, down a pier. The 'march of progress' took us for a ride and here we are, almost at the end. The consensus of those in power deems it necessary to continue building the pier. Available efforts and materials are still being poured into defence and energy production because power is still considered more important than knowledge. The United States talk of 'Peace through Strength' but a true state of peace depends upon every part of life being seen as inseparable from the whole and as East meets West perhaps their facility for introspection will give the West a handle on how to invert the collective consciousness, which, when externalized took us all for a ride. The concern should not be

284

to stand at the end of that pier and plan how to 'keep our head above water', but to learn to fly! We can soar if we do not panic and learn the needs of the time.

Perspectives Blast-off from planet Earth in 1969, free and into outer space: destination moon, was really the external echo of an inner breakthrough, a symbolic excuse for another kind of blast-in to inner space which countless beings on the planet have begun to experience in recent years. As above, so below. In the same sense, art up to the Middle Ages did not have the facility to convey perspective. Essentially, artists of that period were graphically unable to render a three dimensional representation upon a two dimensional medium. However, when an inner change began to permeate the mass mind at the beginning of the Renaissance, it brought forth a blossoming of the human spirit and a fuller perspective on life which was soon introduced into the graphic arts as an ability to portray depth. Likewise, the written forms of the ancient Egyptians were too limited to communicate abstrations or conceptual thought, and this fundamental limitation carried over into their art. The 'sidewalk' is an example of their attempt to cope with the subtleties of perceptual foreshortening in figure depiction. The limitations of modern times have far surpassed the stage of our chaotic art, they are mirrored now throughout the entire planet – chemically impressed, geographically imprinted and genetically etched.

Self as Source The source of all creation, creativeness, creativity, from which to build new priorities, discover new solutions and produce new realities, lies within us, of course. When guided by divine Law and Will there can be no failure. Deep within our psychic being there is a core of light which is the life essence and cosmic connection to Reality. It is the part which is God-given because it is indestructible and in His image. It's called the Self. By learning to use the reverse gear of awareness and focusing within, conscious contact can be made with that point of light. The size depends upon one's spiritual development. As the seeds of openness and attunement to divine impulse are cultivated there is access to more and more of that light. An outward change begins and the consciousness becomes illumined, bringing more wisdom, love and judgement to bear in daily life. The light from the end of the tunnel begins to get brighter and a spontaneous joy can be realized that there IS hope after all, just when it seemed that all was surely lost. With that realization one can learn to fly. It is possible to free oneself from the pull of gravity which anchors existence to physical plane illusion. Breakthrough velocity is needed to guide humanity through the looking glass into the next stage of inner evolutionary development.

The planet is fecund with opportunity right now from those who have made the journey and returned to show the way. These persons are free agents in a world of illusion. 'When the student is ready the teacher appears' is absolutely true, be it in the form of a life-experience, book, personal insight or guru. The true teacher, of course, is the holy spirit. As individuals, guided by the spirit, open to the impetus of new knowledge, love and truth, it must be shared and recycled (just like money) and well used to ensure the continued flow. There are advanced souls amongst us as teachers and guides. For the most part they avoid the dogmas that divided and fanaticised the past. Instead of imposing things from without, they lead by nurturing the finer instincts, inspiring unfoldment from within. The compulsion of many parents and teachers to produce 'clones' or reasonable facsimiles of themselves, their wisdom and world-views is at best a power-trip and at worst a genuine block to human experience. 'How to' books are well sold today because they reflect this feeling that education at its best frees people to be themselves, their own master, and provides fulfilment along the way. True education helps people make the most of their lives, not just memorize facts.

> 'Here is where it is
> Now is when it is
> You are what it is
> Celebrate!'
> *Werner Erhard*

The New Age, of course, is already here. To the extent that each person can feel it, however abstractly, and manifest it according to his/her best vision, it exists. When such people are drawn together into groups, and similarly motivated associations form networks, a powerful and transformational magnetic grid emerges. Because transmutation can only happen via the medium of consciousness first and form later, the new order is being nurtured in its infancy by those focusing more on energy and space. Matter and time are more important to material progress and the old guard who see changes more in terms of outer physical expression, but miss the connection with consciousness. This is not to present the future as a state of abstraction, but rather to indicate that the forms it selects will be conducive for the human spirit to move into a freer, less structured, conceptual framework of existence.

When social scientist Richard Alpert, PhD, parted academic and psychedelic ways with Dr. Tim Leary, he studied in India under a jungle saddhu named Hari Dass Baba. Later, when Alpert returned to America as Baba Ram Dass, his subsequent book, *Be Here Now* blew so many minds and inspired so many seekers of truth that Hari Dass Baba was invited to America. One afternoon at a darshan in a private California home, Hari Dass was asked about the role of LSD in the culture, since it has presaged for so many an earnest and sincere spiritual quest. Hari Dass's answer was simple: 'The West is a very materialistic society, therefore a material substance was necessary to open people up to an awareness of spiritual reality.' It played its part in breaking up the monopoly of matter over the senses, compulsive societal concepts and programmed ways of thinking. Perhaps this is why there is so much expensive merchandising of spirituality in the West. The more money people invest, the less sceptical they become. 'After all, you want to get your moneys-worth, don't you?!'

Flexibility   A beautiful publication of psychic interpretation of coming Earth changes by Associations of the Light Morning,[1] says, 'A new spiritual awareness can not be born within a mind that is firmly attached to old ways of thinking and perceiving. A great flexibility is required. Just as the caterpillar must willingly submit to its near total disintegration of form within the darkness of the cocoon, so must we be willing to release ourselves from that bondage which is created by the limitations of our minds. For transformation can come only through such a release and then the subsequent restructuring.' We are again reminded to simplify our needs, to de-materialize this culture, literally and figuratively. The fruit of simplicity is peace – the result of luxury is more luxury, and inertia. Making the right kind of refinements in physical needs frees valuable time and energy for pursuits more fulfilling to inner needs than just acquiring and sustaining comforts and superficial accoutrements. In the West, happiness eludes many because they believe they don't have enough. In the East they say it eludes them because they haven't given up enough.

The energies affecting our solar system have now shifted into higher gear and will continue to do so. The greatest 'gear' in the universe is turning under the Creator's great cosmic plan. If our own 'gear' can be turned in harmony with that of the divine, we will be in resonance with the unfoldment of that plan and our lives will progress smoothly. The juice is being turned up to prepare everyone for the graduating class. Limitless Love and Truth, the divine force and source of guidance quoted earlier exhorts us to 'be His name'. 'I Am the new heaven in the emotional, mental and super mental realms, now manifesting themselves with increased power. All thought, all feeling now have increased power, either to resolve themselves and disintegrate, or to build themselves through being attuned to the nourishing source which I Am and through that attunement being able to receive New Age energies. These will augment beyond belief the power of thought and feeling to manifest, in your physical realm, things which exist on the inner. You are coming to a time when, to an increasingly greater degree, you will be able to manifest and create through thought and through feeling. You already do this, but your power in this is being augmented. You have termed it instant manifestation; it will become far more instant than you believe possible. Let each man, therefore, make consistent steps, even if small ones, to manifest what I Am, to grow and to expand in His love, in His light and in His Truth . . . '

The vision of the New Age in terms of its potential for human unfoldment, represents a return to harmony under the Law, and resonance with the true Oneness which existence is. The inner vision, held for so long, is already expanding and taking form, becoming externalized upon the planet. The increased vibration of

288

the light is drawing into expression an impulse which stimulates from within the urge toward life, toward the good. A blending of potent energies is being stirred into activity within the alert womb of awareness.

The task of people of good will who form the leading edge of the expanding wave of consciousness is to assist the birth of the new order. It is time to externalize now, through the highest principles, the civilization of the New Age. It's an infinitely creative project which is not focused upon destroying the old ways, rebelling against or retreating from them. It has very much to do with finding and giving energy to ways of releasing new potential and acting in cooperation with others to bring the appropriate ideals into physical form and function. 'Use your energy for, not against' is the key because when you're against 'that', energy which could be used for creating and reinforcing 'this' is lost.

Those who embark upon this course have the expanding energies of the new wave to support their efforts now. Negativity from the Piscean Age, and all that is corrupt and unserving in the existing system, gained power at a time when evolutionary energies were not strong enough to challenge that momentum. Through sheer habit, group agreements and customs which fostered ignorance and self-interest it reached its present hold. That world will continue, of course, until its thrashing is exhausted, living off stored resources like the starving fat person. Endeavours which remain plugged into the dying battery of the old world will increasingly have nothing to draw upon.

The Power and Light Circuit The system which holds the human spirit in bondage is already absolescent because lies have no power except to 'delight the devil' and create confusion. They have no anchor in prior or living reality, but only the shallow roots of words spoken from a lower consciousness. People create their own realities by what they think and believe, and speaking from one's convictions does produce a certain kind of power because its forcefield is self-generating and originates without duality. However, words or actions based exclusively on belief may be utterly fabricated misconceptions. The power they generate has but a closed circuit and only its own emotional juice to

289

draw upon. This becomes more complex when skilful media and vested interests manage to propagate false concepts, perpetrating lies upon entire populations, and this is pretty much the condition of the old system as it has grown over the ages and exists today. However, when Truth is manifested or spoken (the 'living Word') it is cosmically charged with light and living power because it is rooted in the infinity of beingness. Vibrantly alive, it exists in Reality. This is the *power* of Truth. And this is why the corrupt power-structure of the old system will finally crumble. This is also why the new, being consciously aligned and rooted in Truth is the extension of unlimited light and power. To grasp the essence of Truth is to grasp the mythical strand of silk, following it to safety and freedom from the dangerous and delusive confines of the labyrinth.

The Earth has now emerged into Springtime from that bleak progression through the cosmic winter in the constellation of the Dragon. Very little light was available to humanity then, and many hard lessons were learned. Now it is vibrantly alive, scintillating with pro-evolutionary energies filtering from the highest sources – the Creator Himself, the profound forces of the Solar and Planetary Logi, ascended Masters, the many helpers of humanity, and Beings unknown, terrestrial and otherwise. From intradimensional and subtle sources the flow continues through the form the Great Central Sun, blazing in deepest space with silent and unimaginable radiance; our own sun, source and sustainer of all sentient life, and from the many known and unknown planetary influences throughout the universe. What does the old world have to offer? Nothing but its own bagged lunch; dark messy stuff which its propaganda insists is good for it.

Expanding life can no longer remain bound within the chrysalis from which has thus far confined and nurtured it. It has now to absorb and merge with subtler energies and create for itself a new organism more suited to the alchemical transformation through which it must pass before it can emerge into the light of its new world. The new Being is destined to become the essence of boundless freedom and beauty. The dark gestation from which it struggles will produce new form and facility with which to experience that freedom and beauty which it is.

The time is upon us for new lessons and explorations into the territory beyond the vanishing point of the phenomenal world. The way is carefully charted for those who want to start their journey. Beneath its cerebration, the human mind has ever held within its depths the final blueprint and perfect knowledge from which to draw when the time is right. A seed out of season will not grow, but now that acclimation is within us, stirring, straining, with or against the change.

From the sleep of a million starless dreams the pulse of the planet quickens. Restless, and deep within its being a vision from the mists of consciousness awakes. Through myth and symbol an externalizing force uncoils as yawning synapses gently spark silent pre-dawn currents of new birth. In this perfect waking moment all life listens, holds its breath, changing focus as the void of darkness yields its shadows to the young light. The presence of the new day is all around . . . . permeating, invisible, throughout and within. The labour has begun . . . new life awaits.

Take a deep breath . . . .

You are the Infinite One who was lost but now is found. You are the Light and the divine fulfillment of the Father. Know that always there is perfection within and around you and that the Infinite Source springs eternal within your breast.
Be happy. Be successful. Be watchful and be His beloved.

Come home.

References
1. *Season of Changes, Ways of Response* (Associations of the Light Morning, Heritage Press, 1974).

Part Six
Helpful Reading

Awareness Primers *Psychic Discoveries Behind The Iron Curtain,* Ostrander & Schroeder. 1974. Bantam (U.S.);

Supernature, Lyall Watson. 1974. Coronet (U.K.) A natural history of the supernatural

The Tao Of Physics, Fritjof Capra. 1975. Shambhalla (U.S.); Fontana (U.K.)

Frontiers Of Consciousness. Ed. John White. 1974. Julien Press. The meeting ground between inner and outer reality

The Master Game, Robert De Ropp, 1969. Dell (U.S.); Alllen & Unwin (U.K.). If life is an illusion we may as well master its game conditions. A spiritual-psychological approach

Autobiography Of A Yogi, Paramahansa Yogananda. 1969. SRF Fellowship (U.S.); Rider (U.K.) The amazing life-story of the great Yogi who brought Hinduism to the West

The Natural Mind, Andrew Weil. 1972. Houghton-Mifflin (U.S.); Cape (U.K.). New way of looking at drugs and higher consciousness

The Secret Life Of Plants, Tompkins and Bird. Harper & Row (U.S.); Hodder (U.K.). Experiments in plant consciousness

The Magic Of Findhorn, Paul Hawken. 1974. Harper & Row (U.S.); Fontana (U.K.) Human communication with the intelligences of the plant kingdom; its applications and implications for the future

Tao Teh King, Lao Tsu (various publishers) On nature and intelligence

The Rosicrucian Cosmo-Conception, Max Heindel, 1973. Rosicrucian Fellowship.; L.N. Fowler (U.K.)

Shamanism, Mircea Ellade, 1972. Princeton University Press (U.S.); Rontledge & Kegan Paul (U.K.)

Memories, Dreams, Reflections, C.G. Jung, 1973. Pantheon Press (U.S.); Fontana (U.K.) The autobiography of the innermost life of one of the greatest explorers of the human mind.

What Am I Doing Here? Ivy O. Duce. Meher Baba Info. Box 1101, Berkeley, CA 94701 At the instruction of Meher Baba, the author introduces basic spiritual themes, karma, reincarnation, astral phenomena and mechanics of evolution.

Jonathan Livingston Seagull, Richard Bach, 1970. Macmillan, Avon (U.S.); Turnstone, Pan (U.K.) A bird's evolution to higher consciousness!

Introduction to Basics

Toward The One, 1974, Harper Colophon. Edited from lectures by Pir Vilayat Khan. Down to Earth discourses on the nature of the infinite and intriguing graphics.

The Biological Basis Of Religion And Genius, Gopi Krishna, 1972, Harper & Row (U.S.); Turnstone (U.K.) A scientific-philosphical work on the nature and purpose of Kundalini energy as it relates to human evolution and altered states of consciousness

The Impersonal Life, Anonymous, Sun Center Publications, PO Box 54, San Gabriel, CA: On being still and knowing [God within]·

Be Here Now, Baba Ram Dass, 1971, Lama Foundation (U.S.); Neville Spearman (U.K.) The transformational journey of Dr. Richard Alpert PhD, to Baba Ram Dass, seeker of truth. Meditations and recipes for a sacred life.

A Glimpse Of Nothingness, Janwillem van de Wetering, 1975, Houghton Mifflin (U.S.) Allen & Unwin (U.K.) A journal of an American Zen experience

This Is Reality, Roy Eugene Davis, Yogananda Press, CSA, Box 7, Lakemont, GA 30552. A realistic guide to meditation by a disciple of Yogananda

Handbook To Higher Consciousness, Ken Keyes, Jr., Living Love Center, 1730-B La Loma Avenue, Berkeley, CA 94709: On becoming aware, loving and happy NOW. Manual for self reprogramming.

Christian Yoga And You, Evangelos Alexandrou, Christananda Publishing Co. 977 Asbury St., San Jose, CA 95126

The Essene Gospel Of Peace, Edmond Bordeaux Szekely, Academy of Creative Living (U.S.); C.W. Daniel (U.K.) Teachings of Christ translated from 3rd century aramaic scrolls in the Vatican Library

Home Study Yoga Course: 14 lessons by Swami Kriyananda (disciple of the late Paramahansa Yogananda) Ananda Publications, 900 Alleghany Star Route, Nevada City, CA. 95959

Yoga And Self Culture, Sri Deva Ram Sukul, 1947, Yoga Society of America. A scientific and practical survey of yoga philosophy for layperson and aspirant

How To Meditate, Lawrence LeShan, 1974, Little, Brown (U.S.); Wildwood House (U.K.). Bridges the gap between establishment and counter-culture, without religious or cultural bias.

The Chakras, C.W. Leadbetter, 1974, Quest. Understanding the body's vital energy centers

Many Mansions, Gina Cerminara, 1967, Signet (U.S.); Neville Spearman (U.K.). About reincarnation and karma

The Etheric Double, A.E. Powell, 1969, Quest (U.S.); Theosophical (U.K.). Subtle energy body which Kirlian photography can now reveal.

Toward the New Age

The Ultimate Frontier, Eklal Kueshana, Stelle Group, PO Box 5900, Chicago 80,111. An account of the secret brotherhoods and their profound world-wide influence during the past 6,000 years. A guide to the future.

Est: The Steersman Handbook, L. Clark Stevens, Capricorn Press, 1970. Charts the coming decade of conflict and the transformation of all things

Pole Shift, John White, Doubleday, 1980. Prophecies and predictions of the ultimate catastrophe

inner state

Revelation: The Birth of a New Age, David Spangler, 1971, Findhorn Foundation

The Road Ahead, Swami Kriyananda, 1973, Ananda Publications. World prophecies by Paramahansa Yogananda. Guide to the future

Season of Changes: Ways of Response, Associations of the Light Morning, 1974. Heritage. A psychic interpretation of the coming changes related to the Earth and the corresponding transformations within humanity

Insights For The Age Of Aquarius, Gina Cerminara, 1973, Prentice Hall. A scientific analysis of the problems of religion

Passages About Earth, William Irwin Thompson, 1974, Harper & Row. An exploration of the new planetary culture

Aquarian Gospel of Jesus the Christ, Levi, 1975, De Vorss & Co. (U.S.); L.N. Fowler (U.K.)

The Late Great Planet Earth, Hal Lindsey, 1973, Bantam (U.S.); Lakeland Pubs. (U.K.). Correlations between world events today and the prophecies of the Book of Revelation

The Theory of Celestial Influence, R. Collin, V. Stuart: London 1954

Astrological Timing, The Transition To The New Age, Dane Rudhyar, 1969. Harper Colophon

At The Edge Of History, William Irwin Thompson, 1971, Harper & Row. Speculations on the transformation of a culture

The Revolution of Hope, Erich Fromm, 1968, Harper & Row. Towards a humanized technology

The Greening of America, Charles A. Reich, 1971, Bantam (U.S.); Penguin (U.K.) Authentic values vs. the corporate state

The Making Of A Counter-Culture, Th. Roszak, 1969, Doubleday 78-187880, Ira Einhorn, 1972, Doubleday. Technological/stoned insights emphasizing transformational culture
The Psychology of Man's Possible Evolution, P.D. Ouspensky, 1974, Vintage (U.S.); Hodder & Stoughton (U.K.)
Neurologic, Dr. Timothy Leary, 1973, Level Press

Simplification and Survival *Nasha Survival Catalog,* Box 4077, Station A, Toronto, Ont. M5W IM4, Canada (Send 25c) Books to borrow or buy on just about everything
How To Live Cheap But Good, Simple Living Program, AFSC, 2160 Lake Street, San Francisco, CA 94121
Making Do: Basic Things For Simple Living, Arthur M. Hill, Garden Way Publishing, Charlotte, VT 05445
Living Better On Less, Patrick Rivers, Turnstone Press, 1977
Finding A Simpler Life, John C. Cooper, Pilgrim Press. For those seeking a simpler life within the bounds of their present lives
How To Get $50,000 Worth Of Service Free From The U.S. Government E. Joseph Cosman, Frederich Fell, NY
Living Poor With Style, Ernest Callenbach, Bantam
Feasting Free On Wild Edibles, Bradford Angier, 1972, Stackpole
Edible & Poisonous Plants Card Deck, Plant Deck, Inc., 2134 Wembly Park Road, Lake Oswego, Oregon 97034
Survival With Style, Bradford Angier, 1974, Vintage. In trouble or in fun – how to keep body and soul together in the wilderness
An Index Of Possibilities, Pantheon (U.S.); Arrow (U.K.). Ideas and information on energy and power – human, man-made and natural
Crisis In Modern Thought, Swami Kriyananda, Ananda Pubs.
Pathways To Inner Calm, Maria Byles, Allen & Unwin, London
Co-Operative Communities, How To Start Them And Why, Swami Kriyananda, Ananda Publications
Communities Magazine, Drawer 426, Louisa, VA 23093
Communes, Law And Commonsense, Lee Goldstein, c/o NCP, 32 Rutland St., Boston, Mass. 02118
co-Evolution Quarterly, Summer 1974: Food storage issue
Living The Good Life – How to Live Sanely and Simply in a Troubled World Helen & Scott Nearing, Schocken Books
Mother Earth News, PO° Box 70, Hendersonville, NC 28739. A bi-monthly publication with heavy emphasis on alternative lifestyles, ecology, working with nature and doing more with less
See Catalogue Directory listing also
Where Do I Go From Here With My Life? John C. Crystal &

Richard N. Bolles. Ten Speed Publications
1001 Ways To Be Your Own Boss Vivo Bennett & Cricket Clagett, Prentice-Hall, 1976

Social Action

Workforce, 4911 Telegraph Avenue, Oakland, CA 95965. Vocations for social change

The Workbook, Southwest Research Info Center, PO Box 4524, Albuquerque NM 87106. The who, how and why of social involvement for the layperson covering an extensive range of possibilities

Invest Yourself, The Commission on Voluntary Service & Action, 475 Riverside Drive, No. 665, New York, NY 10027

National Center for Voluntary Action, 1625 Massachusetts Avenue NW, Washington DC 20036. Learn who is doing what for whom, where and why

Handbook for Ecology Action, Sierra Club, 1050 Mills Tower, San Francisco, CA 94104

Earth Tool Kit, Environmental Action No. 731, 1346 Connecticut Avenue NW, Washington DC 20036. Useful information on organizing for ecological remedies

A Public Citizens Action Manual, Ross Donald, 1973, Grossman. Step-by-step guide to effective action by individuals and groups from simple letter writing to full-scale law suits.

The Grass Roots Primer, Ed. Robertson and Lewallen, 1975, Sierra Club Publications, San Francisco. How to save your piece of the planet by the people who are already doing it.

The Bread Game, The Realities of Foundation Fundraising. Herb Allen, Ed. Glide Publications, San Francisco. Revised ed. 1974. How-to-do-it handbook for getting funded by a private foundation.

The Organizer's Manual, O.M. Collective. Bantam Books, Inc. 1971. How-to-do-it handbook for getting things done; how to pick issues and get your group together, then how to act from A to Z

Special Committee on Aging Publications List, G-223 Dirksen Bldg., Washington, D.C. 20510. Free. (revised regularly). Excellent source of low-cost information about the problems of old people: health, tax, legal, housing and transportation difficulties.

Open The Books – How To Research A Corporation, 1974. Urban Planning Aid Inc., 639 Massachusetts Ave., Cambridge, MA 02139. How to investigate ownership and control, investments, subsidiaries, stock, holdings, etc.

Task Force Against Nuclear Pollution 153 E Street SE., Washington DC 20003. This group will connect you with reliable information sources (articles, books, groups, people). It has a nation-wide petition campaign. They work on an array of related issues

How To Challenge Your Local Electric Utility: Citizen's Guide to the Power Industry: Morgan & Jerabek, Environmental Action Fd., 720 Dupont Circle Bldg. Washington, DC 20036

People & Taxes, Tax Reform Research Group, PO Box 14198, Ben Franklin Stn., Washington, D.C. 20044: Magazine $4/yr. indiv. $6/yr groups. For folks who want to organize around tax reform.

Media & Consumer magazine, PO Box 6020 Norwalk, CO 06852. $12/yr. If you're looking for projects for your group or individually, this paper has four sections: Clipping Service of trends to provide ideas for local action; Journalism Review, Consumer Action News and Commentary on consumer and media issues.

Food *You Are How You Eat* Donald Law, Turnstone Press 1978. A guide to nutrition and understanding your biological system.

Diet For A Small Planet, Frances Moore Lappe, Ballantine/FOE 1971. It is possible to eat lower on the life-chain and still get adequate protein. Tables for protein combining and much valuable info. about vegetarianism.

Recipes For A Small Planet, Ellen Buckman Ewald, 1973, Ballantine Recipes based on the above book

The Book Of Judgement, George Ohsawa, 1966, The Ohsawa Foundation. Inside story of food, digestion, energy and consciousness. The philosophy of oriental medicine.

Supermarket Handbook: Access to Whole Foods, Nikki Goldbeck, 1973, Harper & Row

Eat Well On $1 A Day, Bill & Ruth Kaysin, 1975, Chronicle Books

Seeds And Sprouts For Life, Dr. Bernard Jensen, Bernard Jensen Publications, PO Box 8, Solana Beach, CA 92075

Dry It – You'll Like It, PBL, Box 234, Longview, WA 98632

Yon Yonson's Primer Or Organic Gardening, The Almighty Publishing Co. PO Box 14094, San Francisco, CA 94114. Primer for beginners with small plots

The Basic Book Of Organic Gardening, Robert Rodale, Rodale Press, Emmaus, PA

Step-By-Step To Organic Gardening, Samuel Ogden, Rodale Press

Raise Vegetables Without A Garden, George & Katy Abraham, 1974, Countryside Books

Food Price Blackmail, Or Who's Behind The High Cost Of Eating: Lobenstein & Schommer, 1973, United Front Press, PO Box 4009, San Francisco, CA 94140

Supermarket Trap: The Consumer And The Food Industry, 1970,

Bantam, Judy L. Kemp. A supermarket survival manual

The Chemical Feast, James S. Turner, 1970, Grossman.A Ralph Nader study-group report on food protection and the FDA. A thorough critique of the FDA Mythology

Eating May Be Hazardous To Your Health, J. Verrett & J. Carper, 1974, S & S. Insider's view of the FDA as a slack custodian of our inner ecology

The Preparation And Organization Of A Community Buying Club, Pennie Monroe, V-Line, ACTION, Washington DC 20525

Food Conspiracy Cookbook And Members Manual, Spring Books, PO Box 4191, Boulder, Colo. 80302

Food Co-Ops For Small Groups, Tony Vellela, Workman Publishing Co. 231 East 51 Street, New York, NY 10022

Food Co-Operatives: How To Start One And Make It Prosper, 165 W. Harvey Street Philadelphia, PA 19144

Gardens For All, Diane Young & Staff, Gardens for All, Charlotte, VT 05445

Gateway To Survival Is Storage, Walter D. Batchelor, 6120 E. Boston Street Mesa, Ariz.

Famine And Survival In America, Howard Ruff, PO Box 5481, Walnut Creek, CA 94596

Stocking Up, Rodale Press. How to preserve the foods you grow, naturally

Family Storage Plan, Bob Zabriskie, Bookcraft Inc., 1848 W. 2300 Street, Salt Lake City, Utah 84120

Indoor Organic Gardening for Survival	Hippocrates Health Inst.
Fasting	25 Exeter Street,
Organic Complete Meal Salad	Boston, Mass. 02116
Survival Diet on 26c a Day	

Food Gardens: The Gardeners' Catalogue, 1975, William Morrow.

International Center For Biological Control (Pest control) Univ. of Calif. 1050 San Pablo Ave., Albany, CA 94706. Offers computerized information-retrieval system covering technical info. on the natural enemies of particular pests. Offers advice & counsel on biological control matters and additional information sources.

Environment *Population, Resources And Environment,* Paul & Anne Ehrlich, W.H. Freeman

The Closing Circle, Barry Commoner, 1971, Knopf

The People's Land, Peter Barnes, Rodale Press. A reader on land reform in the U.S.

The Journal Of The New Alchemists, New Alchemy Inst., 1974,

Woods Hole, Mass. Innovation, alternatives in agri/aqua culture

Church Of The Earth: The Ecology Of A Creative Community, Robert De Ropp, Delacorte

Farmers Of Forty Centuries, F.H. King (orig. plates 1911), Rodale Press. After a few hundred years, US topsoil is almost depleted. Japan and China have sustained far denser populations on healthy land for thousands of years

China: Science Walks On Two Legs, 1974, Discus Books, NY. A revealing look at the unique role and use of science in the lives of China's people. They are involved, not separate from their science

The Limits To Growth, Donel Meadows, 1972, Universe Books. Prophesies the potential collapse of world systems sometime within the next century

The End Of Affluence, Paul & Anne Ehrlich, 1974, Ballantine. A blueprint for the future

The Lives Of A Cell, Lewis Thomas, Viking

Small Is Beautiful, E.F. Schumacher, Harper & Row (U.S.); Blond & Briggs (U.K.)

Silent Spring, Rachel Carson, Houghton Mifflin (U.S.); Penguin (U.K.)

A Sand County Almanac, Aldo Leopold, Ballantine

Living On A Little Land, Patrick Rivers, Turnstone Press 1978. How to avoid mistakes on a smallholding

Health   *Natural Sources Vit B-17/Laetrile*, Moira Timms and Z. Zar, Celestial Arts, 1978

The Home Health Handbook, Copans & Osgood, Garden Way Publishing, Vt.

How To Get Well, Paavo Airola PhD ND, Health Plus, PO Box 22001, Phoenix, AZ 85028

A Guide To Alternative Medicine, Donald Law, Turnstone Press (U.K.) 1974, Anchor Books (U.S.)

Rational Fasting, Arnold Ehret, 1971, Benedict Lust Pubs., NY

The Biochemic Handbook, 1969, New Era Labs, 87 Saffron Hill, London EC1, England. Intro to cellular therapy and practical application of the 12 tissue salts. Homeopathic first aid

Basic Nutrition And Cell Nutrition, R.F. Milton, 1970, Provoker Press, St. Catherines, Ontario, Canada

Back To Eden, Jethro Kloss, 1971, Beneficial Books. A compendium of Herbs & uses

Finger Acupressure, Pedro Chan, 1975, Ballantine. Treatment for common ailments by using finger massage on acupuncture points

Helping Yourself With Foot Reflexology, Mildred Carter, 1973,

Parker

The Well Body Book, Samuels & Bennett, 1973, Random House/ Bookworks US; Wildwood (U.K.)

Bodymind, Don Ethan Miller, 1974, Prentice-Hall. The Whole Person Health Book

Handbook Of The Nutritional Contents Of Food 1975, Dover. Prepared for the U.S. Dept. of Agriculture

Are You Radioactive? How To Protect Yourself, Linda Clark, Devin-Adair

Light And Health, John Ott, Devin-Adair, 1974

You Can Do It! Exercise & Diet Plan, Senator Wm. Proxmire, Cancer Book House, 2043 N. Berendo Street, Los Angeles, CA 90027

Magnetism & Its Effects on the Living System, Walter Rawls, Jr. Cancer Book House, (as above)

Economy   *The Seven Laws Of Money,* Michael Phillips, Random House/Word Wheel

Mental Illness And The Economy, M. Harvet Brenner, Harvard University Press

Small Is Beautiful: A Study Of Economics As If People Mattered, Schumacher 1973, Harper & Row (U.S.); Blond & Briggs (U.K.)

The Entropy Law And The Economic Process, Nicholas Georgescu-Roegen, 1971, Harvard Univ. Press

Economics And The Gospel, R. Taylor, United Church Press, 1973

How You Can Beat Inflation, David L. Markstein, McGraw-Hill. A practical guide for the concerned individual

Seed Money In Action, Jon P. Speller, 1965

None Dare Call It Conspiracy, Gary Allen, Concord Press. A disturbing treatise on monied interests and world power

How To Prepare For The Coming Crash, Robert Preston, Hawkes.

How You Can Profit From A Monetary Crisis, Harry Browne, 1971, Avon

Inflation Survival Newsletter, Oakley Bramble, Hanon Events, 422 First Street, SE, Washington DC 20003

Building Your Future With Silver, Robert Preston, Hawkes Pubs.

Pray And Grow Rich, Catherine Ponder, 1975, Parker

Miracle Power For Infinite Riches, Joseph Murphy, 1972, Parker

Free Enterprise Newsletter: 800 Second Avenue, New York, 10017

Catalogues/ Directories   *Last Whole Earth Catalog* 1971 Random House

Whole Earth Epilog 1974 Penguin Books. Sequel to Whole Earth Catalog

The Many Ways Of Being 1976 Turnstone Press (U.K.) A guide to spiritual groups and Growth Centres in Britain

*Co-Evolution Quarterly,*Box 428, Sausalito, CA 94965. Supplement to Whole Earth Catalog

Psychosources 1973 Bantam Books. A psychological Whole Earth Catalog

The First New England Catalog, Garden Way Publishing, Charlotte, VT 05445 Self-sufficiency products, tools, info.

Nasha Survival Catalog Box 4077, Station A, Toronto, Ontario M5W IM4, Canada. Poverty Survival, Outdoor Survival, Buying guides, Homesteading, Natural Healing, Handcrafts, Money, Fix-it-Yourself, Make-it-Yourself, Food: Hunting, Indoor Growing, Wild Edibles, Nutrition, etc. (send 25c). All their books can be bought or borrowed

The Gardeners' Catalog Wm. Morrow & Co. Inc., 105 Madison Av., NY, NY 10016 Complete compendium of gardening info, plants, seeds, tools and sources

Source Catalog No. 1: Communications Alternative media

Source Catalog no. 2: Communities Survival manual for urban communities

Commune Directory, CPC, Drawer 426, Louisa, VA 23093

Spiritual Community Guide 1975-76, Box 1080, San Rafael, CA94902 State-by-State directly of New Age teachers, Yoga & Meditation Centers, Ashrams, Bookstores, Natural Food Stores and Restaurants. Over 100 descriptions of major spiritual groups

A Pilgrim's Guide To Planet Earth Address as above. Travellers' handbook and spiritual directory

Mother's General Store, 1975. Box 506, Flat Rock, NC 28731. Tools for living the satisfying life

The Connection No. 1. 1974. Prajna Press, Ojai, CA. Alternative life-style technology, literature, bulk foods, tools, gear, etc. at wholesale prices

Somewhere Else. Community Bookshelf, PO Bx 426, Louisa, VA 23093. Alternative living-learning centres and networks

Yellow Pages Of Learning Resources 1972 MIT Press. A resource directory showing how, where and who, with emphasis on involvement

Directory Of Consumer Protection And Environmental Agencies 1973 Marquis Publi.

Earth Guild/Grateful Union Catalog. Earth guild, Cambridge, Mass. 1974. Mail order. Unique selection of tools for mind and hand. Books to change your view of life and the access to tools to help start your own way

Real Time No. 2. Brockman and Rosenfeld, 1973, Anchor/Doubleday Book Reviews cataloguing new ideas and information

My grateful acknowledgement goes to the friends who helped me create this book: Mark Horlings of Friends of the Earth. Bob Berkey and Ron Liggett of the Metaphysical Center in San Francisco, Ralph Palsson of the Astronomical Society of the Pacific. And to those who generously shared their knowledge and time for its compilation: Stewart Walker, Bernard Pietsch and Macelle Brown. Special thanks go to Dr. Daniel Bleise, my early mentor, and to Zach Zar for his support and encouragement throughout, and for buying me a dictionary!

The author acknowledges with thanks permission to reproduce the following illustrations:
Chicago Tribune – New York News Syndicate for the Broom Hilda cartoon; Gahan Wilson for the fog cartoon; Stony Brook Foundation Inc. for the Holocoenotic Environment Complex; National Oceanic and Atmospheric Administration for the Wobbling Earth graph; M. Duke Lanfré for the photograph of Kirlian Pyramid Energy; Ingham Publishing Co. Inc. for the Reflexology Foot Chart; Central Bureau of the International Polar Motion Service for the Polar Motion charts; American Friends Service Committee, San Francisco, for the 'Global Village' calligraphy; and Houghton Mifflin Company, Boston, for the stargazing diagrams after H.A. Rey; and the California Academy of Sciences for the photograph of the Statue of Liberty.

The author also acknowledges with thanks the permission of David Spangler to quote from *Revelation: Birth of a New Age;* and of Llewellyn Publications to quote from *The Fate of the Nations* by Arthur Prieditris.

Readers interested in receiving a newsletter of updates on earth changes, transformation and prophecy, please write the author for details, and include a stamped self-addressed envelope:

Moira Timms
P.O. Box 19
Mill Valley, CA 94142

Errata

On page 171, 2nd line, "described on page 229" should be "described on page 243."

The text on page 227 is in error. The correct text is as follows:

wind is still and the birds no longer sing, because the spirit of the land is heavy with memories too painful to stir the flow of nature. The great herds are gone and the land is now sore. Its once rich potential has vanished and that which remains reminds us only of what must now be and what cannot be changed: aluminum, concrete and plastic. In nature's creation, the dead sustain the living; an exchange of exquisite alchemy. Too many of man's creations contaminate the living, their existence predicated upon perpetuating the production of waste, destruction and death. The great sadness settles over the land with the smog. You see, pollution is somebody's profit.

When urbanites savour the nostalgia of the simple life and the mystical union with nature, and (when there is time) the rhythms of the seasons, they think of Henry David Thoreau. However, it was a visionary contemporary of Thoreau's, one George Perkins Marsh, who probably caused more of an impact on our lives today. Little more than a century ago he discovered the science of the relationships between organisms and their environment, and created the concept of modern 'ecology'. From the trends beginning to take shape during his life in the mid-nineteenth century, he accurately foresaw the dangers and results which depreciation of the environment has now led us to. Related to this, he warned, would be 'the decay of humanity's moral being and the fall of empires.'[1]

This is a drastic but quite accurate prediction when one stops to consider what artists, architects, psychologists and Madison Avenue have been showing and telling us for a very long time now – that consciousness and behaviour can be conditioned by environment, and applied visual stimuli. Consciousness affects the environment and the environment in turn affects the consciousness; it's a self perpetuating and circular process. 'The environment' today is what large-scale ignorance, greed and indifference have produced. Is our moral being now becoming decayed as Marsh predicted? – like our environment? like the Earth? Are the foundations of some well-known empires becoming shaky? In recent years governments all over the world toppled – West Germany, Canada, England, Iceland, Ethopia, the Nixon Administration and Iran.